Marketing Legal Services

Second Edition

Other titles available from Law Society Publishing:

Alternative Business Structures
Iain Miller

Client Service for Law Firms
Heather Stewart

Conveyancing Quality Scheme Toolkit
The Law Society

Leadership for Law Firms
Patricia Wheatley Burt

Lexcel Client Care Toolkit (2nd edn)
The Law Society

Lexcel Business Continuity Planning Toolkit
The Law Society

Lexcel Financial Management and Business Planning Toolkit
The Law Society

Lexcel Information Management Toolkit
The Law Society

Lexcel People Management Toolkit
The Law Society

Lexcel Risk Management Toolkit
The Law Society

Managing People in a Legal Business
General Editor: Jill Andrew

Practice Management Handbook (2nd edn)
Editor: Peter Scott

Strategy for Law Firms
Nick Jarrett-Kerr

Titles from Law Society Publishing can be ordered from all good bookshops or direct (telephone 0870 850 1422, email **lawsociety@prolog.uk.com** or visit our online shop at **www.lawsociety.org.uk/bookshop**).

Marketing Legal Services

Second edition

David Monk and Alastair Moyes

Marketlaw

The Law Society

ISBN-13: 978-1-85328-756-5

First published in 2008

This second edition published in 2011 by the Law Society
113 Chancery Lane, London WC2A 1PL

Typeset by IDSUK (DataConnection) Ltd
Printed by Hobbs the Printers Ltd, Totton, Hants

FSC
www.fsc.org
MIX
Paper from responsible sources
FSC® C020438

The paper used for the text pages of this book is FSC® certified. FSC (the Forest Stewardship Council®) is an international network to promote responsible management of the world's forests.

This book is dedicated to those clients who, over the last 25 years, became friends and heeded these friendly warnings. And, to those who didn't heed them, but survived.

David and Alastair

Contents

Foreword

When I first qualified as a solicitor, it was highly unlikely you would overhear colleagues mulling over their latest strategy for the '4Ps' of marketing: product, price, place and promotion, but times have changed. Solicitors now find themselves in greater competition than ever before. The introduction of alternative business structures early next year has the potential to introduce greater competition to what is already a crowded market.

I believe that many firms have the potential to thrive in the new legal services environment; after all, many modernising trends have been affecting solicitors' practices for some time now, but the latest challenges will need to be met head-on, just as they have been in the past. That means making sure that you promote your business in the most effective way possible.

The most successful practices of the future will be more business-like in their approach and less reticent about what they can offer that other legal service providers cannot. The question as always is 'how?'. Therefore I am very grateful to David Monk and Alastair Moyes for writing a book that encapsulates the practical steps that practices can take to make sure that they stand out from the crowd.

The innovative ideas and best practice laid out in this book will help solicitors across England and Wales ensure that the profession's reputation for quality and leading position in the market will be guaranteed for many years to come.

John Wotton
President
The Law Society

Preface

A lot has happened since the publication of the first edition of this book, early in 2008. Then, the major concern of the legal profession in England and Wales was the changes that were about to be wrought on it by the Legal Services Act 2007. Thus, our book dealt with facing up to these changes and challenges and dealing with what we then termed 'The New Competition'.

To judge by the reactions we received from readers of the book, it was felt to be of help, and much of the material remains intact to assist with the day-to-day marketing of your firm.

So what have been the major changes in the last three years? Perhaps the biggest is the full emergence of non-traditional competition, The New Competition for the provision of legal services to the domestic and, indeed, commercial markets. The promotion of these new providers is no longer limited to regular communications with their existing client and customer bases. They are, in short, all over the media and all over the internet. They are having a noticeable effect. For example, many firms put their reduction in probate work down to the professional and continual promotion of probate services by funeral providers and others.

This is but one example. Practically every matter type has the potential to be eroded in this way by the The New Competition.

In this second edition, we continue to call them 'The New Competition' to differentiate them from other lawyers, the traditional competition with whom, of course, you also have to compete. But they are here to stay and will grow so that perhaps we should now consider them simply 'The Competition'.

Many other changes, unsurprisingly, come courtesy of the internet. People, including your clients, are continually being encouraged to undertake 'DIY law', perhaps with a background online 'mentoring service'. All the major new competitors have excellent websites that are easy to navigate and, most importantly, provide access to legal advice on a 24/7 basis. Then there is the plethora of sites, large and small, offering to put one in touch with a solicitor, and effectively coming between you and your potential clients. In this second edition we look at how to deal with – and perhaps learn from or utilise – these recent market changes.

Other advances in technology in the last three years have continued at a relentless rate and offer new digital marketing opportunities for the marketing-led firm. From the increasingly invaluable Google Adwords to new social media networks, there are ever increasing new ways to contact and maintain relationships with existing and potential clients. While we believe you have to get the marketing fundamentals in place first, the fact is that no forward-thinking practice can ignore these developments.

Many in the profession consider the advent of alternative business structures (ABS) to be *the* major change and, indeed; the advent of new practice ownership may well affect the profession deeply. We discuss ABS and their likely effect in this revised edition, but what ABS will not change is the need for practices – whoever owns them, no matter what their trading vehicle is – to step up their marketing and compete. That is what this book is really about.

Of course, everything has been influenced by the worldwide recession that has been with us since the publication of the first edition. No one knows when or how it will end, any more than its beginning was foretold. But one thing is certain: the correct application of marketing management and of marketing techniques will assist your firm to cope and to prepare to flourish, whatever the circumstances.

We would also like to thank our colleagues Karen Young, Chris Sharman and Leslie Kent for their suggestions and contributions to this new edition.

David Monk and Alastair Moyes
August 2011
www.marketlaw.co.uk

1

'Oh No! Not another marketing book'

This is not just another 'theoretical' marketing book. This is a common sense 'how to do it' book. Each chapter concludes with a series of tasks aimed at the implementation of the book's ideas in your firm. Completion of the tasks should show you where your firm is in the programme towards strengthening your position and succeeding in the new marketplace.

You will not be expected to spend inordinate amounts of money to implement the recommendations in this book. Indeed, it is concerned more with developing and capitalising properly and professionally on the assets that have already been expensively accrued by your firm. This book should grow into a practice development guide enabling the reader to set clear, quantifiable objectives and monitor the progress towards achieving them.

Marketing Legal Services has been written on the assumption that the reader will read straight through the book in its entirety once, before returning to the first chapter and beginning to apply the ideas and tasks to their own firm. Our aim is to minimise the time spent gathering and assessing information, while maximising the results through the book's latter stages.

It is not an exaggeration to suggest that with each chapter and task, your work will build into a marketing manual for your firm, making you far better placed to take on 'The New Competition'.

> *Alteration, change of size, rotation and translation are unimpeachable varieties of change.* – Bertrand Russell

> *Let the great world spin forever down the ringing grooves of change.* – Alfred Lord Tennyson

For those of us who have worked within it, the legal profession in England and Wales over the past 20 years has been full of change. The main premise of this book is that despite what has gone before, the changes in the legal services market as a result of the Clementi review, the Legal Services Act 2007 including the imminent arrival of Alternative Business

Structures together with the appearance of new suppliers are much more profound and far-reaching than anything that has gone before, and can truly be described as 'market changers'.

Market changers have a long-term effect on the existing marketplace. One has only to think of supermarkets, out-of-town retail parks, Amazon, Direct Line insurance or eBay, for example, to see how each has changed the way products and services have been provided and bought, often to the detriment of the traditional supplier.

The legal profession is now in the firing line and, after centuries of a virtual monopoly, is perhaps the least well-equipped to respond to these changes. However, respond it must, and there is little doubt that the marketing discipline will be a vital part of every firm in the future.

The intention of this book is to persuade the profession that things are changing fast and that action must be taken *now*!

It is unsurprising that there is a degree of scepticism about the need to hurry. It seems extraordinary now that prior to deregulation, a mere 25 years ago, the profession was actually prohibited from advertising (in any meaningful sense). Solicitors had little or no interest in strategic marketing which offered little return in such a heavily regulated area.

The Legal Services Act 2007 has been the point around which much of the market-changing activity has been focused. The Act's intention is to open up the market for legal services. However, its contents are directed at the regulatory structure. Alternative suppliers of legal services are already well-established under the existing regulations and it may be fair to say that the Legal Services Act is an attempt to tighten up the regulations to allow solicitors to compete more effectively. One profound change effected by the Act is to enable non-lawyers to take profits out of a legal services firm more easily. This potential new route to profit from general legal services provides both an opportunity and a threat. The opportunity is for new service providers to invest confidently in developing legal services, and for solicitors to attract (and retain) non-lawyer staff to improve their services. The threat is that established legal services suppliers will not be able to compete with the new service providers, 'The New Competition', as their firms, their solicitors' training and their staff are not ready for the predicted shift in the market to more widely publicised, easily available legal services. Whereas, traditionally, the general public and small businesses have been forced to seek out legal services, it is anticipated that these services may in future be offered to such clients alongside their bank statements, telephone bills and grocery receipts.

There is an understandable tendency to react to new threats with a shrug. If the profession has not 'seen it all before', it has almost certainly seen some of it and has easily overcome threats to the 'bread-and-butter' work from estate agents owned by financial institutions, will writing bureaux, licensed conveyancers, 'big shed' personal injury (PI) claims handlers, multidisciplinary practices and others, often by simply doing nothing.

However, Sir David Clementi's report recommended, more strongly than ever before, opening up the supply of legal services, by allowing non-lawyers to own legal practices and, more importantly, by a reduction of the regulations surrounding the supply and promotion of legal services by organisations other than high street solicitors' practices. While there is still some way to go with regard to practice ownership, The New Competition, with its sights firmly set upon domestic and small business's work, has already been unleashed. In a relatively short time, many national 'large brand' organisations have entered the market, or declared that they shortly will, spending millions of pounds on promotions to sell legal services in competition with the majority of solicitors' firms.

Their aim is to capitalise on their established brand names and their huge databases of customer information. Worryingly, these companies are marketing-led to their core, with the skill to pick and choose their most profitable work for the legal organisations they will or have already set up. Their communications will present easy opportunities for their customers to become clients of their legal services division, stressing over and over again the benefits they offer.

For example, in the autumn of 2007, there was a major row between Tesco and the Law Society relating to Tesco's promotion of the idea that its customers would be better off going to Tesco's property (conveyancing) department, which specialised in house sales and purchases, rather than a high street solicitor, who would do 'any old legal work that came through the door'. Instead of emphasising the alternative benefits of local knowledge, local availability, professional qualifications and accountability, along with, in many cases, decades of experience, the legal profession chose to take umbrage at this perceived attack on its professional standing.

While it may seem reasonable to discuss at partners' meetings whether or not people will buy conveyancing services from a grocer, the fact is that they will – unless those consumers are given clear and understandable reasons why the alternative is superior. In part, this book is designed to assist you in organising your firm to communicate that superiority and compete in the new legal services marketplace.

Let us consider who else is entering the legal marketplace. The AA was one of the first organisations to declare its hand, and then formed an association with Saga. The current customers of this alliance comprise 90 per cent of the car owning, home owning, married with children, 50-plus employed/retired population. This is an accurate description of many firms' target consumers! The Co-operative Society, despite its old-fashioned image (or perhaps because of it), has gone from strength to strength recently, and has also declared its intention to expand its existing presence in the legal services market. Halifax bank is merely one of the major financial brands that already operates in the market, and is particularly noticeable because of its powerful and well-presented promotional material.

These and similar organisations are what we term 'The New Competition'. They are also a new threat, new in the sense that they have been regulated and low profile until recently. But this has now changed. Their motivation is to continually expand their ability to provide linked or related services to their current customers, without regard to how such services are manufactured. The legal services market is an exceptional opportunity to tie in more of their customers to their brand, on the basic values of security for the family, home and the future. General consumers or small businesses want their legal problems solved quickly and satisfactorily in a manner that suits them. Marketing-led consumer brand organisations will answer that need in whatever way best fits their businesses.

Professor Stephen Mayson of the Legal Services Policy Institute has suggested that up to 3,000 solicitors' firms may disappear. Other market observers have recently posed the question 'What will your firm do if it loses 25–50 per cent of its private client work?' Your authors have asked this question themselves and have received various answers that boil down to 'Move into commercial work', 'Merge with a larger firm', 'Reduce our operation to maintain profitability', 'Retire!' Another answer was 'Get on one of their panels', but this will mean drastically reduced fees and loss of independence.

We believe there is another way and that's what this book is about. However, before moving on to the more positive, let us consider what it is The New Competition is doing.

The New Competition will have its prime effect on two areas: customer communications and the price of legal services. Organisations are likely to start with a direct mail campaign concentrating, almost exclusively, on the presentation of the benefits of their services, in comparison to traditional legal services. Their brand names are known and trusted by their customers, and they realise that customers and clients can be fickle, and tend to buy their services based on limited information, immediate requirements, quick and easy access, recommendation from friends or colleagues, or even personal whim. Remember that The New Competition is made up of brands that are familiar and recognised by a large percentage of the population. Customers may subconsciously know that solicitors are reliable and have indemnity insurance, but consciously believe that getting a legal problem sorted out by a big brand will be as easy as returning a pair of Marks & Spencer's trousers. While this may not, in fact, be true, it is the perception that matters, and where that perception is ill-founded, it is up to competitors, in this case the traditional providers of legal services (i.e. your practice), to point that out.

The New Competition has started penetrating the bread-and-butter work of the high street solicitor, which we would define as conveyancing, will writing, probate, personal injury (PI) and tax planning. But, with the advent of the Carter report on legal aid procurement and increasingly easy divorce laws, especially along with the push towards mediation, these near-monopoly markets also look vulnerable. And a dive into commercial work may not necessarily provide the lifeboat that some expect.

Banks and a number of specialist providers are already offering elements of legal advice to small and medium-sized businesses. The majority of high street practices limit their commercial work to commercial conveyancing, contract drafting and employment law. These could easily be developed from an established private client practice by The New Competition, in exactly the same way as the traditional solicitors' firm developed such services in the first place. Indeed, while acting for the employer may not attract The New Competition, it is undeniable that the vast majority of employees must be customers of Tesco, the AA, Saga, the Co-op or Halifax, etc.

When new competition enters a marketplace, the increase in supply drives down the realisable price. The price for conveyancing and will writing is already low, and the costs and complexity of PI work are increasing. For many solicitors' firms, this will affect the profitability of the work that underpins their businesses and it demonstrates how essential it is to differentiate the service provided by the traditional legal firm from the apparently similar product offered by The New Competition.

So, how does a general high street firm or small practice compete against nationally known, trusted brands as they bulldoze their way into their chosen new market area, spending millions of pounds on promotion? It would be glib and complacent to say, yet again, that the solution to this problem is precisely what this book is about, but while it is, there is one underlying principle to be addressed at this point, which may bring some relief.

The New Competition, the big brands, has no more methods of promotion or routes to the market than are available to any other organisation. They have no tricks, secrets or special powers that mean they can win business over rivals. What they do have is an understanding of their customers through their databases, access to finance and the people to organise ceaseless and compelling promotions.

But, local, established law firms already have many advantages that cannot be easily replicated by the big brands. These include the ownership of an established legal business with a history of satisfied clients; local offices staffed by highly trained professionals with dedicated and experienced support staff; a trusted brand that can become as big in the smaller geographical market of the average legal practice, as Coca-Cola is worldwide. Add to this the increased promotion and awareness of the need for legal services generated by The New Competition, and it presents an opportunity for a well-organised firm to expand and prosper in its local area.

The task of meeting the big brands head on is a matter of developing marketing knowledge and applying that to the existing business. No revolution is required, just the application of commercial marketing and general management techniques. And, despite the irritation that repetition may cause, that is what this book is about.

This is not just a theoretical marketing book. Indeed, wherever possible, we have avoided, or at least explained, marketing jargon. This is a common sense 'how to do it' book. Each chapter includes sections that illustrate examples of the subjects covered in that chapter and concludes with tasks aimed at the implementation of the ideas in your own firm. Completion of the tasks should reveal to you your progress towards strengthening your position and succeeding in the new marketplace.

The recommendations in this book do not require you to spend a lot of money, nor will you be expected to diversify or look far afield. Indeed, the majority of this book is concerned with looking first inside the firm, and capitalising properly and professionally on your existing assets. This book, and the tasks, should grow into a practice development guide, enabling the reader to set clear, quantifiable objectives and monitor the progress towards achieving them.

The chapters take you through a programme that will lead to a course of action and measurable results, much as you would expect from a marketing manager or consultant. This is hardly surprising as it is based upon consultancy work undertaken within the legal profession over the past 20 years. But one significant difference between a written book and a consultancy assignment is this matter of explanation and clarification. We hope that this does not sound impertinent, but we would propose the following approach to the book.

Marketing Legal Services has been written on the assumption that you will read through the book in its entirety once, before returning to the first chapter and beginning to apply the ideas and tasks to your firm.

We know, perhaps better than any outsider, how busy lawyers, and particularly partners, are. But you have bought this book and we want you to get the best out of your investment. Therefore, read it once straight through and discuss the points raised with your partners if you feel that is appropriate. You may feel your firm has already dealt with several of the ideas outlined in the chapters. If so, you are already ahead of many of your competitors. However, the process of carefully working through this book will highlight areas of potential improvement, and we would recommend that you avoid skipping chapters. Use the ideas in each chapter to judge whether your current arrangements are really providing the returns you anticipated.

When you have an overview of the book's contents, go back to the beginning and work through each chapter in turn, perhaps making notes, including any criticisms or anticipated problems. The task sections then enable you to apply the ideas, with the information you gathered from your firm, to produce clear projects and work plans, with achievable objectives.

Each chapter builds on the ideas or tasks from previous sections, and you may wonder why such detail is required in the early chapters. Our aim is to minimise your time spent gathering and assessing information, while maximising the results through the programme's later stages.

Commitment from your partnership is an essential element for the success of this programme. Although they may not initially be directly involved, your partners will need to be kept informed of what you are doing, and how that will benefit them. It may help to keep the results of the tasks and ideas well documented using the structure of this book. With each chapter and task, the work put in will build into the marketing manual for your firm, providing practical next steps and, we hope, inspiration to achieve marketing best practice. At the end of it you will genuinely be better placed to take on The New Competition. And you should succeed.

In this new environment, success will come most easily to those who complete the tasks. During the Enterprise Initiative Scheme of the mid-1990s, work was undertaken for dozens of practices, reports were presented at workshops, usually with every partner present. An action plan was drawn up and agreed. The partners adopted those recommendations they considered most appropriate and prioritised them. Without exception, they then committed themselves wholeheartedly to implementation.

And what happened next?

Clients happened next. Pressure of business happened next. The latest concern or priority happened next and, on average, following a review five years later, only 50 per cent of our client firms had completed their programme. Ten per cent had done nothing; the rest had done little. It took one firm 10 years to finalise and complete the creation of a database that all 10 partners had agreed was 'essential'. The firm continued to prosper, but not as much as it once had, and it could not have done so in the face of The New Competition.

Our job of updating this book for its second edition is finished. We have proved conclusively that this programme works, and we sincerely hope that it works for you. Change is happening. But change was always inevitable. Don't 'retire' – fight back. Good luck with that fight, revisit the quotations at the start of the chapter, and remember: Bertrand Russell was a philosopher, but Tennyson a poet. The practice of law has always been part art and part science and success will come to those who see inevitable change not as a threat, but as an opportunity.

CHAPTER 1 TASK **Read the book**

For this first task, we would ask you to commit yourself to reading this book once. Allocate time to get through it, so you can retain the ideas within it and then discuss them with your partners. Review your firm's current position, its strengths and weaknesses, and where you would like your firm to be in five years' time.

Having read straight through the book, return to Chapter 1, and undertake a rereading of the chapters and the execution of the tasks appended to each sequentially. Involve colleagues, and ensure that the partnership is committed to the programme outlined within this book. All readers need to understand the immediacy and reality of The New Competition and prepare to face up to it, and what may follow with the advent of ABS.

Ask yourself as you read: 'How will my firm face up to a hypothetical loss of 25–50 per cent of the high street bread-and-butter legal work?' It is worth recognising that this loss to the high street will not be equally shared among the firms occupying it. Analyse and record which firms you consider will lose least/most of this hypothetical figure, and determine where on that scale your own firm sits. How would you mitigate your own defined percentage loss and safeguard your firm? Explore this in the light of the information gleaned from the book during the initial read through.

While initially reading through the book, the reader should also review the accompanying CD-Rom and consider how best to make use of it.

2

Marketing and the legal profession

In this chapter we look at the role of marketing within the legal profession of England and Wales, both historically and currently. We will explain exactly what marketing is and, more importantly, what it is not.

We will relate marketing to strategic plan, business development, staff involvement, and promotion. We consider the winning of new business for the practice and, in recognition of the 'We have more than we can cope with now' syndrome, acknowledge that profitability is truthfully the key, whether it comes from new 'better quality' clients or via the introduction of new services to existing clients. We look at the traditional role of the fee earner and how it has changed, while proposing a skills and interests audit of all staff and partners.

> *So they go in strange paradox, decided only to be undecided, resolved to be irresolute, adamant for drift, solid for fluidity, or powerful to be impotent.*
> – Winston Churchill (on Baldwin's government)

Some weeks before we started drafting this book, I received a telephone call from a practice manager who was anxious that his partnership should take part in the consultancy programme that incorporated the research leading up to the book. He believed that we would both benefit from the association. 'The problem is, David, that the partners move with the speed of a glacier.' 'Tell them the melt is coming,' I suggested, 'because it is.'

The big problem is that many firms, in our experience, move at this speed, but as discussed in **Chapter 1**, The New Competition will change all that. So, it is to be hoped that Churchill's remarks will apply less and less to law firms today, because marketing really can help to overcome Churchill's 'strange paradox'.

What exactly is marketing?

In the library of the Chartered Institute of Marketing, there are, literally thousands of marketing books, the vast majority of which start with a definition.

Perhaps it is the need to define something that causes marketing to be so misunderstood that it can, without care, fall into disrepute. Nowhere is this more true than in the legal profession, which for years was unable to apply even the most obvious of marketing components – promotion. Today, or course, things have changed, although there is still a tendency to mistake marketing for 'promotion'.

However, it is important that every member of the partnership understands marketing, at least in outline, and that the marketing activity involves every member of staff. Therefore, it is important to start with a definition.

Philip Kotler's marketing 'bible', *Marketing Management: Analysis, Planning and Control* (Prentice Hall, 1999) has what is in effect a 16-page definition, concluding with 'the higher purpose of marketing'.

The Chartered Institute of Marketing (CIM) spent considerable time in the early 1990s arriving at a workable definition, which is:

> Marketing is the management process responsible for identifying, anticipating and satisfying customers' requirements profitably.

This definition was used by Matthew Moore in his excellent handbook *Marketing for Lawyers* (Law Society, 1997).

The long out of print *How to Market Legal Services* by Robert W. Denney (Van Nostrand Reinhold, 1984) defines marketing thus:

> Marketing of legal services is the effective execution of all the activities involved in profitably increasing the level of net business by serving the needs and wants of the clients.

The business guru, Peter F. Drucker, whose books *Managing for Results* (Butterworth-Heinemann, 1994) and *Management: Tasks, Responsibilities and Practices* (Butterworth-Heinemann, 1999) are constantly quoted in many of the CIM's library books, provides what is perhaps more of an opinion than a definition, but Drucker's opinion was always worth considering.

> Marketing is so basic that it cannot be considered a separate function . . . It is the whole business seen from the point of view of its final result, that is, from the customer's point of view.

Historically, this has been one of the legal profession's major problems. Lawyers spend far more time looking at the matter from a procedural point of view than at the results of their actions in terms of benefit to the client. To keep it short and sweet, we would propose the following definition:

> If it is not pure production or work or accounts – then it is marketing.

Perhaps, therefore, marketing is best seen not as a discrete discipline, but as a management philosophy, a new viewpoint of the business, an attitude or stance, and a series of management tasks.

The evolution of marketing

To help readers understand what is meant by the 'marketing management philosophy' we can look at the recent history of industry and commerce where, up until the late 1950s, the emphasis of management was on the production and sale of goods and services. What the customer actually wanted mattered not as much as how efficiently goods were produced and sold.

At the time of the industrial revolution, this 'production management philosophy' was perfectly apt. Products were being developed and the customer was seeking them out. While it was true that people would beat a path to your door if you made a better mousetrap, it was fairly soon recognised that you did have to tell people about that mousetrap. Nevertheless, for the most part, and most certainly in the legal profession, it was a seller's market.

However, with greater affluence, greater understanding by the consumer and ever-increasing competition, it became more evident that a manufacturer or provider of services had to explain to the potential customer why the benefits of its product were superior to those of its competitor. It could well be argued that by the mid-1920s, in Europe and America anyway, this philosophy had been fully adopted by all commercial entities and we had already entered the era of the 'sales management philosophy'. It became necessary to sell things and every promotional activity that we understand today has been employed in one form or another ever since. Only where there was monopoly was the need to sell and differentiate oneself absent.

The marketing management philosophy

Today, many legal firms are clearly aware of the 'sales management philosophy' in that they do, now that they are allowed to, promote themselves. However, few have truly adopted the 'marketing management philosophy'. With greater affluence and competition in the consumer world came understanding within commercial entities that the crucial element for success in a business was its ability to recognise and then respond to the needs or requirements of the potential buyer, the customer or client. 'The customer is king' became the byword, embodying as it does the idea that the customer is free to choose what he or she buys, and from where. Therefore, he who presumes to supply the customer with goods or services must clearly understand what the customer actually requires or needs, and how these needs may be satisfied by the purchase of those goods or services on offer.

In short, commercial organisations learned to define and present the benefits they offered to their potential customers, and how to differentiate their company, products and services.

Companies who did not recognise the change in the market and the growing power of the customer, or who failed to adapt accordingly, fell into difficulties or fell by the wayside. Caveat emptor may remain enshrined as a legal principle, but commercially, caveat vendor became and remains a more appropriate maxim. It is this recognition of the importance of determining and ultimately satisfying the needs of the customer or clients that may be said to define the marketing management philosophy.

If we look at the recent history of the legal profession, we find that it is the last to come to terms with how to accept this philosophy. For the most part this is due to the peculiar and 'artificial' market in which legal services have historically been supplied. Until comparatively recently, firms were not allowed to advertise and competition was restricted to within the profession. In other words, legal services were not supplied in a free market.

Realistically, and with the possible exception of some publicly funded litigation matters, this has not been the case for some years. Authorised probate practitioners, licensed conveyancers, mediators and the conciliatory approach, arbitration, no win no fee arrangements, the reduction in value of publicly funded work and high profile compensation claim processing companies have all in their turn been heralded as likely to inflict enormous damage on the traditional high street practice. But they are as nought when compared with The New Competition.

Without doubt, solicitors will need to become more proactive, and perhaps more aggressive, in their approach. To understand and adopt the marketing management philosophy is the first stage.

Marketing and the legal profession

In his introduction to *Marketing for Lawyers*, Matthew Moore quoted the American marketing academic, Theodore Levitt. Levitt introduced the concept of 'marketing myopia' in which he proposed that dead and dying industries fell into a downward spiral through failure to comprehend that they were part of a wider scene. This in turn produced a misunderstanding of the customer's requirements. He famously cited American railroads and movies. The railroad companies got into massive difficulties because of their failure to recognise that they were in the transport business, not the railroad business, and took knocks from both the enormous increase in private car ownership, and the development of low-cost airlines. Similarly, Hollywood insisted that it was in the film industry, and not part of the wider entertainment world – its response to television, for example, being far too little too late.

Interestingly, through the adoption of the marketing management philosophy, both were able to reverse their fortunes: the railroads went into part-ownership of airlines and holiday companies; the film industry benefited from the development of television production companies, the huge market for videos/DVDs, merchandising and theme parks.

We have seen, in the past 15 years, an enormous change in the legal profession, much of it as a consequence of deliberate government policy. Initially, the market for legal services was well defined within its traditional, 'accepted' boundaries. Legal firms were strictly controlled in their ability to communicate with their clients and in their means of competing with others.

As a consequence, firms had little opportunity (or even need) to influence their own destinies. Both lawyers and potential clients knew what solicitors did, when they needed to be instructed and under what circumstances. Most firms did not find it necessary to seek business beyond the usual Rotary Club social connections and, indeed, were positively constrained from doing so by the Law Society rules.

Almost overnight the entire situation changed. Deregulation of the traditional bread-and-butter residential conveyancing market, initially by allowing non-solicitors to practise as licensed conveyancers, and subsequently by extending that right to powerful financial institutions, radically changed the market and the 'base price' obtainable.

Most recently, we have seen the publication of the Clementi report and the Legal Services Act 2007. As the impetus for government change has been the desire for greater consumer choice the subsequent changes within the profession will, in our opinion, have a greater and more far-reaching effect than anything that collectively has come before. Unfortunately, at times of change, there is usually a period of uncertainty – witness the recent confusion over the ill-fated HIPs. Uncertainty provides the perfect reason for inactivity, based upon a 'wait-and-see' attitude.

This book is dedicated to the belief that there is no longer time to wait and see; firms that wish to survive and grow in the new environment must begin to take action now.

From now on, previously clearly defined boundaries between the services offered by the solicitor, the accountant and the insurance broker are being dissolved. No longer is it clear, either to members of the profession themselves, or to the larger part of their market, the public at large, who is able to give best advice, to coin a phrase, about what.

The days of the traditional family solicitor or even longer established 'man of affairs' are gone; the market is becoming more sophisticated and is daily being educated through the media and specifically the larger financial institutions on the availability of alternative choices. The New Competition can only accelerate these present trends where demarcation lines between the professions are less obvious, and where it will become increasingly less necessary to engage the services of a solicitor to carry out, for example, residential conveyancing. There are already many areas of conventional legal practice that the public are encouraged to believe they can handle themselves, through books such as Fenton Bresler, *Law without a Lawyer* (Century, 2000) and 'legal packs' available from most stationers.

Again, The New Competition will promote this attitude, together with the benefits of their services, to the detriment of both the standing of solicitors and their ability to charge fees. It is already evident that at the lower end of the spectrum of services offered by the profession both prices and margins are being squeezed by competition, further deregulation and (specifically in the case of legal aid) by government intent.

Perhaps the most attractive end of the spectrum is the higher end, i.e. those areas where high levels of skill and specialist expertise are required, and paid for. But even here there will be some form of new competition as solicitors in general, reacting to the pressure from The New Competition, will seek out new markets for firms in areas that they have not traditionally targeted.

Litigation and other work involved in the administration of justice (i.e. the courts) will clearly remain the sole province of the traditional legal profession, but as already noted, the profitability in these areas is questionable except for the specialist firms (e.g. legal aid franchise holders, etc.). Barristers' chambers can already advise the public directly in some limited areas, a trend that we anticipate will continue to grow.

On the non-litigation side, it is evident that your firm will have to work harder for the private client work, obtaining it in the first place, maintaining the profit levels and retaining the client subsequently. This will require greater emphasis on the benefits of using your firm: you need to recognise that the majority of the public do not understand what it is lawyers do, and therefore will inevitably, unless corrected, go for the cheapest price. By contrast, corporate or industrial clients will assume a greater importance as clients that require the most sophisticated and specialist services (although, as noted above, these too may come under competitive pressure).

However, change inevitably brings opportunity! The firms that succeed will, in the future, be the ones that keep a detailed eye on change and react swiftly to it. Beyond all else, practices will have to become outward looking and consider the needs of their clients before the demands of 'production'. This goes far beyond providing best advice or putting the client's interest first. It is largely to do with the proactive recognition of customer demands and needs, and an improvement of communications between client and solicitor. In short, we see a future full of opportunity for the marketing-orientated firm but a future in which competition will be fierce. Being a solicitor or a firm of solicitors will no longer be a guarantee of security or success. The latter will accrue to those firms that are able to identify what the market requires and then 'deliver the goods'. It is this, precisely, that marketing is about.

Inevitably, there has been and will continue to be restructuring of the profession. The smaller firms have been under threat for some time and only the most sophisticated have survived profitably. There have been larger numbers of mergers and takeovers, and regrettably, some failures, even of established practices. This process will continue – even merger is unlikely to be the complete answer.

To survive and prosper, these smaller and merged firms will need to be able to target their market segments and focus their resources on the provision of services for those segments. Conversely, larger broad-based firms, provided they use the advantages of size appropriately and manage themselves efficiently, are well placed to face the future challenges.

It is important to end this section by re-emphasising that nothing said in this book, or relating to any part of the marketing proposals, should be considered as a lack of recognition that professional standards and quality of work are paramount. Although it may seem a reactive statement, legal firms are, and have to be, client driven.

However, the partners of a legal firm must recognise the necessity to stand aside from the production of work, and allow time to consider the firm's strategy, its goals, practice development and increased profitability. It is this that marketing is all about. It is true that 'if it isn't pure production or accounts – it is marketing'!

The traditional role of the fee earner

The basic role of the fee earner has changed little from the days of the family solicitor or the 'man of affairs'. Perhaps there is a little more emphasis on the gaining and retention of clients but primarily the role is to produce high quality legal work in a timely manner.

Unfortunately, this skill alone is no longer sufficient for a successful legal practice. Indeed, it could be argued that this skill, on its own, can be detrimental. It is the solicitor who continues to look primarily at the matter, rather than at the client, who has led to the creation of 'dead files' rather than client databases.

We will consider databases in detail in **Chapter 6**, but suffice it here to say that the majority of firms with which we have dealt in the past do not truly have a database, and even their mailing list is frequently corrupted by incomplete or inaccurate information. Files show the address from which the client moved, not the one you moved them into. Salutations including 'Mrs Jones – Deceased' or 'Mr John Smith Esq' are not apocryphal. They stem, at least in part, from the fee earner's traditional role.

Because the fee earner's traditional role has always been defined by matter type, he/she seldom considered the other needs of the client and therefore rarely recommended any other services provided by the firm, unless prompted to do so, often by the client. In short, cross-selling was not the concern of the fee earner, production of legal work was. The future of the firm did not matter, the completion of 'the matter' did.

In many ways this attitude is unsurprising. Fee earners are trained to produce legal work. They are usually measured, and frequently rewarded, by their billing. Their future career depends on the growth and development of the firm and increasing profit retentions, although these are matters that are left to the partners and seldom discussed by the partners with fee earners. Many partners are, of course, fee earners, and at least some will fall into the category of traditional fee earner.

Of course, not everyone can take responsibility for the business strategy, the marketing and development of a firm, or its promotion, but in the first of our practical tasks in this book we will ask you to consider what skills and interests each member of your fee earning staff actually has (see the end of this chapter).

We also need to look at the partnership. In due course, we will strongly recommend that the partnership should appoint a marketing partner to take responsibility for the marketing management function within the practice. We will go into more detail about the role of the marketing partner later, but we would recommend that all partners are included in the skills audit, while considering who will fill the role of marketing partner (assuming that the firm has not already appointed one).

To conclude this chapter, before the task below, you might like to consider our irreverent descriptions of the type of partners we have met over the past 20 years:

- The dedicated lawyer who genuinely believes that it is only essential to do good quality legal work for the firm to survive and prosper.
- The 'anti-marketing' partner who believes that undertaking marketing, or even in some cases promotional activities, is unnecessary and possibly unethical ('We are not in trade, and work will come to us as it always has').
- The 'anxious but insecure partner' who believes that something should be done in the field of marketing but does not know what. Almost always confuses marketing with promotion.
- The 'salesman solicitor' – they may not be a partner, but are good at promotion. The danger is to define what percentage of his time (and this type usually is a 'he') is spent on promoting himself and how much on promoting the firm. It is also worth recognising that often this type of fee earner has much lower billing than other staff. This may be acceptable if part of his job description is 'selling the firm' and may be necessary as this type is often the least good at the production of legal work. They can be very valuable but need management. The role in this case is promoting the firm and gaining new work for others to execute.

- The 'modern' solicitor – this term probably best describes the emerging solicitor of today, who is certainly the type that should be sought out by your practice. He or she completely understands that there are three essential ingredients for success in the current practice of law:
  - professional ability;
  - management skills;
  - marketing understanding and application.

The skills and interests audit

Marketing manuals frequently start by looking outside the firm at its environment through market research, client analysis, and a study of competitive activity and communications analysis. All these are important and will be covered later in this book. However, in preparation for your marketing activity, it is necessary to look first inside the firm.

As already noted, we will be recommending that you appoint a marketing partner to oversee the marketing management function. This must be a person in the organisation who can genuinely and willingly assist with promotion and who has an interest in, understanding of, or is prepared to develop an understanding of marketing. A formal skills and interests audit will assist in this and in developing your own 'informal' observation. An example form is included at the end of this chapter, and on the accompanying CD-Rom.

There can be few areas of endeavour that can be called more 'people-based' than the legal profession. If the marketing management philosophy is truly adopted, then the firm will become more focused on the client rather than production of work and will begin to view itself and its activities from the perspective of that most important group of people – its clients. But the firm is also people. The firm's greatest asset is its partners, fee earners and support staff.

Too often in researching this book, we have found that support staff feel they are not considered or involved and, as a result, a deep well of experience, resources and goodwill is left untapped. Similarly, fee earners are, understandably, measured primarily if not exclusively by the quality of their work and the value of their billing. However, like the partners, all members of the firm, be they fee earners or support staff, have a potential to influence the marketing of the firm via the impression of it they create and the way they represent the firm to clients and also friends, relations and associates.

The audit will highlight those most suited to participating in the marketing activity, and may, if it is not already obvious, assist in the selection of the marketing partner. However, the audit is also important for those who are not selected or suited to managing or participating in the marketing activity, in that it will help everyone to understand what the marketing function is. In many ways this is a perfect example of how marketing influences all aspects of a practice. The skills and interests audit is primarily seeking information to assist the marketing function, but the results will obviously have relevance to practice development and personnel issues.

The professional side of the audit is also extremely useful. When skills are laid out on a chart, gaps and overlaps (many of which may have already been suspected) quickly reveal themselves. So do the obvious opportunities for product packaging and cross-selling. These subjects are dealt with more fully later in the book.

Including address and family details that are undoubtedly held already in personnel may seem pointless, but where the person lives is more than just the address. For example, people living one side of the city are less likely to be involved in activities on the other side. People with no children are hardly relevant to the local parent–teacher association, and someone with a low golfing handicap is unlikely to give that up to join a tennis club.

The questions about preferred types of client are also revealing, and as with every other section of the audit, there is no right or wrong answer. Some people are better suited to dealing with an undemanding client, while there are many lawyers who enjoy the cut and thrust of a challenging client. The question about prospects, almost on its own, will indicate which people are thinking about obtaining new clients for the firm and which are not. Again, this is not a criticism. People with no prospective clients may never have given the matter any thought, or have been trained, managed or encouraged to do so. The questions relating to promotional or marketing activity that is currently being undertaken by individuals is often another eye opener. Frequently, there is more promotional activity going on in the firm than is generally realised. Unfortunately, this also indicates that it is uncoordinated, and perhaps even haphazard in nature. It is, nevertheless, a starting point.

There are other revelations to come, for example, a lengthy and enthusiastically filled out form will illustrate an energy and a concern about the firm's future. Conversely, a form with many blanks may well illustrate someone who would prefer to do their day's work and go home. Not everyone is suited to marketing.

It is ideal to get as many forms completed as possible and the most effective way of doing this is a personal interview with each member of staff. However, this may be overly time consuming. On the other hand, if this interview is conducted after the forms have been completed, and is based on them, it need not occupy more than a few minutes for each interviewee. Once the forms have been completed you will have an interesting and increased knowledge of the attributes hiding within the organisation. We have already touched on how this information can be used, and the subject will be enlarged upon greatly throughout the book. However, as an anecdotal illustration, a skills audit of this type produced the unrecognised information for one firm that one of its conveyancers was, at that time, the British Archery Champion. Although his name was known only to a few people in his home town, it was known to a specific market niche (the archery world) nationally. A very successful personalised promotional campaign resulted in a considerable increase in conveyancing business, and new clients.

Keeping staff informed

Because your people are important to the firm and because you will be requiring assistance from them, it is absolutely vital to keep every member of your staff involved and informed at each stage. Therefore, before the skills audit form is distributed (ideally, a couple of weeks before), a memo should be circulated to all staff to inform them of the reasoning behind it. It is important that your staff does not find the questions intrusive and that they maintain control over the information given. It is for this reason that we have included the introductory paragraph on the skills and audit form.

CHAPTER 2 TASKS **Perform a skills audit**

Quite clearly you are capable of writing your own memos, and will undoubtedly prefer to use your own words. However, for illustrative purposes, and for your adaptation, a draft informative note and memo are reproduced below together with the skills and audit form. This material is also on the CD-Rom.

Skills and interests audit

Draft informative note for staff

The partners are currently involved in planning the firm's strategic development and growth over the next few years in the light of the Clementi and Carter reviews.

It is a policy decision to involve all staff in this planning process and you will in due course be asked to complete a questionnaire that will be discussed with you individually.

The value of this exercise should not be underestimated. The results, once analysed, will be published, along with the strategic decisions that have been made as a result of the findings.

It is very important that no one should view this exercise with doubt or suspicion. It is, and is intended to be, both positive and forward looking as well as a prelude to a period of growth. You will be kept informed at each stage, and it is part of our stated objective to improve the security, working conditions and future of all employees. If you have any queries relating to this letter, or to the form that will be distributed within a week or two, please do not hesitate to ask me personally.

Staff memo to go with audit form

Dear

Further to the memo referring to the firm's strategic planning programme, I have pleasure in attaching the skills audit form referred to in that memo.

There are no right or wrong answers. Please take only 10–15 minutes to fill in the form. Brief answers are perfectly acceptable.

Skills and interests audit form

Please note this is a voluntary exercise. Your help would be greatly appreciated. However, do feel free to leave blanks on the form if you feel that the question is not appropriate.

Name:

Job title: Department:

Specialist area of law (if fee earner):

Specialist area of work (if support staff):

Home address and postcode

Spouse's name: Spouse's occupation:

Children's names and ages:

Have you any other work or previous employment experience whether in the legal profession or not?

Are you involved in any other work or professional activities, e.g. boards, committees, directorships, trusts or council's activities?

Trade association memberships:

Club memberships (theatrical, chess, reading circle, etc.):

Sports club memberships:

Charitable/community/civic activities:

Spouse's memberships and activities:

Other interests and hobbies:

Spouse's interests and hobbies:

Favourite clients by name, by type:

Key prospects:

Personal strengths:

Ambitions:

Please return this form to [*name of partner*] by [*date*]. Thank you.

Information provided in this form is held on an informal basis and will form no part of your employment record or be used in any way as an appraisal.

Analysing the skills and interests audit form

The first analysis to be undertaken is the number of forms returned, and why those that weren't returned were not. While it is not intended that this audit should form part of a performance appraisal, it does provide an interesting insight into the attitude towards the job, particularly if the submission, or more importantly non-submission, of the audit form is discussed in a face-to-face interview.

Review of the department in which people think they work, particularly in the case of support staff, can be very illuminating. Similarly, specialist areas of work or law can lead to discussion relating to aspirations.

As noted above, the home address and postcode may seem irrelevant, until they are pinned out on a map. The geographical spread of staff can lead to considerations relating to activity within a particular area.

Similarly, knowledge relating to the spouse's occupation may lead to promotional thoughts, and the children's names and ages will provide a talking point for the interview, and perhaps illustrate how much non-working time an individual member of the firm may have available. Questions related to previous work experience and other professional activities are geared to provide a list of organisations or companies with which at least one member of the firm has a direct contact.

Trade associations can, through membership, often be turned into professional contacts that can, with the right persuasion, provide recommendations to potential clients. Similar comments apply to club membership and associations with sporting activities. Charitable, community and civic activities are perhaps some of the strongest contacts within the community that the firm seeks to serve.

Although it needs to be handled delicately, the interests, activities and memberships of a staff member's spouse can also lead to contacts within the community.

The answers to questions relating to favourite clients by name and type and key prospects will illustrate what level of new business activity can be expected from this member of staff, and finally, comments under personal strengths and ambitions are not only important, but are quite often the first occasion on which a member of staff has been asked such things since their recruitment interview.

The statement on the bottom of the form, 'Information provided in this form is held on an informal basis and will form no part of your employment record or be used in any way as an appraisal' must, of course, be a true statement. On this occasion you are seeking help from your staff, and perhaps an opportunity to motivate them. You are not seeking another tool to manage or monitor them.

If there is any doubt about this, that final paragraph should be excluded from your form.

Register of skills

Following the skills audit, some firms have found it useful to produce a 'register of skills' indicating which fee earner specialises in which activity and on some occasions in which specialist niche market or area, for internal use, to encourage cross-selling. In due course, this can, once refined, be useful for external communications.

The selection of a marketing partner

Many firms may already have a marketing partner. If this is the case, it is important to define the role, and ensure that the partnership does not consider the marketing partner's role to be solely concerned with promotion. Other firms have a marketing committee where roles and tasks need to be assigned equally across the members and coordinated by an individual so the committee acts together.

Whether there is an existing incumbent, or this is a new appointment, the partnership needs to consider the following:

- Who is most/least suitable for this role?
- Does any one member of the partnership stand out as an obvious candidate?
- Is he/she an equity or salaried partner?
- If a salaried partner, will they be given the authority?
- Number of years with the firm?
- Number of years as a partner?
- Department head responsibilities?
- Other existing partnership responsibilities?
- Experience in marketing?
- Training in marketing?
- Perceived marketing training needs?
- Current involvement in the firm's marketing planning?
- Why is this candidate particularly appropriate for marketing management?
- How well can the marketing management be integrated into the overall management of the firm?
- What outside assistance (consultants, agencies, etc.) will be required?
- What is the marketing budget?
- Is there any suitable person who really would like to do this job?

As a result of this chapter, you and the partnership should resolve to understand more about the discipline of marketing (in its true sense) and adopt the marketing management philosophy.

The partnership should appoint a marketing partner with management responsibility and a willingness to learn more about the discipline.

The marketing partner should employ marketing skills throughout the firm and, if necessary, seek temporary or permanent outside help to do so.

The firm should undertake a skills and interests audit of all partners and staff.

The groundwork has now been set to enable the firm to move forward in its overall marketing development plan.

3

Reviewing your firm's current position

It is important that everyone within your organisation has an understanding of marketing and, ideally, enthusiasm for it. Therefore, those actually charged with managing the marketing function need to begin to explain to other members of the firm what marketing really is.

In this chapter, we demonstrate why marketing is needed; why it is needed by your firm; how the management of the marketing function works and fits in with other management tasks. Then we begin reviewing the firm's actual position via a simple sales analysis, an initial profit analysis, a review of technology, a simple client analysis, initial market information and how this can be used to face up to The New Competition.

Most problems do not get solved. They get superseded by other concerns. – Thomas Sowell, Economist

Perhaps the greatest concern for any practice faced with The New Competition is the organisation and implementation of the marketing management within the firm.

Maybe, in the light of **Chapter 2**, the partnership has already appointed a marketing partner or is considering doing so. However, it is really important that everyone within the partnership and, indeed, within the firm understands, and is ideally enthusiastic about, marketing. While everyone throughout the firm has their part to play in the marketing effort, it is unlikely they will be involved in the management of the function. Indeed, it would be uneconomic and probably unhelpful if they were. However, it is vital that everyone has full knowledge of what is being undertaken and that those actually charged with activity under the marketing function have the full support of their colleagues.

In this chapter, and to help with that understanding, we discuss why marketing is needed, why it is needed especially now, and why it is needed within your firm.

The individual discussion following the analysis of the skills and interests audit proposed in **Chapter 2** provides an ideal opportunity to ensure that every member of staff is fully conversant with the principles of marketing, their place in the overall marketing scheme, and why it is important to their own future, as well as that of the firm.

We will then propose a brief review of your firm that covers the current management structure, the organisation and administration of the firm, your use of technology, your budgets and budgetary control and the current understanding and management of the marketing function.

There are many books on the subject of market research and analysis, including the excellent manual by Lucy Adam, *Marketing Your Law Firm: A Solicitor's Manual* (Law Society, 2002). This, among other things, provides a detailed guide to an in-depth approach to collating marketing information.

However, with The New Competition, time is now pressing. Many firms will already have undertaken market research, client and matter type analysis and possibly a profitability study. Even those who have not will probably have an intrinsic understanding of their firm's current situation, and that may well be sufficient for our immediate purposes.

What we seek to do in this chapter is discuss how sales and client analysis can benefit your business, and how to go about it. We will show you how to collect and collate the necessary information and provide a format that will enable you to do it quickly, the analysis of which should provide an 'overview' of your firm's current position.

Why marketing is needed

The quotation at the beginning of this chapter could as well have been written by a perceptive lawyer as by an economist. In recent years, changes and perceived threats to the stability of an independent legal profession have appeared, only to be superseded by new concerns.

Deregulation, the Solicitors' Code of Conduct 2007, Rule 2 (previously Solicitors' Practice Rule 15), legal aid franchises, licensed conveyancers, will writing bureaux, compensation claim 'factories', financial institution-owned estate agencies, divorce by consent, increased small claims court thresholds, etc: these and other factors have arrived, been dealt with, and/or superseded. The legal profession may be a slightly different 'shape' but it is still there and it is still powerful. The profession has, by and large, successfully overcome these issues.

But is there a danger of complacency with the acknowledgement of this fact? Or is the Legal Services Act 2007 recognised at last for what it really is – a market changer? Market changes happen every so often, and things are never the same again.

An example already used in **Chapter 2** is Theodore Levitt's review of the American railroads and movie industry. What the legal profession cannot afford to be now is myopic. The changes to the market for legal services are, and will continue to be, as profound as anything faced by the railroads and the movie industry.

More recent market changes are the out-of-town shopping mall, the development of hypermarkets, Direct Line insurance (a major influence on the high street insurance broker) and eBay (a direct attack on the small ads section of local newspapers). The changes triggered by Sir David Clementi are as dramatic in your own, smaller world. Never before has the discipline of marketing (in its true sense) been needed more urgently by the profession. The marketing discipline and its management is the route by which to face up to The New Competition.

Any standard marketing textbook will tell you that marketing is needed because of the following:

- increased competition;
- the need to identify clients;
- the need to segment clients;
- establishing the nature of the 'product';
- to make the client more aware of benefits;
- the need to make a profit.

Increased competition

Competition doesn't come only from The New Competition referred to above. Your traditional competitors – other solicitors – will be aware of the imminent changes and the need to take action. Indeed, some already have by joining forces with like-minded firms in groups such as Quality Solicitors and Lawnet. This is one response but not the only one open to forward-thinking practices. Those firms that do not take action for themselves, through marketing, will be left behind by the firms that do. You may have already begun to notice this.

This applies also to the existing 'non-solicitor' competition. Halifax, the AA, the Co-op and the many other non-traditional providers of legal services are not going to stand by and see their hard-won market taken over by, for example, Tesco or Virgin Legal. They will increase their activity to defend their position at the same time as The New Competition enters, or increase their activity within the market with innovative approaches, having the financial and (especially) the marketing clout to do so. This is the threat that the legal profession faces and it is not going to go away.

Most of The New Competition businesses are service-based organisations where the move into domestic and small business legal services is a natural extension of their current activity. The services tie in accurately with their customers' needs, and will improve the customers' view of their brand's usefulness. It must be remembered that from a customer's point of view, accepting a new service from a trusted brand presents an easy option compared with finding a solicitor. And people will most often take the first and easiest option to solve a problem.

The New Competition is truly a market changer, and it is why marketing must become the predominant feature of your firm's management.

The need to identify clients

The days when clients loyally returned whenever they had a legal need are long gone. You have an absolute requirement to identify your clients so that you can communicate with them, predict their likely needs, serve them better, try to engender some form of loyalty, even if it is only through client satisfaction, and actively seek recommendation from these satisfied clients.

Identification of your clients' needs will enable you to ensure you have the production resources within the firm to meet the current and future demands of your clients. You also need to understand the client's chosen method of delivery of your services, and the delivery method used by your competitors. It is a very simple change, but one that seems so profound to many in the profession as to produce scepticism. The change is simply explaining to a client that they have a need for which you can supply a solution, rather than telling them about a service you could produce if they ever wanted it.

The need to segment clients

Market segmentation is extremely important. We cannot talk to all our clients individually all the time, and must therefore devise methods of speaking to smaller groups with similar interests in one go. Market segmentation allows for this. It also provides an opportunity to promote a specific range of services for which we have a resource available with the intent of increasing volume of production of that service to maximise the usage of the production resource we have. A specifically targeted campaign, rather than general promotion can assist with this. We deal with market segmentation in more detail in **Chapters 4** and 7.

Of course, a refinement of segmentation is the development of a market niche, which will become increasingly important, because it is an area that will be difficult for The New Competition to service. Niche marketing is also discussed in **Chapters 4** and 7.

Establishing the nature of the 'product'

People do not buy 'products'. They buy the benefits they perceive they will enjoy from the tangible product, and even more so from an intangible service. This is so obviously the case in the legal profession, but the analysis and the presentation of benefits are poorly understood. We return to this topic in **Chapter 7**. However, it is never too early to learn the vital lesson that your clients buy the benefits of the service you provide, not the features or procedures of it – to make clients more aware of benefits. In many ways this is the prime reason for marketing. It is without doubt the raison d'être of all promotional activity, needs to be understood by every member of staff who comes into contact with clients or prospects and should be the guiding light of all activity. All activity! Imagine how your firm would prosper if every member of staff were to ask themselves, regularly, this question: 'What benefit does the client/prospective client gain from the action I am about to take?'

To make the client more aware of benefits

A considerable part of this book is concerned with the definition and presentation of the benefits that a client or prospect will derive from using your firm. Notably, **Chapters 5** and **7** refer to the differences between features (of a product or service) and the benefits to be gained by the client. It is a fundamental part of marketing to encourage partners, fee earners and support staff to think not only about features – what the service is, how it is produced – but essentially in terms of benefits: what is it that the client gains from purchasing this service from us? Indeed, why should they pay us at all?

The need to make a profit

This goes without saying! Hopefully!

Overcoming hostility to marketing

In *Marketing Management: Analysis, Planning and Control* (1999) Philip Kotler acknowledges that there is some hostility in many areas to the whole concept of marketing, even suggesting at one point that it is an old-fashioned discipline that perhaps needs renaming. In consultancy, we have for a long time 'pussyfooted around' words such as marketing and, even more, selling. But the gloves are off. The New Competition understands and uses these business disciplines and those words, and therefore so must you.

Although it is increasingly less prevalent today, we have for years in consultancy come across comments from the more sceptical partners that boil down to: 'We don't need marketing' (although they need promotion, usually) 'because we have enough work already.'

Kotler proposes that this hostility, or scepticism, can be repudiated with the following arguments:

- The assets of the firm have little value without the existence of clients.
- The key task of the firm is therefore to create and hold on to 'customers'.

- Customers are attracted through promises and held through satisfaction.
- Marketing's task is to define an appropriate promise to the customer and to ensure the delivery of satisfaction.
- The actual satisfaction delivered to the customer is affected by the performance of other departments.
- Marketing must have influence over and understanding by these other departments if customers are to be satisfied.

The assets of the firm have little value without the existence of clients

And the assets of a legal practice are what? Skill, training, and experience – we could go on and into great detail (which we will when we analyse benefits) but this will suffice as an illustration. The assets of the firm are not its premises, which are probably owned by a section of the partnership anyway, its computer system, furniture or, especially, its history and goodwill. The assets of the firm, as understood by a client, are only the skills of the people to solve their legal problems.

In fact, in the case of a legal firm, assets have no value at all without the existence of clients, and clients, your clients, are under threat from The New Competition – marketing can help.

The key task of the firm is therefore to create and to hold on to customers

'Customers!' Along with marketing and selling, this is a word that you should be considering internally. Not externally as it will confuse the client, but within the firm so that the true position of the client is understood, by every member of the firm. Without the customer there is no firm. Without the firm there is no job. Without the job there is . . . well, it's obvious. Marketing can help here.

'Customers' are attracted through promises and held through satisfaction

Make no mistake about it, The New Competition will be holding out very attractive promises to your clients. They will not be confined by tradition and professional conduct rules in what they say. They will make direct comparisons with the alternative. The alternative is you.

But 'customers' are held through satisfaction and here The New Competition may have a disadvantage. Marketing can help you survive the comparison and capitalise on another's disadvantages.

Marketing's task is to define an appropriate promise to the customer and to ensure the delivery of satisfaction

People buy benefits. Once we have analysed the benefits (see **Chapter 5**) we can begin presenting them (see **Chapter 7**) to our clients, our prospects and our professional recommenders. But first, we have to ensure that every member of the firm fully understands and appreciates what the benefits are and that they are real benefits to the client.

The marketing discipline will have no problem in defining the appropriate promise, but will need management authority to ensure the delivery of satisfaction.

The actual satisfaction delivered to the customer is affected by the performance of other departments

It is marketing's job to be 'the Man from Mars' – to view the firm as if for the first time. Every aspect of the firm matters: your telephone system (You might be the best lawyer in the world, but I don't want to hear Vivaldi on the telephone); your support staff (I may trust you but I am damned if I'll face up to that haughty receptionist again); your facilities (Why can I never park my car/why are the spaces filled by the partnership?); and your style (I'm happy with the job, but do I need a bill that is expressed so haughtily and so dismissively?). There are so many areas like this. What else applies to your firm?

Marketing must have influence over and understanding by these other departments if customers are to be satisfied

In essence, this book has a very simple message. If marketing is really understood, it will be seen, automatically, as the most important management discipline, and the only way to face up to The New Competition. If that is accepted, the marketing authority over other departments to ensure customer satisfaction is guaranteed.

It is not too early in this book to say, once again, that the most successful firms we have worked with or researched this book with have been run by fairly autocratic managing partners. Without exception, in our experience, they have a marketing bias.

The day-to-day running of the marketing function may well be delegated to another partner, but the senior management of the firm must understand, adopt, implement and fully support the marketing philosophy to compete with The New Competition. And then, marketing can help.

The American view, from Mr Denney, is far more direct (*How to Market Legal Services*). Denney believes that marketing's chief objective is growth of the firm, and counters anyone who says 'We are already too busy and can't handle the work we have got, so why should we spend time and money planning for more growth?' with the following fundamental needs for growth:

- To survive
- To develop
- To keep up with inflation
- To provide resources for development
- To be able to service more clients
- To increase
- To provide security
- To provide room and opportunity
- To replace clients
- To enable the firm to continually upgrade its client list
- To provide continuing professional challenges
- To enable the firm to direct and control its future
- To provide an appealing environment

To survive

Peter Drucker has a well-developed theory that the first objective of any business entity is survival. Periods of growth have a way of stopping almost as quickly and mysteriously as they started; then a firm is left with a lot of problems and expenses that actually threaten its ability to survive and to continue in business. The financial crisis and subsequent recession from 2008 onwards proves this.

Nowhere is this more apposite than in a highly competitive environment or one in which competition is increasing. As with each of these headings, marketing is the key to growth, but in this case it is also the key to survival.

To develop

A firm needs to develop the ability to handle larger and more complex matters, which are usually more profitable. Again, if there is a diminishing of the traditional private client market because of The New Competition, and estimates put it as high as a 50 per cent loss of turnover, legal firms will need to be able to develop and handle 'better' matters.

To keep up with inflation

It is extremely unlikely that the costs of staying in business will do anything but continually rise. This is why, among many other reasons, the firm needs to plan for growth.

To provide resources for development

Resources are needed to develop new services, new areas of law which the firm will require in order to keep up with the changes in the profession, and the changing needs of its clients.

To be able to service more clients

This broadens the client base and lessens the dependence on a few historic clients. Once again, this is particularly relevant when historic clients are under threat. Volume may not be the only key (having fewer clients but with more profit per client is just as acceptable), but the ability to handle new clients and new client needs is an imperative.

To increase

Few will argue that growth is needed to increase, for example, the partners' income.

To provide security

Security for retired partners, and for existing, past and future staff is also important. If the profession is to go through a hiatus, it is likely that the best professionals will be looking for the most secure and rewarding positions. Firms need to retain their best staff, and not just end up with those that no one else wants. Marketing can help with this.

To provide room and opportunity

This is required for the younger lawyers in the firm. These people are the future of the firm. They will leave if the picture becomes static and there is little opportunity to move up in your firm. They are also most likely to be closest to the real problems faced by the firm as a result of The New Competition and to be target recruitments of The New Competition. You must provide quality opportunity.

To replace clients

Clients who have been lost to The New Competition will need to be replaced – as will clients who have been lost by attrition; clients who have outgrown the firm; and clients you no longer want to deal with. When reviewing legal practices' marketing plans, we frequently see an objective that states: 'Get rid of dross work'. Dross work is seldom defined. We would define it as clients you do not wish to deal with – for whatever reason.

To enable the firm to continually upgrade its client list

Any firm that is static, or even shrinking, is naturally hesitant to subtract less desirable clients from its client list. While this is clearly the opposite side of the attracting new clients coin, it is just as important. It is dross work again, by another name; it is unprofitable work, almost certainly. It should be removed from the client list. But it will need replacing – which is where marketing can help.

To provide continuing professional challenges

The professional challenge, together with greater recognition for their improving level of work, is partly what people go to work for, i.e. 'the ego factor'. But, it is also relevant to the firm's future. If the firm is to lose up to 50 per cent of its historic private client billing, it will have to seek more interesting work. This in turn will offer the continuing professional challenges that growth demands and provides.

To enable the firm to direct and control its future

Marketing can help to enable the firm to direct and control its future – or, to be fair in a constantly changing environment – to control as much of it as is possible to do.

To provide an appealing environment

A firm that has a stated growth policy is an appealing environment to a new recruit, especially at a time when The New Competition will inevitably be forcing the contraction of some firms. New recruits tend to be attracted to a growth environment and this ensures that the best applicants choose you. Never forget that recruitment is partly a sales job. You must sell your firm to the best applicant as much as he/she needs to sell themselves to you.

And finally, plan for growth because the competition is doing it: The New Competition; the old traditional competition; the non-professional existing competition – all are doing it. You must do it too . . . and marketing can help.

Understanding the management of the marketing function

To go forward with this book, we must now assume that your firm has appointed a marketing partner who is strong enough to establish marketing as a central management discipline of your firm and will take responsibility for the strategic planning and management tasks involved.

In its simplest form, there are three areas of management in any enterprise:

(a) production management;
(b) resource management (time, money, people); and
(c) marketing management.

It is likely that the senior or managing partner will coordinate the management of all three areas. In fact, this is a task that will be assisted by the marketing partner, who must, by definition, have an influence over the areas of both production management and resource management.

Production management

The influence that marketing must exert over production is considerable. The marketing analyses will indicate the 'products' that are profitable, those that are not, those that should be developed, those that are prime products and, in the final analysis, those that should be dropped.

Marketing, when properly applied, will also indicate what products should be packaged together to provide a group of services for a specific market segment (i.e. the older client, or the 'owner/driver' businessman) and will also have a major influence over how products are presented.

In many ways, this is one of the most difficult aspects of marketing to grasp. The legal profession has always produced and provided a quality range of legal services. Why therefore should it be packaged and presented differently now? The answer is that the marketplace has moved on and it is essential for the provider of any services, or indeed products, to talk to their potential or existing marketplace in a language that they, the customers/clients, understand. Without doubt, this is what The New Competition will do and so will the successful private practices.

This is why the selection and support of the marketing partner is so important. You need, with trust and understanding, to allow the production manager (or managers – most partnership structures allow for departmental heads who are primarily production managers) to continue in their normal role of ensuring quality and timeliness.

It is the marketing partner's job to turn the numerous positive features of the production department's work into understandable benefits to the client. But in addition to this, it is part of the marketing partner's brief to define through their research and analysis what it is that clients and potential clients actually want, how they want it presented and how they require it to be delivered.

In other words, the marketing function of a practice should have a major influence over the production department. This is, of course, not unusual. There are few tangible products that have succeeded in the marketplace without having been developed as a result of the marketing department's activity. Similarly, there are very few commercial enterprises where the production of product, services or work is produced by the people actually charged with selling them. Generally, products are produced in a factory but sold in a showroom or shop by an entirely different team. Similarly, most services are produced at a central 'production' facility (factory!), but sold via trained and dedicated teams in offices and call centres. Yet solicitors, and perhaps management consultancy practices, believe that the client must meet and approve of the production personnel in advance of placing the order. These types of practices have failed to divide production and marketing management.

Resource management (time, money, people)

Resource management is generally the responsibility of the managing partner (or the partnership through the managing partner). Here again the importance and influence of the marketing management cannot be overstressed.

Time, in the legal profession, is traditionally used as a method of calculating costs. But, if the marketing management philosophy is truly adapted, it is the marketing department that will set price, through a combination of the cost-on science and the art of establishing 'what the market will bear' given the added value due to better overall customer service.

Thus, the marketing department has a major influence on money. Many of the practices we reviewed in researching this book had very detailed expenditure budgets, but left the development of the sales budget to a simple percentage increase on last year's figures.

A key task for the marketing management of any practice is to establish realistic sales budgets, not just in global terms across disciplines within the firm, but individually for each product, department and, indeed, fee earner. These sales budgets need to be related not only to last year's turnover, and existing production resource, but also to the marketplace currently, and the specific promotional activity that the marketing department plans to initiate.

People are the prime asset of any legal practice, and are also, as has been noted above, despite being primarily production workers, in constant contact with clients and therefore, like it or not, represent the firm's 'sales force'. As such, it is essential that everybody presents the same image, the same message and the same relevant benefits and adopts pre-agreed client handling methods. All of this is the responsibility of the firm's marketing management.

The message that the management of a firm must make clear to everyone within it when dealing with 'understanding the management of the marketing function' is that marketing is far more than just promotion.

Does it work?

Of course, the introduction of a marketing-based management philosophy within any endeavour works. We have already said that during the past 20 years of management consultancy within the legal profession, those firms that have been the most successful are those that have been run autocratically; run by powerful management that fully adopts and understands the marketing management philosophy. An anecdotal example comes from about 10 years ago.

EXAMPLE **Profitable practice**

Two firms were almost identical in nature – the same size, the same partnership numbers, the same number of fee earners and other support staff. Their geographical catchment area was very similar including a relatively wealthy residential area, a considerable development of light industry and retail parks and a long-established section of the community drawn from ethnic minorities. That one firm was on the northern side of London and the other the southern side of Birmingham made very little difference and the total billing of the two practices (in excess of £1.5 million per annum) was almost identical. And yet the profits remaining for division between the partners were four times as much in one than the other, even after paying considerably higher salaries to fee-earning staff.

The reason for this disparity was entirely down to marketing management. Although the turnover was similar, the product mix was very much biased in one case towards profitable products. The volume of these 'products' was greatly increased by the targeting of that type of work through promotion. All staff were trained to consider the clients' needs fully, and therefore the volume of cross-selling and additional income was considerable. And the staff had been motivated to achieve this. Because the firm was divisionalised more along market lines that production demands, the productivity of each fee earner was far higher because work was charged for properly and executed efficiently. Every member of staff with client contact had been trained in benefit presentation and cost justification. In short, the most profitable firm knew its market, its competition, its clients, knew how to communicate, how to charge, how to execute the work, how to gain additional work and recommendations and, on the rare occasions that they happened, knew how to handle complaints. The management of the firm knew the strengths and weaknesses of each member of staff and played to the strengths, while only occasionally bolstering the weaknesses.

Although your author worked with both firms for some time, and indeed the most successful over a number of years, I would take very little credit for their success. In fact, many of the suggestions, and some of the techniques within this book, are based on methods we developed together.

A word about partners' meetings

If the management of a practice is structured along the lines of a board of directors, with a managing director, a marketing director, production director and accounts director, it makes sense to structure partners' meetings along the lines of board meetings.

First, partners' meetings should be formal, regular and run to a predetermined standing agenda, obviously allowing time for extraordinary or other business. Those members of the partnership charged with the executive responsibilities outlined above are, in effect, appointed by the full partnership to carry out that executive responsibility and report back to the partnership.

This is precisely the process that happens with a board of directors, and it works. As such, the executive officers will have full authority within the parameters agreed, and should be required only to report back on progress against a predetermined plan. Committees can work, but the one most likely to succeed is the committee of one.

A good chairman (managing partner) will institute an annual 'away day' which should not be a junket, but a time dedicated to developing and reviewing the firm's strategic plan and longer-term goals. This is, quite obviously, a process in which the marketing partner should be deeply involved.

Initial sales analysis

In our experience, most firms have a very accurate expenditure budget, and control it well.

However, few seem to have the same accuracy with their 'sales' budget. In part, this is because the profession has historically dealt with income by way of total billing targets, with little specific thought given to individual fee earners, matter types or even, in some cases, departments. This historic attitude is in part a throwback to the pre-deregulation period, where the work would automatically flow through to the firm; exactly what type of work it was remained irrelevant provided there was sufficient of it. This whole approach was exacerbated by the pre-divisionalisation approach that accepted that most fee earners undertook a variety of different matter types, and additionally 'dabbled' with other work. Many lawyers considered the client to be 'their' client, for whom they would undertake any work, rather than 'the firm's' client, who should be passed to an expert. The truth was that in many cases, firms were actually a loose collection of sole practitioners.

Obviously, this approach to work is no longer acceptable, and is being positively legislated against, but often income analysis is undertaken in a similarly haphazard way. Therefore, perhaps as the first stage of the marketing function, there is a need to begin to understand the sales budgetary control within your firm and to put some actual figures to the detail. See the tasks at the end of this chapter, 'Financial assessment of your firm' for a suitable list.

Where there are obvious anomalies (e.g. a very low figure for one fee earner), it is important to understand why. For example, does that fee earner have considerable managerial duties over and above fee earning, or have they perhaps only worked for the last three months of the year? This information is extremely important to strategic planning and future developments, and should probably form the basis for discussion between the managing and marketing partner prior to the first strategic planning away day.

You will now have an overview of the total sales fees of your firm for the last three years broken down between branch, division, matter type and fee earner.

We must now turn to an analysis of profit.

Initial profit analysis

In **Chapter 5** we look at profit from the point of view of the '6Ps'. But from an analysis point of view, we need to make some judgement related to the profitability of the firm, branch, department and each fee earner.

The simplest way is to apportion fixed overheads as a percentage of the firm's total turnover that each branch/department/fee earner produces. Then variable overheads can be calculated and added to the equation based upon actual usage, which is presumably recorded in the accounts department.

Firms have many different approaches to the calculation of profitability. Which method you choose is less important than the action being taken, and it being applied consistently. Obviously, profitability is a key factor, and a predominant aspect of the marketing function.

In *Marketing Your Law Firm*, Lucy Adam expands greatly upon the theme of initial sales analysis and profitability. It is well worth a read. However, in our task of facing up to 'the new profession' the above will suffice.

Most software packages include features that can undertake the majority of the marketing functions outlined in this book. However, the vast majority of the firms researched for this book do not make use of such marketing facilities. In the worst case scenario, client information, account information and case management are kept on separate systems that do not 'speak' to each other. In today's environment, and faced with The New Competition, this really is unacceptable.

An early task for the marketing partner is to understand clearly exactly what the firm's current technology can, and cannot, do. In many cases, providers of hardware and software systems talk in a language that is not clear, and expect an understanding that is not always there. There is no harm in having a Luddite moment. Call in your suppliers for an interview, and ask them to assume that you know nothing about computer systems or their usage. (If you feel embarrassed by that, show them this book and tell them you are doing what you were told.) Then ask them to avoid or to explain each piece of jargon, reminding them that that is precisely what you have to do when talking about the law to your clients and prospects. (A useful lesson here: remember that your clients will be as bemused by legal expressions, as you may be by technical ones.) Too often, communications relating to information technology (IT) fall down because of the assumption by the expert of a level of understanding from the client, and the embarrassment that – at worst – leads to a pretence of understanding by the client.

Assume ignorance. As for clarification, explain what you require from the system and it can almost be guaranteed that your requirements can be met once the system has an input from the marketing department as well as production and accounts.

Initial client analysis

If the IT system had been put into operation 10 years ago, there would be no problem in undertaking a full client analysis. Unfortunately, few practices got their marketing information together that long ago despite, in most cases, their systems having the facility to do so. In researching this book we thought that the old joke from some 20 years ago, that only the legal profession had 'dead files' where everyone else had a 'user base' was itself long dead. Not so. A client we had advised to develop a database (12 years ago) had only just started it (two years ago) and even then only because they had called us in for another assignment. The truth is that most firms who think they have a database do not. At best, some have a mailing list, and this is often unreliable.

Clearly, we will be recommending throughout this book that this situation must be addressed now by your firm, especially in the light of The New Competition with their massive computing power and understanding of it.

Essentially, what the marketing partner needs to do is to ascertain exactly what is available within the firm and its IT system for immediate usage, and how long the IT experts within the firm estimate it would take to get a mailing list cleaned, and ultimately a database usable. We will discuss databases in very much more detail later in **Chapter 6**, but here we are concerned with an initial survey to produce, once again, an overview.

Notwithstanding our snide remarks above, many firms do produce excellent financial/accounting figures. However, the information available is not always looked at from every angle, or in the most useful way, especially from a marketing point of view.

By way of an example, it is useful to consider the manufacturer of the ubiquitous 'widget'. It may be useful for the manufacturer to know that last year it achieved a turnover of £100 representing the sale of 75 units. How much more useful, however, would it be to be able to identify that the total of 75 comprised sales of 50 standard models at a unit price of £1 and 25 deluxe model widgets at a unit price of £2. Perhaps because the services provided by solicitors do not easily segment themselves into different widget 'models' as is the case with a manufacturer, the profession has shown a marked reluctance to record what it sells in anything other than the common denominator of money, and an overview of the firm or, at best, the department. In consequence, many firms are not really aware of what they actually sell (i.e. 'product analysis'), nor are they aware of who buys what they sell or why (market and client analysis). Most firms currently have the technology to achieve this, but perhaps have not yet seen the value of doing so. It is sincerely hoped that this book will help illustrate just how great that value can be. Part of the problem is that, while it is useful to understand the profile of the client coming to the firm, it is more important to understand the profile of the client coming to a specific department.

The classic marketing categories would group clients according to e.g. gender, age, work status, social profile. The tasks section at the end of this chapter has a more detailed list to assist you in your analysis.

It is interesting to note that along with 'getting rid of dross work', most practices would claim that they want more 'clients of wealth', from the AB categories. However, few actually set out to achieve this objective, even if they knew how to.

A similar exercise should be undertaken in relation to commercial clients to record their status as sole traders, partnerships or limited companies, and their turnover (again, see the tasks section at the end of this chapter). Additionally, and particularly relevant for niche marketing is a consideration of their areas of operation or expertise. Not every manufacturer produces widgets.

If it is possible, it would be ideal to relate the type of service/matter type purchased with the client who commissions the work. Our experience shows that this is unlikely to be practical from historical records, although it is most certainly something that should be instigated by the marketing partner for the benefit of the future of the firm.

More important is to make some assumptions and observations.

First, we need to begin to look at the individual client, and understand their individual needs. For example, there is a vast difference in the needs of the first-time buyer, who almost certainly just wants quick access to their new home and the 'last-time' buyer, who is probably viewing the purchase of a new (possibly smaller) property as part of an overall financial restructuring, which should include investment advice, inheritance tax planning, will writing, lasting powers of attorney and other considerations.

What do we offer both groups? Conveyancing!

Initial market information and analysis

An obvious extension of individual client analysis is a review of the overall market.

Historically, the profession has not chosen to distinguish between the different markets it serves. Implicitly, there is recognition that there is no 'overall' or homogeneous market for legal services, but little formal acknowledgement of this. Effectively therefore, this is a lack of comprehension of 'marketing'. In fact, there are many different markets for legal services and each one of them could be segmented to provide clearer targets, ultimately leading to discrete niches.

The first and most important distinction to draw is that between private individuals (private clients) and business organisations (commercial clients). The initial task for the marketing partner in this area is to confirm the numbers of each, and try to categorise them further as outlined above.

At this stage it is also valuable to see if there are any links between the two initial markets. An obvious one would be private client work undertaken for the directors of a commercial client, or the opportunity to seek new commercial work from a private client who happens to be a director of a company, or in another way responsible for the placing of legal work for his firm. Strangely, it is extremely rare to find consideration being given to this by legal practices, without considerable encouragement to do so by an outside source such as a consultant.

Many, particularly large city firms, have given up private client work to concentrate on commercial, and in extreme cases, international legal work. The advent of The New Competition is likely to precipitate further change. Private client firms who will see a diminution of their market are likely to pursue commercial work, particularly at its lower levels. It is essential to know where your firm stands now, in relation to markets. To understand, if only in outline, the opportunities for cross-selling between the two markets will be vital to the survival and development of your firm.

There is another reason why the distinction between private clients and commercial clients is particularly relevant. Although clients from both markets purchase legal services, what they purchase is usually different; what they are able or willing to pay is different. Their motives for purchasing are different, as are their procedures for selecting suppliers. In short, the differences between the types of clients are marked, and sufficient to demand a different approach by the provider and seller of these services.

Beyond this 'first level' of differentiation, there are many other possible segments, sub-segments or marketing niches, which may be usefully identified for the purposes of planning and marketing. We shall return to this subject in more detail in **Chapter 6** which covers databases. Suffice it to say at this stage that the profession seems to make little distinction between markets or market segments, which results in the profession dividing itself along 'production' rather than 'market' lines. As an example, fee earners often think of themselves as contentious or non-contentious, and yet a client, and particularly a commercial client, may well require services that are provided by both litigation and non-litigation. What a commercial client needs is a solicitor with the understanding of his or her industry to provide a total legal package, covering all services and, where appropriate, being proactive in recommendations and preventative law, such as reviewing terms of employment before trouble arises.

The commercial client has a set of needs entirely different from those of the private client. Although they would never express it as such, what they really want is the old 'man of affairs', someone who will take care of the legal requirements of living in this day and age, in a proactive form, in a supportive form: 'a friend in a hostile world'.

What tends to happen is that the two sets of clients are treated similarly irrespective of their individual needs, and at no point are their overall differing needs considered. This however, is something that the marketing partner must tackle. You want your clients, both commercial and private clients, to think of you as part of their team. Why should 'my solicitor' no longer apply when 'my doctor', 'my dentist', 'my bank manager' and in commercial terms, 'my accountant' still do? The answer is that, even in the medical profession, and particularly in the private sector, the skills of marketing have been adapted to the profession and used.

It is also true that marketing has been adopted by some members of the legal profession. They are few and far between. They are notable because of their high profile and success, but there is no reason why a marketing-minded practice, even a small practice, should not adopt such practices that have already been proven elsewhere to themselves, and become a big player in a small pool even if it has no wish to become a national brand.

This is the key to survival in the face of The New Competition, and the prime purpose of this book.

CHAPTER 3 TASKS **Review your firm's current position**

Use the lists in this section to assess your firm. At this stage, the analysis requires only short answers as the detail will be added in later exercises. This analysis will give you the starting point data that will underpin your firm's further development.

Financial assessment of your firm

- Income per branch (assuming the firm has more than one site)
- Total income per division (assuming the firm is divisionalised from a production point of view)

- A list of matter type definition used within your firm (probably instigated by accounts and used for new file opening)
- A breakdown, for the last three years, in sterling and percentage terms of the fees earned by matter type (percentage refers to the percentage the matter type has contributed to the firm's total turnover)
- A list for the last three years of the fees earned in sterling and percentage by each individual fee earner
- Fixed costs across the firm
- Variable costs across the firm

Your firm's accountant or accounts department should be able to help you with these figures.

Client records database

The IT manager and partner responsible for IT should be able to help you understand what marketing capabilities your current system has, or could have with little additional work (see **Chapter 6** on databases).

- How many client records do you have? (Accounts system billing contact details in the last three years.)
- What proportion of these records is in paper or electronic form? What is the potential duplication between these sets of records?
- Are those records split easily between domestic and commercial? (By 'easily' is meant: can you generate an up-to-date, separate list of domestic and commercial clients without it taking more than one hour? As yourself, would you be happy and confident to send each contact a Christmas card?)

As an initial assessment, review the client information your system currently holds and compare that view with the list of required information below.

For domestic clients, in addition to their contact details and purchasing history, do you hold or have the ability to record this information:

- gender;
- marital status, which these days should include divorcees and civil partners;
- age – usually subdivided into five bands: 18–24, 25–34, 35–44, 45–64, 65+ although it is increasingly relevant to define the 65+ group in more detail with the increased longevity and demographic changes;
- working conditions – employed, self-employed, retired;
- social groupings:

  AB = professional, senior and middle management

  C1 = junior managerial and all other non-manual workers

C2 = skilled manual workers

DE = semi-skilled and unskilled manual workers, people dependent on state benefits and those with no regular income

For commercial clients, in addition to the primary contact for the company and its purchasing history, do you hold or have the ability to record the following information?

- All directors and company offices
- Accountant
- Year end date
- Number of employees
- Turnover
- SIC (Standard Industrial Classification) code or business type
- Size – number of sites
- Shareholders or owners
- Bank branch
- Main matter type of work
- Estimate of the percentage of the legal work instructed to other firms
- Number of directors or employees also known as private clients to your firm
- Do you distinguish professional contacts that refer work to your firm?

At this stage, brief answers will be useful in getting an overall assessment of your firm. Once complete, please retain these details for further use in later chapters.

IT system

For future reference you may find it useful to have this system information available. For combined systems please give details of the practice management elements.

Practice management and/or case management

- System vendor
- System title
- System version
- Date of installation
- Date of last updates

If your IT system is less than five years old, it may also be useful to have the sales information given to your firm by the systems vendor. Compare the benefits of the system listed with the general use currently and ask your system vendor to help you gain the most from the system you have bought.

The marketing partner should use the material in this chapter to impart information to all members of staff to ensure their understanding of why marketing is needed and where they fit into the scheme of things. The partnership should declare a growth strategy for the firm.

The firm should undertake a brief initial analysis of matter types and client profile as a prelude to further work later in this book.

The completion of the tasks in this chapter will ensure an understanding of the firm's current position prior to undertaking a marketing audit of the firm.

4

A marketing audit of your firm

In this chapter we continue to look at the firm's current position, and introduce a speedy and simple way to undertake a marketing audit of your firm. In this, we will include the firm's scope of activity, geographical coverage and markets by both client type and matter type. We will also look at market research as it is appropriate to your firm and discuss market segments and niches. A wide range of management information, as it is applied to marketing, will be addressed and we will touch again on strategic options.

In addition, we will provide advice on a client survey, staff communications and involvement, departments and teams and even premises and first impressions.

Finally, we will encourage you to look at new ways of using a SWOT analysis and either undertake one or update the one you already have as part of your firm's business plan.

Be more than you seem. – Frederick the Great

Many legal practices express concern, when undertaking a marketing or promotional exercise, that they may start to promise more than they can deliver. This is not just scepticism, it is a genuine and well-founded concern.

In every marketing or promotional activity, your firm must be clear and truthful. It is for this reason that we would emphasise again that the timely production of high quality legal work is of paramount importance and must come before everything else. However, producing the work but not telling anyone about its benefits or how it competes is as bad as promising something you cannot deliver.

You should therefore aim to follow Frederick's advice to be more than you seem. When your clients receive more than they expected, they are doubly satisfied – more likely to use you again and to recommend you. When they receive less, the quibbles and grumbles about service and price occur.

While organisations of The New Competition are less likely than you to be inhibited in their promotional stance, they may well have difficulty in maintaining the quality standards, universally, that they claim. We are talking here about a 'mass produced product'. Your own must be more 'bespoke'. Perhaps this, more than anything else, is the starting point for differentiating the legal profession from The New Competition. You must now start telling clients, prospects and professional contacts about these differences.

In this chapter, we will deal with an essential activity that, frankly, too few firms undertake. The aim is to establish where, from a marketing point of view, your firm currently stands. Only then can you decide where you want it to be going. To achieve this we will discuss how to look at your firm's geographical coverage, its scope of activity, the markets you serve – by both client type and matter type – and take a limited look at market research. We will also discuss market segments and market niches along with the strategic options available to legal firms.

We will look at client surveys, staff communications and involvement, departments and teams and a new way of using a SWOT (Strengths, Weaknesses, Opportunities, Threats) analysis, either by undertaking one, or by updating the one that you already have.

At the end of this chapter, and replicated on the CD-Rom, you will find questionnaires and worksheets to help you swiftly through the process.

Geographical coverage

It is fair to say that at least some legal work will travel. There is no constraint on a lawyer working for a client in a different part of the country, and this often happens, particularly with past satisfied clients. The development and use of Internet and email facilities make this even more practical and the principle of working at a distance will undoubtedly be highlighted by those of The New Competition who will be (and, indeed, are) promoting themselves nationally but executing the actual work centrally. It is, perhaps, less important than before to know how many of your clients live, for example, within 10 miles of the office.

However, if marketing is about anything, it is about targeting, and quite obviously a geographically defined market can be the first target.

Knowing the geographical make-up of your area is more important than knowing specifically where your clients live. The demographic profile of, for example, a particular housing estate, will illustrate what types of legal services are likely to be required by the residents. The difference between the requirements of a sink estate and a stockbroker belt are obvious, but there are many subtle degrees between the two extremes.

For this reason among others, it is important to consider geographical coverage department by department. Again, the most obvious split will be between commercial and private client work. The key purpose to geographical area definition is to avoid dissipation of effort. From the promotional point of view, practical geographical limitations need to be applied to the firm's activities: while it would be fair to say the distribution of a newsletter could be to anywhere, the offer of a home visit could not.

Part of the strategy of The New Competition will be to promote, develop and play up the brand image. A brand image simply means that one knows from the name the type, quality and to a certain extent, cost, of the service being offered. This The New Competition will do nationally. There is no reason why your firm should not develop a similar brand identity within your own smaller geographical area – especially if you target that geographical area more tightly by the application of industry category, size of company, existing clients, etc. or, in the case of a private client, employment, location, wealth and age. With effort, your 'brand' can be as recognised and as clearly understood to your chosen limited audience as Coca-Cola is worldwide.

The first tightening of the target market therefore is geographic, although that is not to say that you should ever turn work away from outside your chosen area.

Range/scope of activity

In **Chapter 3** you were encouraged to list the matter types undertaken by your practice, and we noted that the matter type definition was probably instigated by the accounts department.

Using this list, the marketing partner should consider that range of activities, and whether it is too wide, or not wide enough. The percentage figures of total billing for each matter type will indicate its current position and value to the firm. Consider the range of services your firm offers compared with the services of your local competitors and those that a client might expect or want. Whether your firm is a specialist or general practice you should use this analysis to determine the gaps in the services offered.

Apart from range, the other area to consider is the scope of activity – which matter types could be improved or increased, which areas have a capacity for expansion, and which are your firm's prime products.

Prime products are those for which the firm has the resource to produce, and the capacity to increase, the volume of current sales, either from existing staff or from reasonably predictable recruitment. They must be matter types that have a proven market, and the marketing partner needs to be clear how that market will be approached with a view to expansion.

Historically, firms have been inclined to be all things to all men. This overall service approach has been reduced by the need for specialists and specialisms, the development of such things as legal aid franchises and, of course, competition which has frequently eroded profits. This competition, as we have noted throughout the book, is set to increase greatly.

The legal profession has been largely reactive; it is now, perhaps, time to be proactive. The marketing partner must discuss with the partners what the range or scope of activity should be for the firm, as so often the tendency seems to be for polarisation. There are firms that concentrate solely, for example, on conveyancing. The recent downturn in the property market makes this approach vulnerable. There are PI firms, and a number of commercial practices have actually ceased doing general private client work. It is most likely that these firms have made decisions as a result of considering their existing range/scope of activity and looking to the future of the marketplace.

Markets by client type

The above study of the matter types executed within the firm will show what work is being undertaken for clients, but does not necessarily help with defining the profile of those clients. In defining the client type we start to understand where legal services can be promoted in the future.

For example, one may be instructed to do a large amount of commercial conveyancing, but does the work in fact come from a number of independent retailers needing many small transactions, or from a national retailer buying up small shops, or indeed a manufacturer moving into the area, producing only a few large bills?

Another reason why a study of the client type is important is so that you can identify how strong the firm's hold is over its existing clients, and on what that hold depends. Is it because a single fee earner or partner has a personal relationship with that client built up over a considerable amount of time? What will happen to the client when that person moves or retires?

Linked to this is an analysis of the skills within the firm and the attributes that are likely to be critical to a particular client. Does the firm have the resource and spread of skills to enable it to grow as the client grows? Consideration also needs to be given to how dependent the firm is on a particular client/small group of clients/market segment.

In **Chapter 3**, we looked at client analysis and will, in due course, look at databases (see **Chapter 6**).

However, the brief analysis proposed here would allow the marketing partner to divide the domestic market clients according to relevant marketing factors, such as:

- geographical;
- demographic;
- matter types bought;
- potential matters to buy;
- affluence;
- potential future profit for the firm.

For commercial clients, classification should be according to factors such as size, industry type, matter type required/provided, whether or not they are a 'multi-user' and their position as a referrer of others.

Segments and niches

The marketing partner needs to consider what segments of the market the firm is currently serving. Can these then be broken down further into small niches?

For example, the firm might already work for a number of charities, and as a result of this experience and 'speaking the charities' language' be able to attract more charities. Perhaps a partner has a special knowledge of the intellectual property law relating to computer software. If so, there is a growing niche for such expertise that will clearly not be confined by geographical limitations. A knowledge of a particular industry or area of activity which enables the lawyer to understand and speak the language of that entity is in itself a niche.

At this stage we are looking for an initial review. We will return to the subject in more detail in later chapters, where we will look at developing niches.

Market research

Remember, we are dealing here with the current situation as it pertains to your firm. It is likely that the firm has to undertake some research, however informal, and this should be reviewed by the marketing partner. Similarly, simple local knowledge can be applied while making this review; consider use of the most recent population census for the defined geographical area (if this has not already been assessed). The local library or town hall can usually provide a range of data about their/your area that goes beyond demographic issues – the projected structure plan, for example.

Your firm's stance

Ultimately, the partnership, guided by the marketing partner, needs to decide the markets and clients to be served and the relative volume to be expected from each identifiable category of client, the types of products to be offered and the relative mix, and the basis (or bases) on which the firm has chosen to compete, i.e. its competitive advantage(s).

Essentially, there are three approaches that can be taken:

1. A full-line all-market strategy wherein the firm offers all products to all markets and attempts to portray itself as a general practice. This stance is typical of that held by most average practices.
2. A market specialist strategy wherein the firm chooses a particular market or market segment and attempts to provide the full product range required by that market or market segment. Examples of this would be a firm choosing only to serve the commercial market, or only the matrimonial segment of the domestic market.
3. A product specialist strategy wherein, for example, the firm chooses to offer litigation to all types of clients, and possibly subcontracts its litigation services to local non-contentious practices.

Traditionally, many firms in the profession have chosen a full-line all-market strategy. This may no longer be appropriate for some firms in today's more competitive, and less 'protected' world. It is certainly difficult with this strategy to maintain a realistic and significant competitive advantage, or to promote it effectively. The changes to the publicly funded sector also apply pressure to the full-line, all-market approach.

Partner to fee earner ratio

What is this ratio? There is, of course, no right/wrong answer to this question, but increasingly we need to consider what might be termed the 'pyramid of production'. Most certainly, The New Competition will be ensuring that all work is done at an appropriate level, with a high emphasis on technology and operatives who are not necessarily legally qualified.

Your firm needs at least to consider a similar approach. The partners need to take time out from fee earning to manage their business, plan its strategy, develop its markets and undertake the marketing activity required. Therefore, the partner to other fee earner ratio is relevant to the growth of the firm, as is the role of support staff.

A good example of this is a small firm known to the authors who, through the use of technology, including the digital outsourcing of all typing facilities, have developed to a point where only the receptionist, legal cashier and cleaner are not fee earning staff, at one level or another. Indeed, the receptionist is also the database manageress. Of course, all work is supervised by a partner, but surprisingly little actual legal production work is undertaken by the partners who, in addition to maintaining quality standards, concentrate on client liaison and practice development.

Departments and teams

Departmentalisation is so obviously the right approach, forming as it does centres of excellence, that it is rare indeed these days to find a firm that is not departmentalised in one way or another. The marketing partner needs to consider the departments that currently exist within the practice and determine what, if any, marketing or promotional activity these departments undertake for themselves.

The problem with departmentalisation is that it can lead to compartmentalisation, limiting the cross-fertilisation between departments, limiting the services offered to the clients, and ensuring that matter type considerations come before the true consideration of all the clients' needs. This is a perfect example of the production management philosophy (see **Chapter 2**).

The other problem facing the marketing partner is the promotional activity undertaken by individual departments. Does this impinge on the overall image of the firm? Can the activity of one department damage the image of the others? Some years ago the Law Society instigated an initiative called 'Will Power'. This used a Batman-like figure to encourage the making of wills. It must have confused the serious-minded commercial clients of the practice, who saw newspaper coverage of the firm's senior partner prancing around the town centre on a Saturday morning dressed as a turquoise 'Will Power'.

Marketing spend to billing ratio

In many commercial enterprises this is a vital ratio for assessing the current and future profitability of a product or service. The amount of money spent marketing the product or service is always included in any profitability study. An analysis should be undertaken of the marketing spend by a department or on a specific matter type, including a proportion of the firm's overall promotional budget, on such things as newsletters, leaflets, etc., so that a benchmark can be established. Material at the end of this chapter and on the CD-Rom will assist you in making this assessment by relating the firm's turnover to its expenditure on marketing or similar activities. We would then suggest that you break down this overall figure, item by item, to ensure a full understanding of what this money was spent on.

Again, at this stage, there cannot be any right/wrong answer, but an analysis of this type will initially indicate an over/under-spend situation, will enable the marketing partner to propose an increase/decrease in the marketing budget to the partnership, and will ultimately provide a year-on-year comparison against profit. All marketing activity should be quantifiable and have a measurable success level. This is the first stage of that process.

Staff communications

As has already been mentioned, staff are an important part of the marketing activity, and it is useful therefore to consider at this early stage the prime methods of communication with them. In analysing this area there are several questions to consider:

- How regularly are staff meetings held?
- Are these meetings departmental or firm-wide?
- Are the staff managed by memo, by email or face-to-face meetings?
- Does the firm have an appraisal system?
- What is the conduit for ideas to be passed up from the staff?
- How are new initiatives, such as the introduction of a newsletter, introduced to the staff?
- How au fait are the staff with the principles of marketing and the firm's growth plans?
- When and how will the partnership declare the results of the skills and interests audit to the staff?

In our experience, firms often consider that staff appreciate social events, but sometimes there is an overemphasis on this. In many firms we have introduced the concept of what we term 'quality circles'. These originated in Japanese industrial production where workers were asked to contribute to the well-being of their factory and product.

The same concept can be applied to your practice. Groups of staff should be invited to speak openly about the firm and how they would improve it. If these meetings are held on a regular basis, say quarterly, they can provide a very good forum for information to be passed to the management of the practice, and at the same time provide a conduit for information the other way: a perfect forum, for example, to introduce a new marketing initiative. Initially, these meetings often provide the opportunity for well-known grievances to be repeated. However, once the discontents have been dealt with, the meetings can establish a valuable way for the partners to understand more about the workings of their own business.

Different firms organise their 'quality circles' in different ways. Some exclude partners, and have a chairman (one chairman who covers all the quality circles) who reports findings back to the partnership and provides the answers given by the partnership at the beginning of the next quality circle meeting. Others use a partner to chair the meetings on a rotation basis, which is fine as long as no member of staff feels inhibited.

Ideally, all staff should have notice of the agenda of each meeting, and minutes should be taken and circulated.

Competition

Although the legal profession has always, quite rightly, seen other solicitors as colleagues, they are, nonetheless, also competition. The marketing management philosophy requires consideration of this competition with specific reference to those who are taking a particularly strong marketing stand and/or have had considerable success in developing their practice. The questions listed in the questionnaire in the tasks section are designed to help you.

In our experience, most practices do have a reasonable understanding and knowledge of their immediate traditional competition. As part of adopting the marketing management philosophy, making the effort to note this information, even if it is just gossip, gives a useful record of the market position at a particular time. It can be revisited and reviewed to provide an indication of local market movements and help develop your firm's strategy.

Unfortunately, there is far less understanding of The New Competition. These firms, from outside the profession, are the ones who are 'cherry picking' your clients. It is a hard question to answer, but the marketing partner needs to consider how the firm would cope if it lost 25 per cent of its bread-and-butter work. It is safe to say that The New Competition will target high-volume domestic services by offering a commoditized (i.e. simple, stripped down) product.

The intention of this book is to ensure that that does not happen to your firm. However, a 'what if' scenario should be played out within the partnership to understand the potential changes. Perhaps making a note of these discussions provides the ability to analyse and review them in the future.

The recession that occurred between the first and second editions of this book has already subjected some firms to this level of contraction. But it has also held up the planned expansion of The New Competition. We believe, as we move out of recession, the cherry picking will resume with added vigour and will require a return to the thinking discussed above. 'What if' games are good. If things turn out better than planned, so much to the good. But if things are worse, they will be doubly worse for lack of planning.

Client survey

The introduction of a client satisfaction survey seems to be the recommendation of every marketing book, yet it can be fraught with dangers. While it is an undeniably valuable marketing tool, it almost inevitably has to be introduced professionally to get meaningful results. Remember, there really are lies, damn lies and statistics.

Also remember that without giving an incentive, you will get responses to your questionnaire only from the sycophants and your detractors.

If the firm has undertaken such a survey recently, or is doing so on a continuous basis, the marketing partner should review the results and decide:

- What action should be taken as a result of the survey?
- Is the process worth continuing?
- What value did the survey bring to the firm?

If you have not done a client satisfaction survey, we would specifically advise you not to do one at this stage. If, when you have read this book, you still consider a client survey to be worthwhile and it fits within the marketing planning, we would recommend you employ a professional customer survey company. It will be able to give you not just the responses from your clients, but also a view of how these fit within the legal services arena, including, ideally, both The New Competition and consideration of your geographic market place.

Strategic planning review

It is likely that the regular partners' meetings, and perhaps the annual away day, have dedicated some time to strategic planning. Hopefully, these meetings will have been minuted, and it will be extremely useful for the marketing partner to collate the minutes over, for example, the past three years and then write a brief report to the partnership on how much has been achieved, and why the rest of the objectives and decisions have not been implemented.

While the previous sentence sounds very negative, it does not reflect on your firm, but is simply the result of the authors' 20 years of undertaking such reviews. In fact, if your firm has achieved more than 50 per cent of your plan in the past three years, you have achieved more than the majority of firms and are in an enviable, tiny minority. If that is the case – forge ahead. If not – catch up.

Mission statement

It is very strange that the phrase 'mission statement' has fallen into such disrepute that it is almost unused today. However, we want to reintroduce the idea, for if a mission statement can be created within the firm, it in itself can be a measure of almost everything the firm does.

Our own favourite example of a mission statement comes from Robert Townsend – the author of *Up the Organisation* (Coronet Books, 1977) and who, following a stint as Chief Executive Officer of American Express became the CEO of Avis. Having built it from relatively nothing into the second biggest car hire company in America, he had the wisdom to leave it second biggest (to Hertz) in the recognition that 'there was no profit in pioneering'. The danger with this policy was that his staff could take a 'me too' attitude. His mission statement blew that approach out of the water. It was:

> We try harder in the business of renting driverless cars from airport sites – profitably.

'We try harder . . .' the rest is successful history.

SWOT analysis

Perhaps your firm has already undertaken a SWOT analysis, in which case an update may be appropriate. However, more likely it has not been done for some years and now, in face of The New Competition, is the time to reinvestigate it.

At the end of this chapter and on the CD-Rom, you will find forms that will assist the marketing partner in the process. It is not, however, something that can be left to the marketing partner alone. Indeed, a SWOT analysis should come as the result of conversations between the people who know the firm well. This is not always just the partners. Support staff, practice managers, the IT managers and even selected clients' opinions can be very illuminating. The end product is four lists of words or phrases that identify the strengths and weaknesses of the firm and the opportunities and threats to the firm from the external environment. Sometimes, the same phrase can be repeated under different headings. IT systems can appear under all four!

This is a very basic but useful business analysis tool and starts with an examination of how the business is now, the business that has been bequeathed to you by the decisions, actions and results of the past, and past partners.

Your firm is indistinguishable and undividable from the legal profession, and therefore we start by listing, briefly, what we see as the SWOTs of the legal profession. The findings of your own firm will then need to be overlaid on this.

SWOTs of the legal profession

Your practice is, inextricably, part of the highly institutionalised legal profession which is governed, in England and Wales, by the Solicitors Regulation Authority and under the influence of the Law Society and the government. Actions taken by an individual firm will always be in the larger, overall context of the profession itself, and it is therefore essential to look first at the SWOTs of the profession.

Strengths

- Independence
- Known integrity
- Known strict code of conduct
- Respected
- Some 'monopolies' (e.g. crime)
- Obligatory negligence insurance

Weaknesses

- Restrictions of code of conduct
- Historic dependence upon bread-and-butter products (conveyancing, probate, etc.)
- Perceived inapproachability
- Relative lack of commercial skills
- Non-specialist tradition
- History of regulated (monopolistic) markets
- Fragmented structure
- Slow to change
- Ignorance of The New Competition
- Uncertainty/lack of response to The New Competition
- A focus on matters and not on clients

Opportunities

- Established and growing market for legal services
- Complexity of the legal environment
- Europe/increasing globalisation
- Scope for innovation
- Association with or forming of multidisciplinary practices
- Legal Services Act 2007 (including ABS)
- Consumers' and small businesses' ignorance of the value of a solicitor's work
- Branded networks
- Third party referral agents
- The Internet and social media

Threats

- New, commercially aware competitors
- Consumers' and small businesses' ignorance of the value of a solicitor's work
- Aggressive promotional stance of competitors (deliberately challenging the traditional legal practice)

- Loss of bread-and-butter matters (potentially coping with a 25 per cent reduction in billing for these services)
- Legal aid franchises and rates
- Small claims court
- Carter, etc.
- Legal Services Act 2007
- The Internet

To summarise, the major strengths of the profession at large are the public's known view of the profession, that it is regulated by a strict code of conduct, is independent and is composed of persons of trust and integrity who carry insurance.

The major weaknesses of the profession are the restrictions imposed upon it (but certainly not imposed upon The New Competition), its fragmented structure, making concerted action or reaction difficult or near impossible and its long history of operating in restricted or highly regulated (monopolistic) markets. Very recently, the profession has begun, slowly, to recognise the need for change and to be more proactive.

The profession's major opportunities lie in the vast market for legal services in today's increasingly complex and ever-changing world, the scope for innovation in law and the provision of legal services, the development of 'product packages' and the potential of Europe and global business.

The major threats to the legal profession are provided by The New Competition, coming, as it does, from outside the legal profession and its regulations and bringing with it, as it will, an aggressive approach to marketing and promotion. While the Legal Services Act 2007 can be seen as an opportunity particularly on the funding and multidisciplinary practice fronts, it is above all a major threat.

Not to be ignored is the constant barrage of criticism and 'knocking copy' directed at solicitors and the legal profession by the media. Lawyers are seen, usually wrongly, as 'fat cats' and the public just don't like that or supporting them, and this in itself makes them highly susceptible to the promotional stance of The New Competition which will deliberately play upon this bias.

Your firm

Each practice is individual, although all firms share some similar attributes, many of which from a SWOT point of view have been covered above in the SWOT analysis of the legal profession in general.

The following is designed to assist the marketing partner in undertaking, in consultation with other members of the firm, an individual SWOT analysis specifically for your firm. Our guidance can only be indicative, although it is hoped that the form at the end of this chapter, and on the CD-Rom, will assist the process.

Opportunities and threats

The objective here is to ensure you are aware of the major opportunities and threats that face the firm's existing product ranges. The purpose of this analysis is to enable you to identify:

- new opportunities for existing products, e.g. in new areas, for new clients or in new applications;
- opportunities to serve existing clients with new products;
- future threats to the firm's market position and profits;
- the firm's intrinsic knowledge and understanding of its own market and marketplaces.

Such identification requires careful analysis of the environment in which the firm operates. At the end of the chapter, and on the CD-Rom, you will find a series of questions to help you. The answers to these, plus other questions pertinent to your own specific firm, should pinpoint the major product and market opportunities that now require evaluation. They may also provide warning signals regarding which present product or market activities to consider for scaling down or possible ultimate withdrawal.

An alert and innovative marketing partner should, following the analysis of familiar products and clients, now look for new opportunities in other product and market areas. As a general rule, it is more advantageous to take action to develop opportunities than it is to counter threats – not that threats, especially those posed by The New Competition, can be ignored.

Once an opportunity has been identified, the firm must ensure that it has sufficient production resource (fee earners and support staff) to expand the capacity to take advantage of the opportunity, or be certain that recruitment will allow this to happen. This is part of the identification of prime products.

An opportunity may provide the momentum to begin packaging legal services together to emphasise their strong points. For example, work out the different needs of the first-time/last-time buyer and how the firm can market each section effectively. This not only demonstrates the benefits of coming to your firm, but provides a differentiation over the majority of your competitors. It is indeed part of an opportunity recognition scenario that will enable you, without 'knocking copy', to promote yourself against The New Competition. You are then in a better position to establish the firm as an authority and leading light in your area and, of course, you need to establish a promotional programme.

Reacting to threats is not dissimilar. One can invest in promotion to compete; one can reduce prices and work to increase the number of clients. But both these actions will have a major negative effect on the profitability of a product or service already under threat. Possibly, it is a better strategy to move resources away from these areas and concentrate them on opportunities or to look at ways of reducing the cost of providing the service to maintain the margins while repackaging the particular service with others. Repackaging can both reflect market trends and also add value to a particular product – a power of attorney might be offered with a will, for example.

Strengths and weaknesses

The above analysis should identify a range of opportunities which probably will require evaluation and narrowing down. An analysis of the firm's resources (those currently or potentially available) will identify major strengths and weaknesses, knowledge of which enables the initial evaluation of opportunities to be developed.

The basic question the marketing partner needs to ask is 'How well equipped is the firm to face the future?' Specifically, the following areas need to be addressed (detailed questions are included at the end of this chapter, and on the CD-Rom):

- financial position;
- market position;
- management and personnel;
- physical facilities;
- general.

Once again, this is not intended to be an exhaustive list. Your own firm must and will have peculiarities and individualities that need addressing.

The marketing partner will now need to summarise the information gathered under this and under the opportunities and threats section. The major opportunities should be evaluated and prioritised according to identified strengths (or potential strengths). Threats should be examined in conjunction with identified weakness (or potential weaknesses).

Competitive advantage

No business, of any kind, can survive unless it maintains some kind of advantage over its competitors. To be effective in the marketplace, the firm must possess a meaningful competitive advantage. Never has this been more necessary to a legal firm than today in the face of The New Competition.

Identification of the firm's competitive advantage is vital, since it will determine the most appropriate direction to follow in the future – this being in those areas where the firm can differentiate itself from its competitors and offer and deliver measurable additional benefits.

A competitive advantage is found by comparing the firm's strengths and weaknesses with those of its competitors, both traditional and The New Competition. It can take many different forms, from a convenient location relative to a certain type of client (e.g. the only firm in a given location), to an advantage based on a preferential supply position (e.g. where a firm in the form of its personnel is in a position to offer specialist services which others cannot).

Examination of the following areas will help identify the firm's competitive advantage (existing or potential):

- preferential marketing position;
- technological superiority;
- preferential catchment area;
- physical advantages; and
- personal competence.

Again, your own firm's individuality needs to be considered, but as a starting point, detailed questions are included at the end of this chapter, and on the CD-Rom.

Factors may be different for different market groups, e.g. a factor that enables the firm to compete well in the commercial market may give no advantage at all in the domestic/private client market. Competitive advantages need to be clearly defined, as they should, in large part, determine the future direction of the firm.

Two basic rules are universally applicable:

1. Always lead from strength – exploit competitive strengths as far as possible.
2. Concentrate resources where the firm has (or can readily develop) a meaningful competitive advantage.

Earlier in this chapter we have looked at client, sales, matter type and market analysis. As part of the marketing partner's SWOT analysis, and certainly prior to reporting his findings to the partnership, it is worth considering the following in the light of the SWOT analysis:

- Which markets (defined by type of client) is the firm currently servicing? As a first step, consider the three main markets of commercial/ domestic and criminal.
- What percentage of turnover does each market represent?

- What resources are used to serve each market?
- How profitable is each market?
- Which products are sold in each main market and in what proportion?
- How profitable are these products?
- If a product is not profitable, are there other reasons for retaining it (such as completing a range of products to service a major client or retain criminal defence or family unprofitably to support private practice)?

Review again and summarise sales by:

- client;
- product;
- department;
- office location.

Completion of the analyses outlined in this chapter should provide a marketing audit of your firm, and an adequate overview of the firm's current position. The intention is to develop objectives for the future, and define the firm's future scope of activity. Your overview therefore should include statements relating to:

- the markets and clients to be served and the relative volume of business to be expected from each identifiable category of client;
- the type of products to be offered and their relative mix;
- the basis (or bases) on which the firm has chosen to compete, i.e. its competitive advantage(s).

Having determined the firm's major opportunities, looked at its strengths and developed its competitive edge or advantage, you should find it comparatively easy to produce quantifiable objectives. Numerical performance specifications need to be established for the firm's desired rate of growth, market penetration or share and profitability. Such quantification serves two purposes.

1. It provides target objectives for all to try to achieve.
2. It assists in making future decisions regarding use of resources, provided that you pay attention to the monitored results.

The limiting factors such as, for example, the number of qualified personnel available, the difficulty in recruitment, the availability or lack of cash resources, or even space, plus other weaknesses and threats must be recognised.

CHAPTER 4 TASKS **Assess your market**

Marketing audit questionnaire

1. Geographical coverage

Use this list to identify the geographical coverage of your firm. List area, towns, villages and postcodes.

- What is target geographical area coverage for commercial clients?
- What is target geographical area coverage for private clients?
- Within these two major markets are there any geographic variations by department or by product?
- What are the major departments' or products' geographic coverage and how do they differ?

2. Range or scope of activity

Using the matter types sold list previously generated, assess the list and the percentage figures to produce a list of areas of legal work that could be increased or are missing in comparison to local competitors or from the viewpoint of what a client would expect. Also consider what your firm would like to offer the client.

Based on your product analysis (matter types) and the percentage contribution to turnover, rate each category as follows:

- Should it/can it be increased?
- Is it trading at about the right level?
- Should you consider dropping this activity (or keep it for the sake of a complete range)?
- As with product range/scope above, which clients/client type would the firm seek to keep, expand or attract?

3. Segments and niches

In comparison to other local general practice firms, does your firm specialise in serving the needs of a particular type of client? Use these questions to analyse it further:

- What segments of the legal services market does the firm currently serve (e.g. professional practices, engineering companies)?
- Can these be broken down further into small niches?
- Does any partner or fee earner have any particular industry knowledge and experience?

- Does the firm serve any particular market niche(s) at present, where the niche is part of a larger market segment (e.g. patent agents (professional practices), agricultural machinery manufacturers (engineering companies))?

4. Market research

- Has the firm undertaken any formal market research in the past three years?
- What informal market research has the firm undertaken in the past three years?
- Does the firm have the census information for its target market?
- Is there any formal review of the local council's planning or structure strategy for your geographical area?

5. Marketing spend to billing ratio

As an initial step, take the total marketing budget and the total gross billing figure for the previous full financial year. If information is available, do the same for quarterly periods in this financial year. Break down each item of expenditure and calculate its ratio to the particular department's turnover or to the firm as a whole. This will produce a list of marketing items with a ratio to their related turnover. From there a variance can be calculated from the general marketing/billing ratio or from a comparison with other departments.

Table 4.1 Simple ratio calculation tables

Total billing	Total marketing budget	Ratio

Department	Department turnover	Marketing item	Ratio of item to turnover

6. *Staff communications*

Use the questions below to assess your firm's current communications methods.

- Does the firm have firm-wide staff meetings?
- What formal staff meetings are held? Are they department by department?
- When the firm has departmental meetings:
  - Are they department-wide or split between fee earners and support staff?
  - Are these meetings recorded by agendas and minutes?
  - Are they regular or as required?
- Does the firm operate a 'quality circle' approach to staff meetings?
- Does the firm have a formal approach to staff social events?
- Does the firm run a formal staff appraisal system?

7. *Competition*

Looking at the geographic areas defined earlier, now consider the competitor firms within that area.

- How did a local competitor achieve a strong marketing image or high profile development?
- Which local firms are in the ascendance and which in the decline?
- Is there a specific reason why (partner retirement or service changes)?
- Which firms are a threat to your practice?
- Which are supportive?

8. *Strategic planning*

It is important to include management work already done by your firm.

- Have you undertaken any strategic planning reviews or away days in the past three years?
- Are the minutes available? Use them to collate a list of targets set and whether those targets have been achieved.

9. *Mission statement*

- Does the firm have a mission statement?
- Does the firm have an implicit if not an explicit mission statement? Please attempt to sum up what your firm's mission statement could be.

10. Competitive advantage

When considering your firm's competitive advantage, use the list of questions below to assess your firm's market position.

PREFERENTIAL MARKETING POSITION

- Does your firm possess any control over its environment, or any part of it, through any of the following factors (or other influences)?
  - Long-term reputation
  - Price advantages
  - Monopoly location
  - Readily available products
  - Personal relationships with clients
  - Superior promotional activity
  - Affiliation/joint venture
  - Others
- Does the firm differentiate its products in any way?
- Can the firm differentiate its product range, or part of it, to provide a competitive advantage?
- Can your firm package products together to provide an overall service for a niche market (e.g. the provision of services to the older client)?

TECHNOLOGICAL SUPERIORITY

- Does the firm provide technically superior products?
- Are products offered at exceptional price/quality/value ratios?
- Is the firm innovative in product design?
- Is the firm a leader in product innovation?
- Does the firm possess special facilities/relationships/personnel through which to tailor and promote its services?

PREFERENTIAL CATCHMENT AREA

- Is the firm physically located so that it is better able than its competitors to appeal to clients/potential clients?
- Does the firm have a number of locations which offer any particular advantages?

PHYSICAL ADVANTAGES

- Does the firm possess superior facilities?
- Does the office provide a convenient location?

- Does the firm offer superior/comfortable offices?
- Is there convenient access/parking?
- What other related physical advantages can the firm offer?
- What high technology assets does the firm have which offer special appeal/benefits to clients/potential clients?

PERSONAL COMPETENCE

- Does the firm possess superior management?
- Is the firm organised managerially so that it has a competitive edge or can it be so reorganised?
- Does the firm possess particular skills in its personnel in production/marketing/accounts?
- Is the firm particularly skilled in client relationships?

SWOT analysis

Start with an examination of the business as it is now. Future results will be obtained by exploiting opportunities highlighted, not by solving problems. Resources, to produce results, must be allocated to opportunities rather than problems.

Opportunities and threats

- What are the activities of The New Competition?
- What threats do our existing competitors pose?
- How significant do these appear?
- What are the plans of our direct competitors within the profession?
- What threats does The New Competition pose to us specifically?
- What are the strengths and weaknesses of our traditional competitors?
- What are the strengths and weaknesses of The New Competition?
- How will the Legal Services Act 2007 affect us?
- What new legislation is expected and how will it affect existing products/clients?
- Which segments of our market will exhibit increases/decreases in demand for our services?
- What changes in society are taking place which may change markets/products?
- What changes are taking place within our commercial market?

- What changes are taking place within our domestic market?
- What changes are occurring within our defined geographical market area in terms of new commercial/residential/industrial developments, for example?
- What is the impact of new technology likely to be on the availability/cost/profitability of new/existing products?
- Will such changes in technology favour us or our competitors?
- How is the structure of the profession likely to change in light of the Legal Services Act 2007?
- Will the future environment favour the large or small firm, the generalist or specialist?
- How will recruitment and retention of key fee earners affect our firm's ability to service the future markets we identify?

Strengths and weaknesses

FINANCIAL POSITION

- How strong is the firm's financial position?
- How able is the firm to provide financial resources which may be necessary to fund future activities?
- What credit is available if required?

MARKET POSITION

- Is the firm a leader in any of its chosen markets?
- How do the firm's 'products' compare with those of (a) traditional competitors; (b) The New Competition?
- How does the firm define its markets?
- What is its market share in each area and is this growing or declining?
- Which are currently the most/least profitable markets for the firm's legal services?
- How strong is the firm's hold on its existing clients?
- How vulnerable is the client list?
- On what does the hold on clients depend?
- How strong is the firm in the skills and attributes that are critical to its chosen markets/market segments?
- What is the firm's reputation/image with (a) clients; (b) staff; (c) professional contacts; (d) the general public?
- Are there constraints placed on the firm that are not necessarily placed on its competitors (this will apply specifically to The New Competition)?

- How dependent is the firm on a particular client/small group of clients/market segments?

MANAGEMENT AND PERSONNEL

- How capable are the senior managers of the firm in the commercial knowledge and skills required to direct and manage the firm's strategic and marketing plans?
- How appropriate is the organisation structure to current needs?
- To what degree is management limited in its viewpoint by tradition or preconception?
- Is management sufficiently flexible to deal with the new situations that are arising, and specifically The New Competition?
- Does the organisation structure facilitate or hamper rapid evaluation of problems and decisive action?
- How is the planning process carried out?
- How are the firm's objectives and goals defined and subsequently evaluated?
- Are there any monitoring processes in place, other than in the production of work?
- Are there sufficient skills in the management structure to manage the functions of marketing, finance, personnel and general management?
- Does the organisation structure facilitate the management of these functions?
- Does the firm have sufficient technically qualified personnel or can they be recruited?
- Does the firm have a relatively stable, loyal staff or is its turnover high?
- Is the firm heavily dependent on a small number of highly competent individuals or is technical talent evenly spread?
- Is the firm, or any member of the firm, uniquely talented or capable in any way?

PHYSICAL FACILITIES

- How is the firm situated relative to its clients?
- How is it situated relative to other important bodies and institutions, e.g. the law courts?
- Is the firm well equipped in technologically advanced office facilities?
- Is the number of office locations compatible with the existing market product?
- What image is presented to clients, the general public, competitors and staff by the physical facilities and assets of the firm?

GENERAL

- To what degree is profitability dependent upon:
  - personal relationships?
  - product availability or convenience?
  - technical competence?
  - product design and innovation?
  - availability of capital?
- Would the firm be strengthened by merger, acquisition or joint venture and are such opportunities available and, if so, at what cost?

The partnership and departmental heads must recognise the role that marketing plays in every aspect of the firm's activities, and having begun to understand the role of marketing within the legal profession, reviewed your own firm's current position and undertaken a marketing audit, your firm has very nearly completed the information gathering and analysis stage that is essential for the firm to move forward.

This will be completed once your firm has accepted that marketing is not an add-on, but is a central management philosophy, and as we will see in the next chapter, a series of management tasks.

5

Marketing and management

This chapter concludes the process of collating the information regarding your firm's current position and management. We will then begin organising in preparation for implementing the strategy your firm has decided upon.

We will look at the current management philosophy of the firm; consider the three areas of management; introduce the concept of the '6Ps' approach to marketing management; relate this to the firm through individual departments; and consider what benefits, including unique benefits, your firm has to offer its clients.

We will also introduce the concept of reviewing the discrete services you offer as individual 'products' along with their attendant benefits.

> *A committee is a group of people who individually can do nothing, but as a group decide nothing can be done.* – Fred Allen, US humorist

Of course, the above quote is not true of all committees, but it certainly is of some. Frequently, a partnership effectively becomes a committee and, as we have already seen in earlier chapters, one of the biggest threats to a legal practice, faced with the Legal Services Act 2007, is inertia. In research we have often seen the attitude expressed in partnerships that 'Something has to be done – but what?'

This chapter deals with understanding the different elements of management philosophy and how to use it to distinguish between the varying management styles in a firm. It expands into the application of the '6Ps' (see below) and how a firm can use them to define its marketing position and identify areas for development. Completing the tasks will help you to assess:

- the management philosophy of the firm;
- the firm from a marketing management philosophy point of view;
- the '6Ps' and how they apply to a firm and individual departments;
- the benefits the firm delivers to its clients;
- the application of 'product life cycle' and how it can inform marketing decisions.

In any enterprise there are three areas of management that need to be fully and continually addressed:

1. Production management
2. Resource management
3. Marketing management

Indeed, the predominance of one or other of these three areas will quickly identify the style of management employed within the organisation and the progress that has been made by that firm along the evolution of marketing (see **Chapter 1**).

Production management

Clearly, production management is to do with a firm's ability to produce the services that define being a legal practice: the ability to provide professional legal services to appropriate clients. This must include the recruitment of sufficient people with appropriate skills and qualifications, allow for development of the skills through training and the maintenance of quality control through management and monitoring.

While it is obviously vital to maintain the quality of professional work, which is indeed the finest advertisement any firm can have, the firm that is led from a production stance is likely to be more driven by outside influences such as the availability of a certain type of fee earner rather than market considerations such as, 'What is it the market requires, that we can provide profitably?'

Of all enterprises, a firm within the legal profession is one of the most closely regulated, monitored and, indeed, expensively insured operations within the business spectrum. Therefore it should apply, though rarely does, that production of work and the maintenance of its standards should be the last of the commercial managerial considerations. So why is this not the case in the majority of firms encountered during researching this book?

We would say it is because solicitors are basically production workers. They chose the legal profession with the intention of providing (producing) legal services. They are measured by their clients and their peers by the standard of the work they produce. They are rewarded primarily by billing for the results of their production endeavours; they are applauded and recognised not, or seldom, for their general management skills, or even the acquisition of a new and important client, but for the resolution of a knotty legal problem or the completion of a perfect job.

But this is unsurprising. Few people went into the legal profession to become general/industrial/commercial managers. They wanted to be lawyers. This is not to suggest that the partners within the firm do not understand the need to manage their firm – it is the emphasis we are concerned with. However, a production-biased management committee will be more concerned with the production of work than with the client who purchases it.

The production of legal work and the maintenance of the highest quality standards are of paramount importance and a vital management task. But they are not the only task.

Resource management

Essentially, resource management is the control and best use of time, money and people. This is a mathematical discipline, and one that is frequently run by an accountant or an accounts-minded manager.

As with production, all resource management is vital. Having the right number of people with the right qualifications available at the right level to fulfil the needs of the firm's clients is an obvious prerequisite for ensuring credit control, money on account of costs, interim billing, prompt payment of fees and a managed expenditure budget. It provides the lifeblood of any practice. Time is frequently quoted as the most precious commodity of all, and time recording, time management, and billing on account of time are all areas that have, at least in part, been pioneered by the legal profession.

Once again, this is an inward-looking management philosophy. Even if it is all-encompassing, this management philosophy will stop short at producing a sales budget, designed to show in global figures where revenue is coming from. In fact, one of the most often recognised failings of this management philosophy is that the expenditure budget will be minutely detailed, while the sales budget (where the money is coming from), is based largely upon a percentage increase in last year's billing, with little or no consideration given to the change in market forces, competition or even production resource. At best, this management philosophy would be indicated on the evolution of marketing as 'the sales management philosophy'.

Marketing management

Perhaps now is the moment to briefly reread **Chapter 2**, where we quote various definitions of the marketing management philosophy, our own favourite being 'If it is not pure production of work or accounts – then it is marketing'. Marketing is as all-encompassing as that, and firms led with a management philosophy based upon marketing are usually the most successful.

So, marketing is a business management philosophy, perhaps *the* business management philosophy, but it is also a series of management tasks.

The production and resource management within a firm is often well-organised. However, marketing management is often not clearly defined and its elements split into different areas of a firm's management arrangements. Profitability is seen as a management accounting question, numbers of matters are dealt with as a resourcing issue and the firm's brochures as a marketing issue. A clear, complete picture of the firm as a business and of the firm's philosophy needs to cover all aspects of the firm from the perspective of each philosophy. Think of it like the four-colour process used to print pictures. If one colour is missing or out of register, then the picture is not clear or accurate.

For example, a trainee is about to qualify and be taken on as a full-time fee earner within a department. That change in personnel modifies all three elements of the management philosophy within that department. Each element has a view of the change and together they form a complete picture of how to proceed and maximise the return from new staff. This approach should be scaled up as a view of the whole firm and scaled down to each department's products.

Figure 5.1 The three elements of management philosophy

The quote at the beginning of this chapter may seem a little harsh. Nevertheless, it is a fact that the most successful firms we have seen in the past 20 years are either those that are run autocratically by a powerful senior or managing partner, or those that have developed a structure, common in industry, where the senior partner has a coordinating role with the three areas of management outlined above delegated to individual partners. This is nothing new. In industry, the roles would be filled by the managing director, the production director, the company secretary/accountant, the marketing director. In this scenario, the managing partner/managing director's role is one of coordination but this coordination is likely to be steered by his/her own affiliation to, or understanding of, production, accounts or marketing.

We would not seek to change people's attitudes if we did not genuinely believe that, with the advent of the Legal Services Act 2007 and the new, well-funded and aggressively promoted competition, an understanding and application of marketing, in its true sense, is essential to the survival and growth of the average legal practice in England and Wales.

Hopefully, the firm will decide to appoint a marketing partner who may, and should, seek outside assistance from qualified professionals. However the management tasks associated with marketing are undertaken, it is essential that initially all partners, and subsequently all relevant members of the firm and its staff, should understand the principles behind the tasks of marketing.

Nowhere is this more important than with department heads, or those responsible for specific disciplines within the practice. Although there must be a coordinated and firm-wide/corporate approach to marketing, it will become evident that different departments will have different needs specifically when related to promotional activity. Therefore, a wide understanding of marketing could be described as essential.

To assist with this understanding, we have extended the commonly used '4Ps' to our own '6Ps':

- Product
- Place
- Price
- Profit
- People
- Promotion

Under each of these headings we would invite, first, the managing/marketing partner and subsequently each departmental head to consider their own departments in relation to the 6Ps.

In his book *Marketing Management: Analysis, Planning and Control* (1999), Philip Kotler uses an anonymous quote as the introduction to his chapter on 'The strategic management and marketing process'.

> There are three types of companies. Those who make things happen, those who watch things happen and those who wonder what has happened.

With the Legal Services Act 2007, the advent of The New Competition and ABS, it is hoped that all legal practices in England and Wales will fall into the first of these three categories. At the very least, the aim of this book is to ensure that no reader falls into category three.

Product

What is it that the department sells? Of course, you know that what you sell is a range of legal services, but it does no harm to consider, for the sake of this exercise, that your services are discrete products. This is important because it will lead you to begin to consider the features of your products and this in turn will lead to a definition of benefits. It is benefits that clients (or customers) buy, and for too long the profession has talked to its clients about procedures and how things are achieved with a disconcerting emphasis on what the client has to do, rather than referring to the benefits that the client will derive from having the work done successfully by the practice. This exercise will also help you to consider:

- whether all different services of the firm/department are bought for the same reason (unlikely);
- what benefits the clients derive from the purchase of a specific service from you. The benefits must vary between matter types and, as most firms work in departments from a production point of view, it is quite logical that benefits analysis and definition should be discussed on a departmental basis;
- whether or not the client understands the benefits (an external communications analysis will tell you this); and
- whether you are expressing the benefits both internally and externally in the best possible way. We will deal with this in later chapters.

Under 'product', each department should consider the following:

(a) features and service;
(b) options;
(c) style;
(d) quality;
(e) capacity;
(f) brand name and branding;
(g) packaging;
(h) warranties and returns.

Features and service

As noted above, clients do not buy products, they buy benefits. However, before you can begin to define the benefits the client will derive, you need to fully understand the features of your individual products.

The legal profession is actually quite good at telling the clients what they do (features of their service), but not necessarily relating them to benefits to the client. We will discuss benefit presentation in **Chapter 7**, but it is worth starting by listing the features of each product offered by each department. The benefit analysis form will be found at the end of the chapter and covers the following:

1. What are the benefits to the client of coming to a solicitor (as opposed to another provider of legal or pseudo-legal services)?
2. What are the benefits to the client of coming to your firm (as opposed to other solicitors or providers of legal services)?
3. What are the benefits to the client of coming to your specific department?
4. What are the benefits to the client of commissioning this particular product from your firm?
5. What additional benefits do you consider the firm should offer?

It is worth undertaking this exercise through a questionnaire along these lines with all members of staff at all levels. It is often illuminating what insight can be gained from reception or other members of support staff, including, for example, the office junior who may well see more of the firm running around it than a fee earner will do in their office.

The benefit of analysis of this type has another advantage for the firm. The returned questionnaires will help to demonstrate an understanding of the firm by individual members of staff, which may indicate an attitude to their work (e.g. job versus career) and perhaps highlight training needs. Using this as a basis for discussion at a staff or departmental meeting can have great advantages both by involving staff and in such matters as cross-selling and seeking recommendation.

A service is basically the business that you are in. But how well do you actually serve the client who is buying a particular product from you? By adding additional service features to your product, you are enhancing it and differentiating it. For example, part of the product that the client is buying may be peace of mind. But how good are you at ensuring that peace of mind is maintained throughout the transaction? This will at least partly dictate a client's opinion of your product, their satisfaction with it and whether they will use you again or recommend you elsewhere. The benefit analysis referred to above should ideally incorporate such ill-defined matters as peace of mind, friendship, and care and support.

Options

If clients buy services for different reasons, it is evident that some will require a basic service and others a lot of optional extras. This is a concept that we are all used to in other areas of industry and commerce, but at first seems alien to the legal profession. Why is this?

First, because it is a profession, and its practitioners are used to telling their clients (customers), or at the very least advising them. Fine! But there is evidently a vast difference in the needs displayed by, for example, the first-time buyer and the last-time buyer. As mentioned in **Chapter 3**, what they require is totally different: a quick, easy, inexpensive move into their first home in the first case, and quite probably, a total rearrangement of their financial position in the second case. What the profession normally offers is – conveyancing.

The ability to provide various options for different clients can greatly enhance and differentiate the status of your practice. It is also a benefit that is unlikely to be available from The New Competition. However, this is dependent on those options being clearly understood by the staff and presented in a form that is understandable to the client.

Style

Every person has a profile – a style, if you like. So does every organisation, including a legal practice. For too long and in many areas, the legal profession has tried to be all things to all men. Like it or not, the firm will present a profile to the outside world and that is something that should be a strategic decision and not an accident.

In the most simplistic terms, you need to consider whether your firm is 'young and thrusting' or 'staid and reliable'. Ninety per cent of firms questioned would say that they are somewhere in middle. Ninety per cent of firms are wrong!

Consider estate agencies. Consider supermarkets. Consider car dealerships. Consider clothing outlets. Is your firm a fashionable boutique or an 'outfitter'? There is nothing wrong with either, but 90 per cent of the profession is wrong in trying to be both. The departmental heads and marketing partners should consider the style of their products and the firm.

Quality

Your firm, almost by definition, must maintain quality standards, be they those of the Legal Services Commission, the Law Society's Lexcel quality mark, Investors in People (IIP), or rules set out by the Solicitors Regulation Authority or as yet unseen frontline regulators. But the quality of your product, its place in the spectrum of choice, should be a strategic decision not an accident.

It is evident that big city firms can charge far more for what is essentially a similar service than can a small rural practice. Why is this? It is, of course, partly a result of the stance the practice takes, but more importantly, it is also an indication of the client's willingness to pay. Price is frequently used to differentiate qualities and we are conditioned to believe that 'the more we pay the more we get'.

However, it is not just a matter of pricing. The quality of 'feel' has more to do with the level of service than the execution of work. The firm/department needs to consider, product by product, the true quality level it can realistically offer.

We look at quality related to price under the 'Price' heading in this chapter.

Capacity

It is important that the firm should consider its production capacity in any given area. In later chapters, we will talk about 'prime products'. These are products that you will choose to promote and, by definition therefore, they must have the capacity to increase the volume and billing within the discipline either from existing (presumably underused) resources, or from resources that are demonstrably easy to recruit.

Brand name and branding

In many areas of commercial endeavour the brand name and image of the company are extremely important and valuable. While highly protected brand names, such as Coca-Cola or McDonald's, actually identify the product, branding is even more necessary with products that are difficult to differentiate. This is why petrol companies, for example, spend so much promoting their brands.

Clearly, a legal firm is unlikely to be a multinational on the same scale. However, branding in a more localised context is still important. What does the name of your firm mean to potential clients in your catchment area? How does it reflect the range of products you offer?

Some firms have considered branding a particular product from their range of services. The idea was developed from observing, for example, 'Your Move' as an estate agency name or the branding of various will-writing bureaux or compensation claim organisations, etc.

Generally speaking, to use branding to promote a specific legal product would be both expensive and potentially confusing. It will also most probably have a detrimental effect on cross-selling between disciplines and departments. That said, part of the purpose of all promotional activities must be to raise the awareness of your firm's name, and what that name stands for and provides, in your geographical area. There is no reason why within that area, and specifically with your past satisfied client base, you should not be as high profile as The New Competition will seek to be nationally.

Packaging

Perhaps this seems even more irrelevant than branding. It is not. While with some consumer products 'packaging' may include a review of what the product is wrapped in, this is probably better placed under 'promotion' and does not address the issue that is important to the legal profession.

'Packaging' also means bringing together in a single package several appropriately linked products. The incorporation of the various products in a home computer system is a perfect example. Of course, the products are available individually, but they can also be packaged together to increase the awareness of each component. By a slight variation of the component parts of the package, it, the package, can be tailored to different market niches.

Thus it is with the legal profession. By linking together 'last-time buyer' conveyancing with financial and inheritance tax planning, will making and other appropriate discrete services, one has a perfect package to offer to the older client. By linking together the various services available to the small businessman, a package can be developed to assist in infiltrating this comparatively lucrative market.

Warranties and returns

What 'guarantees' do you offer on your products? You are obliged by the Solicitors' Code of Conduct 2007, Rule 2 to point out to a client what you will do when something goes wrong, which without care gives the impression to a client that you are so used to things going wrong that you already have a system in place to deal with the problem. What do you do to reassure the client? Surely, a guarantee of service is not unreasonable, and is certainly one of the benefits clients will be seeking when they purchase a product from your firm.

Of course, a client is not going to return your work in the way that we might return a faulty washing machine. But it is the nature of business life that some things will occasionally go wrong. Beyond what is required by Rule 2, what procedures are in place to handle these product quality problems and, equally important, what plans are in place to win back the goodwill of a disgruntled client?

Product life cycle

Fifteen years ago we would never have thought to consider product life cycle in the context of the legal profession, but now some firms are giving up legal aid while others specialise in it. For a long time there were many firms in the middle who did nothing. Some didn't even know how to make the decision. Similar and different life-cycle pressures are happening in most areas of legal and financial work today. The marketing partner and departmental heads need to be aware of this and of the position on the life cycle of their individual products or services. Perhaps then the firm should decide department by department what should/could be dropped and what should/could be developed. In his excellent book *The 10-Day MBA* (Piatkus, 2005), Steven Silbiger gives a simple four-stage illustration to show how the product life cycle affects sales over time.

His four stages are:

1. Introduction
2. Growth
3. Maturity
4. Decline

Silbiger defines *Introduction* as the 'What is it?' stage, where awareness and education are needed for either a new product or a new market sector. This would be particularly relevant with regard to new legislation that might affect a small business operator. Perhaps the introduction of a total service for care-home owners might fall into this category, as most certainly would the promotion of a package of services aimed at the elderly.

Growth is described as the 'Where can I get it' stage, and Silbiger recognises that the second part of the growth period, together with the first half of the maturity period, is possibly a product/market peak.

The *Maturity* stage is the 'Why this one' stage – when the market is well-educated to its needs, and is differentiating between suppliers. This is clearly a stage already reached with standard conveyancing or personal injury compensation services, which is why product differentiation and target marketing is so important for these and similar products.

The fourth stage – *Decline* – is defined as the 'How much?' stage. Most solicitors would agree that at least some of their products have now reached the 'How much?' stage.

However, products can be regenerated by a re-launch, a restatement of the relevant benefits, perhaps by product packaging – linking with other appropriate services, and by the introduction of these services into new markets.

In the case of a legal practice, this does not necessarily even mean new market niches. It may simply mean taking a proactive approach to groups of people to whom, until now, we have simply reacted, and it is here and in areas like this, where the marketing management philosophy can really begin to pay dividends if properly applied.

Product differentiation

So how can you try to make your product stand out? Few people actually want to buy the products offered by a solicitor. The client's objective is to move house or make a will, to get divorced or to secure their future. To do so, he may choose to use a solicitor but the need for that solicitor is derived from the client's objectives outside the control of that solicitor. The solicitor sells the products only because of the derived need of the client.

For clients, especially those who have only infrequently used a solicitor before, it is very difficult to differentiate between the services offered and the firms offering them. Therefore, you need to consider for yourself how to differentiate each individual product, and indeed the firm itself, on behalf of the client, before you can even begin to promote your products to them.

The benefit analysis referred to above, and the use of its results, can have a major positive input in this area. It would be worth revisiting some of the headings above and considering them from a different point of view. Quality and features/benefits/service could, upon analysis, illustrate the capabilities of the firm and its staff to fulfil specific needs. Product packaging and, indeed, capacity provide differentiating product links and usable capacity. Service and brand naming can imply timeliness, courtesy and accuracy, all vital to solicitors.

And then there is fit and styling. How do the services you offer fit with the specific market niche and its profile? You can demonstrate that you understand clients and wish to serve them by, for example, avoiding or explaining legal jargon thus making your presentation less ambiguous and easier for the client to understand. Remember, nothing is gained by scoring points with your superior knowledge or making clients feel uncomfortable because they do not understand but are afraid of losing face by asking.

Additional guides to differentiation, and indeed the building of product packages perhaps leading towards niche markets, can be defined by reference to demographics. There is a growing elderly market. How is this affecting your geographical area? Single parents, gay couples or business women are all obvious niches in general terms. However, there may well be other specific niches in your catchment area or in your client base. Defining these, and indicating clearly how you can serve them, will greatly help to differentiate your product.

Can you present your products in a way that will appeal to specific members of the community (e.g. Urdu and Polish speakers)? Are you situated in a university town? Is there a dominant local manufacturer or similar organisation? Is yours a military town?

All these, and many other factors, can enable you to package your products carefully, differentiate them accurately and in due course profitably aim them at a specific niche.

Prime products

Of most importance to this whole analysis are 'prime products'. You need to define accurately your prime products and promote these, allowing other products to be a service support to the prime products. Prime products are products that are definably profitable on a stand-alone basis, in respect of which the firm needs to have:

- the production capacity (allowing for expansion);
- a defined market or market niche;
- a proven access to this market or niche.

Place

The second of our 6Ps is place. Perhaps this is more a corporate matter than a departmental one. It is nonetheless important that departmental heads consider how the firm is presenting itself from the point of view of their department. Again, the marketing or managing partner's role is one of coordinating these views.

It is evident that the action of one department can influence, sometimes negatively, the image of another department. Departmental managers should therefore consider this when they are looking, with their partner's hat on perhaps, at the presentation of the firm. Nowadays, of course, you have to consider not only the physical presentation of your 'place', but also your place in cyberspace – your website.

Our headings in this section are by no means exhaustive. The purpose of 'place' is to get you to look at your firm with outsiders' eyes. In other words, perception (rather than reality). Consider how it appears to your client and professional contacts. Indeed, it does no harm to ask them from time to time. We are in no way proposing a formal piece of research, but the occasional conversation can be most illuminating. Similarly, it is extremely worthwhile to get an outsider to telephone the firm and report back.

Two brief anecdotal stories will illustrate this point.

EXAMPLE **Gaining access**

First, an extremely successful firm in the Midlands had noted how many clients had begun to miss meetings or be late for appointments and how commercial clients were increasingly reluctant to come to the office. No one had the time to investigate this, but the answer proved quite simple. A refurbishment of the office coinciding with a rerouting of a ring road had left clients, even those who had visited the offices before, being spun out on to the ring road next to the refurbished building and past it in the heavy traffic by the bus station before they had realised they had gone too far. Typically of a modern town, this meant travelling around the entire area again, frequently for the same thing to happen. Thus, private clients were late, having also missed the entrance to the multi-storey car park, and commercial clients were seeking other firms with easier access or demanding home visits. For 12 months no one had taken responsibility for resolving this problem, which was in fact quite simple. The repainting of the end gable in white and the erecting of the largest sign permissible by local planning regulations ensured that the firm was eye-catching and easy to access. It took an outsider to recognise this. You have to be your own outsider.

> The second tale illustrates a very common situation following acquisition of new technology. Frequently, and for some time after installation, it is unmonitored, and perhaps even not fully understood by the fee earners. In this case it was a new telephone system. Our client was adamant that the new system was working perfectly and yet on 50 per cent of the occasions we telephoned the firm we were told by the receptionist that we would be put through to our contact's voicemail (perfectly acceptable) only to find that the extension just rang out continually (totally unacceptable and very frustrating). Another firm, whose receptionist knew our voices well, would say 'Yes, just putting you through,' only for us to discover that we got not our client, but the voicemail. Of course, we are the supplier to that practice and therefore how we are handled is less important (perhaps!), but we were not being singled out. Clients, too, were finding the same problem and once it had been brought to the firm's attention, the problems were quickly rectified.

But will your suppliers tell you? Probably not; and probably your clients won't, but they may well vote with their feet. Someone within the firm needs to be the firm's outside eyes, but they also need to be the outside ears.

How does your office look?

Remember, you are so used to your premises that you probably don't see them at all. What impression does the building give? How well does your reception area function? How much privacy is provided for clients? How tidy are the public areas, including the corridors and offices visited by clients? What does your literature look like? How old are the magazines in the waiting area? What are the loos like, and how are they equipped? Does the smell of soup from the vending machine permeate through the place?

If you had never walked into the building before, what would you really think?

It all seems so obvious, it is almost embarrassing to talk at such a basic level to qualified professionals, but these matters are important and these days we can no longer afford to be above such things.

Telephone

The telephone is often the first, and ultimately the regular, client contact with your 'place'. How good are you at handling clients on the phone and passing messages between each other? How likely is the anecdotal story above, or something similar that could be applied to your firm? Who is responsible for finding out? What will the procedure then be for sorting it out? Who will do that?

Differentiation

Does your place provide any unique features such as disabled access, town centre parking, a crèche, which provide additional benefits and ease the task of differentiating your overall presentation?

Where else?

Where else could you present your services? What is your policy behind home visits, clinics, seminars, joint ventures and presentation of your private client services to the employees of commercial clients?

Joint ventures

Should you consider joint ventures, especially relating to niche markets with, for example, accountants in inheritance tax planning, or the licenced trade?

Seminars

Have you the capability of presenting seminars either individually or as part of a joint venture? Have you the opportunity to present seminars, and have you the resources available, including the people who are able to present?

Location, location, location!

There is another aspect to 'place' that is outlined in Matthew Moore's *Marketing for Lawyers* (1997). Apart from touching upon the appearance of the office and the impression it gives, he also, importantly, points out that location does or should play a major part in the development of the range of products offered. This is particularly important when considering prime products. Moore's examples are illustrative, but are, of course, not exhaustive. He suggests that there is little point in offering a first-rate tax planning service in a depressed residential area, or establishing a criminal legal aid firm in a wealthy commuter village. While this is true, the likelihood is that the firm is where it is and will have to stay there, and most probably has a range of services that it will continue to offer. However, as we shall see, there is a vast difference between offering a service and promoting it. You should only promote prime products, and your prime products should be relevant to the environment in which you work.

One final point on 'place' which has already been touched upon already. You should keep a watchful eye on the changes taking place in your own immediate environment, changes in demographics relating to the population, changes in planning regulations and development, changes in local attitude and of extreme importance at the present time, and changes in the competition.

Price

This third 'P' can raise some thorny issues. Historically, the legal profession has taken a 'cost on' approach to pricing, which leads to a presentation of prices as an hourly rate. The Law Society's three-thirds approach is an extension of this 'cost on' method.

It has been said that pricing is part art and part science. If the 'cost on' and hourly rate are science, then the artistic part comes from the marketing approach of 'What will the market bear?' or 'What is the client willing to pay?'

We must emphasise the word 'willing'. It is hard to justify a price without the appropriate presentation of benefits. We will be dealing with benefit presentation and cost justification later but as an introduction, the client might be described as willing to buy at that moment when the benefits understood by the client outweigh the price being asked.

As with many marketing activities, it is worth considering pricing on a departmental basis, since 'willingness' will vary between matter types and this whole approach to pricing will assist in leading towards profit accountability department by department.

The main concern from a marketing point of view, having established that the department is trading profitably, is the method of price presentation. As a rule, the profession is poor at price justification. You should prepare in advance, and throughout the transaction, an atmosphere that leads to the client feeling they have received value for money when the bill is presented. Wherever possible, present the benefits to the client of using your services in writing, right up to the ultimate bill, rather than as currently, presenting the facts relating to the work that has been undertaken. Cost justification should be a continual process.

Strangely, the larger the bill, the simpler the presentation of price seems to be. A commercial lawyer may have little problem in justifying a £150,000 bill because it is small beer to someone who has just spent many millions of pounds. By contrast, the conveyancing department may have a considerable problem in giving a £500 quote to someone ringing round for a competitive price. This is even more the case when the potential client is searching the Internet. See 'Fixed Fees' below. This illustrates the difference in attitudes between market sectors, and why pricing and price justification training is a matter that should be undertaken department by department. However, in all cases, the principles are the same, and depend upon the client's understanding of the derived benefits.

How to assess the price

In their book, *Creating Value* (Butterworth-Heinemann, 2001) S. S. Mathur and A. Kenyon clearly link pricing strategy to product differentiation and rightly note that with well-presented differentiation (and added benefits) prices can be increased with little or no reduction in turnover, plus both improved customer satisfaction and a simultaneous decrease in complaints.

Similarly, Philip Kotler reminds us that price makes a quality statement, but also that the price–quality relationship defines your firm's or department's competitive market positioning (1999). That position adopted by your firm is a guide to potential clients when they consider your firm's products or services in comparison to alternatives from other firms or, increasingly, elsewhere. Price and quality can be varied to reposition a product or service when market conditions change.

To present your services in the best light means considering what message the price/quality position sends out to the clients.

High price + High quality = Long-term premium service strategy

High cost, high levels of service, with a high perceived value for the client.

High price + Medium quality = An overpricing strategy

This could say 'We are such busy lawyers, we couldn't possibly take on any more work' or 'You are too cheap'. However, both these positions will affect potential in the long term.

High price + Low quality = A hit and run strategy

This is not a position for any solicitor who wants to keep practising long term.

Medium price + High quality = A market penetration strategy

Highly laudable and not to be confused with discounting. It is fine to be building a market share, and obviously the strategy leaves room for price rises later. However, remember that this is almost certainly the strategy that will be adopted by The New Competition or at least those who do not actually set out for a bargain basement strategy.

Medium price + Medium quality = An average quality strategy

A middle of the road (often lazy) strategy, probably most suited to non-prime products.

Medium price + Low quality = A shoddy goods strategy

Shall we be frank? In our experience this is a strategy that is never recommended, never acknowledged, but often delivered.

Low price + High quality = A super bargain strategy (N.B. Not a loss leader)

There is still a profit element and this is an excellent strategy for penetrating or developing a new market, or filling excess capacity while enhancing a firm's standing in other commercial sectors and maintaining its demonstration of quality – e.g. providing low-cost private client services for the employees of important commercial clients. However, as noted above, beware: this is probably the strategy of at least some of The New Competition.

Low price + Medium quality = The 'pile it high and sell it cheap' philosophy

This has been used frequently over the past decade by sections of the legal profession, or their competitors within it, for example, cut-price 'bucket shop' mass conveyancing, will writing and personal injury claims.

Low price + Low quality = A cheap goods strategy

A perfectly reasonable strategy for a market trader, but with little place in the legal profession. However, some competitors such as Tesco's legal services are purporting to provide just that.

As noted throughout this chapter, the response when facing any of these strategies must be the promotion of added benefits and a clear cost justification. It may be depressing, but we should remember that a vast majority of the public genuinely believe the old joke that 'a lawyer has been defined as a man who helps you get what's coming to him'. You have to overcome this attitude.

Remember, as Matthew Moore says in *Marketing for Lawyers* (1997), 'The quality of service offered by all parts of the firm to the client is axiomatic to establishing a good marketing identity' – absolutely!

Fixed fees

It is, perhaps, appropriate here to discuss a current conundrum – that of fixed fees.

Most lawyers we meet seem to feel that fixed fees have been forced upon them, though by whom exactly is unclear as fixed fees have been around even longer than The New Competition.

From a marketing viewpoint we should be applauding them, the open-ended cheque of the hourly rate is clearly a put-off, especially for 'standard services' like conveyancing. But the effect of fixed prices is twofold. It seems that it is a downward pressure on profit margins, and an excuse or alternative to presenting benefits.

When the proposition is simply based on price, the customer will obviously, always, go for the lowest. (We discuss benefits and their presentation in **Chapter 7**.)

If a matter type is locked into the downward spiral that is fixed price, there is another alternative and one that surprisingly will both improve margins for your firm, while at the same time offering fairer value to your client.

We call it the application of 'optional extras'.

Optional extras

Every matter type will have a base service. This is absolutely not the least you can get away with doing for every client, but the essential part of the service that this individual client requires.

Take, as an example, conveyancing. The simplest service one can offer is, possibly, the purchase of a property with clear title for a cash buyer. That is your fixed fee and the price that is published. It is a low price and perfectly fair to that buyer. Why should he be paying for things he doesn't need? A price list is then drawn up for the additional services that may be required for each individual client. Dealing with a lender. Dealing with a management company. A flying freehold. Special covenants. There will be many more. Our first client needs none of these – why should he pay for them?

You will, of course, set your own base price, and draw up your own list of extras. What is essential to establish, and for you to establish with your clients, is that this is not 'switch selling' (promoting something lesser and then selling up from it) nor is it an underhanded way of increasing your prices, but a fair way of establishing a price for an individual client dependent on that client's actual needs. This principle can be applied to most matter types.

Profit

This, our fourth 'P', is, of course, a need with every firm, and an objective. Nevertheless, within many firms we have associated with, there has been an urgent need to increase profitability.

To achieve this, it is sensible to consider a profit analysis department by department. Strangely, many firms baulk at this. But it is something that we strongly advise. Perhaps your internal or external accountants have a formula to achieve analysis. If not, follow an extremely simple one as a starting point.

Assume that the firm would continue with all its buildings, IT and partnership expenses. Consider these, and other unmoveable expenses as fixed costs. These fixed overheads should be divided between the departments pro rata to their percentage of the firm's turnover. This is considered a fair measure as a small department may create a large turnover, but will still have to maintain its contribution to the overheads even if a larger department with a small turnover were to disappear – in fact, of course, it would have to increase its percentage.

Then allocate the total cost of staff, consumables and other variable overheads to each department concerned. By deducting the total overheads of a department from its turnover, the partners will have arrived at a profit/contribution for each department. The department head can then apply a similar approach to find the profit or contribution for each product. This greater understanding of profitability will help define prime products and also raise questions about pricing.

There are, of course, reasons for continuing to offer loss-making products – to complete the range, or to enable the firm to service important clients fully, for example. However, in every case, the partners should know which products are profitable and which are not, and by how much.

People

If there is one enterprise that can truly be said to be based on our fifth 'P', people, it has to be the legal profession.

We include people (and profit) along with the traditional 4Ps of the marketing mix, because of the uniqueness of the profession. Undoubtedly, the quality and training of the people that make up the firm are vital to the firm's stability and growth. Indeed, it could be argued that the aspirations of the individuals within the firm will power that growth. Matthew Moore notes in *Marketing for Lawyers* that 'an increasing number of partners have left firms in recent years to join practices where there is a greater will to develop and grow'. And it is not just partners. The best people at every level will seek out the best firm wherever possible and we have repeatedly found when talking to applicants for jobs that they would most like to work with a firm that they considered was in control of its own destiny. No one has ever used the phrase, 'marketing-led practice' but this is what it amounts to.

It is depressing therefore to note that in a vast majority of our client firms (even the friendliest), we still hear repeated complaints about the old 'them and us' syndrome as it applies between staff and partners. Subsequently, it is often denied by partners, but we believe whatever the truth, the perception of staff in many firms is that they are kept ill-informed. This often leads to a feeling of underlying suspicion, and a lack of appreciation.

As an aside, it is worth considering that most staff, in many different organisations, believe that they have a full and complete picture of their organisation. The truth is that very few are as well-informed as they could be, and inevitably there will be areas of information not available to them. These gaps, these missing parts, are often filled with gossip and speculation and this can lead to the staff having a view of the firm and its aspirations that is very different from the view held by the partners.

We would suggest a formal approach be taken to staff communications and think that perhaps the introduction of quality circles, or perhaps something similar with a different name, should be considered. In essence, these are regular staff meetings which, if handled properly, can provide a valuable two-way conduit of information, opinions and ideas.

From a marketing point of view, however, the marketing/managing partner should consider the following:

- What do staff say to clients?
- What do staff say socially about the firm?
- Do the staff share the partnership vision?
- Do they understand their role in this vision?
- How are they rewarded (this is not just a question of money)?
- Are they the first or the last to know about a new promotional campaign?

Again, this is only intended to be an indicative list, but our recommendation in all cases is that it is important to keep the staff informed and involved. Staff like to be included and this can be particularly significant in areas such as strategic and promotional planning.

The skills audit undertaken as a result of **Chapter 2** will be of invaluable help in addressing staff interests, issues and training requirements.

To maintain crucial staff quality level, successful recruitment is vital. This is covered in a later chapter of this book, but at this early stage we would point out that too often firms neglect to 'sell themselves' to the applicant they most desire who, almost by definition, will be attractive to other firms.

Promotion

Let's be truthful. Promotion is what most people in the legal profession think marketing is. As an example, we have worked for a firm in the south of England who had a 'general management committee' and a 'marketing committee'. Fortunately within this firm, it was just semantics. The marketing committee was really an advisory committee on the subject of promotion, and indeed had some very good ideas, while the general management committee was much concerned with the 6Ps as described in this chapter. Both the senior partner and the managing partner who, of course, sat on this committee, were instinctive marketers. Sadly, neither would consider themselves as such and continue to mistake marketing for promotion, believing rather in 'general management'. However, they are still extremely successful and profitable so in this case it really is 'a rose by any other name'.

Regrettably, not all firms are like that, and although the profession has come a long way from sitting behind a brass plaque and referring to its past satisfied clients as 'dead files', it still has a long way to go in matters of promotion and needs to move at increasing speed in view of The New Competition.

Fortunately, most firms do now consider their 'dead files' to be their potential 'user base' and this change is a great advantage, as the basic principle of promotion for the legal profession (and, indeed, its expansion) must be to look first inside the firm. Unfortunately, many firms who believe they have a database in fact have no more than an 'un-cleansed' mailing list. Later in the book we shall show how to put this to good use, and the whole of **Chapter 6** is devoted to this subject.

Much of the second half of this book is devoted to the practical matters of promotion, but first some vital ideas that underpin both theory and practice. Promotion can involve many things, from office presentation, stationery, leaflets to personal selling, direct mail, TV advertising (see the list in the questionnaire in the tasks section of this chapter).

In the ominously numbered Chapter 13 of *The Professional Adviser's Guide to Marketing* edited by G. Humphrey and Norman Hart (Mercury Business Books, 1990), Robert Hall writes about 'marketing in practice for solicitors'. It is an interesting read. Nowhere does he mention promotion. He has a clear understanding that marketing is far more than that, and that promotion itself comes at the end of the marketing chain.

Nevertheless, promotion is relevant unless you are a partner of the largest firm in the world with over 470 partners and more than 1,400 lawyers operating in 50 offices throughout Europe, the Middle East, North and South America, Australia and the Pacific Basin, and you can bet they used a lot of promotion to get there.

Or unless you are one of the number of respondents who answered the question 'What will you do in the light of the Legal Services Act, and The New Competition?' with 'Retire!'.

CHAPTER 5 TASKS **Assess what your firm offers**

Assessment of the 6Ps

As you will see from earlier in this chapter, we have found it helpful to look at the marketing management tasks as the 6Ps (Product, Place, Price, Profit, People, Promotion).

It is under these headings that we would invite each department head to consider their own departments in conjunction with the marketing partner. The form below should be circulated to each department head.

An important part of this exercise is identifying from the clients' point of view the benefits they receive from using the services of a law firm. See point 5.

Once completed, the responses will need to be collated and a conclusion drawn for each department. It is recommended that the marketing partner arrange a marketing development session with the department heads to work through the questionnaires. The aim is to generate a marketing review document based on the questionnaire and discussions with department heads to be used as a baseline for further developments.

Marketing communications and promotional audit form

This questionnaire is intended to identify the 6Ps of marketing within the firm and, specifically, individual departments.

Where a question does not appear to be relevant, please write 'n/a' to indicate that the department head has considered the issues. Please use as many copies or additional pages as required.

1. What is it that your department sells to the client? List the 'service products' or 'physical products' your clients buy.
2. For each of the products identified, please provide a comment on the following attributes of the service or product. Each comment should reflect how the department head would like their clients to feel about the service/products offered.
   - Quality. What is the view a client would have of the quality of the products or services you offer?
   - The features. When buying a product or service, what is included in the price?
   - Options available. What potentially is charged as an extra feature of that product or service?
   - Style. The public face of your department. Where are the products or services on a scale from 'stylish boutique' to 'traditional gents'

outfitters'? How does your department differ from others in the firm in its style?

- Branding and brand name. Is the firm's name associated as a brand with one product or service, like conveyancing or PI?
- Packaging. What products or services do you link together and sell as a 'packaged' service?
- Size or capacity. With each product or service, what level of service, that is, time and thought does the client require?
- Services. For each provision of a product or service how do you measure the client's satisfaction?
- Warranties. Not just Chapter 1 of the SRA Code of Conduct; not what happens if things go wrong. What positive steps does your department take to provide 'guarantees'?
- Returns. Beyond Chapter 2; are there explicit procedures for maintaining or re-establishing a client's 'goodwill'?

3. Are all the different services offered by the department bought for the same reason?
4. Is there a combination of product/services across departments or with additional attributes that might be 'packaged' together to provide a differentiated product to the potential purchaser?
5. What benefit does the client derive from their purchase of our service? Draw up a shortlist of benefit statements for each product. Each statement should contain the phrase, '. . . which means that . . .'. See the additional questionnaire form on benefits analysis. Example:

   We have many years' experience in this area of law which means that you can be confident we will quickly and knowledgeably deal with your matter.

   . . . which means that we save you time and money.
6. How does the client understand (or have communicated to them) the benefits of the product or service?
7. What feature, advantage or benefit of a product or service could differentiate it in the view of a potential purchaser? Use this question to understand what is a feature of the service, and advantage of your firm's service and the resulting benefit to the client.
8. Does the department have a 'prime product'?
9. How does the firm's office look? What impression does the building give to potential clients of your department?
10. Does the firm's office provide any unique features such as disabled access, town centre parking or proximity to a crèche?
11. How good is your department at handling clients on the phone and passing messages to other departments regarding potential further work? Is there a formal or informal procedure?

12. What is the department's policy towards home visits, clinics, seminars, joint ventures and the presentation of our private client services to the employees of our commercial clients?
13. Is the information for your department on the firm's website current and accurate? How often is it reviewed?
14. Using the table (Figure 5.2) below, place the identified products or services in the area most appropriate. Use the external choice of products or services a potential client has to gauge the relative quality or price your department offers.
15. How are costs or prices discussed with the potential clients of your department? Is there a set procedure followed?

Figure 5.2 Quality vs. price

16. Do the firm and departments have profit and contribution information available? Are there any planned loss leader products or services? Please provide details.
17. What areas of promotion does your department currently use to communicate with potential and current clients?
    - Brochures, standard
    - Brochures, tailored to clients' position
    - Press and public relations
    - Newsletters and booklets
    - Telephone answering and messaging systems
    - Direct mail and leaflet dropping
    - Articles and lectures
    - Seminars
    - Client entertaining
    - Advertising
    - Directory advertising
    - Posters
    - Television and radio
    - Videos, PowerPoint and presentations
    - Website
    - Social media
    - Direct selling
    - Personal selling
    - Cross-selling
    - Actively seeking recommendation
    - Sponsorship
    - Other, not covered by the categories above
18. Have there been any problems or promotional errors?
19. Additional information and comments.

Please add any further information you feel relevant to the products and services you provide.

Benefits analysis questionnaire

Attached is the draft text of a memo to all fee earners to help them analyse the benefits they see from the services they offer.

Ideally, each person should be encouraged to complete the form alone. Clearly, this will produce a lot of repetition, but it will also provide an opportunity to see which member of staff has given real consideration to the subject and which has just dashed to get it out of the way. Analysis of the returned questionnaires can provide an indication of where further explanation, or possibly even training, is required.

To help identify benefits, there is a list of reasons why people or companies use solicitors. We will be using this list again in **Chapter 7** when we look at practice development issues. It may be useful to retain the notes made at this point for use in **Chapter 7**.

Draft memorandum – benefits to clients

To: All fee earning staff

From: Marketing partner

WHAT IS IT WE DO FOR OUR CLIENTS?

As part of the continuing work on [*marketing management/practice development*] we are looking at the benefits to our clients of our firm's work. To understand this better, we need to ask each fee earner to think about what it is they provide for the clients by way of benefits derived from our services. The aim is to produce a list of benefits to be used across the firm and in future promotional activity.

Below is a questionnaire section that outlines what it is we are looking for. Once completed, [*name of partner responsible for marketing*] will be collating the questionnaires so please write as many benefits as occur to you. Since everyone will be completing this form, we understand there will be repetition from people in the same department. We would expect you to spend half an hour or less. If you get 'writer's block' please call [*named person*] for inspiration.

To help identify benefits, below is a list of reasons why people or companies use solicitors.

A client is looking for a combination of the following:

- Help in solving problems (getting out of trouble)
- Help in preventing problems
- Money – ways to save it, keep it or make it
- Background – experience of or expertise in a particular matter
- Background – experience or expertise in the client's industry or field (in the case of commercial clients)
- Attention and respect
- Availability
- New ideas
- Timeliness
- Confidence that provides the client with peace of mind
- A big name in the area or a recognised expert in their field

- Being kept informed throughout
- Follow-up
- General business counsel (in the case of commercial clients)
- General personal counsel (in the case of private clients) – as it was in the days of the family solicitor or the 'man of affairs'
- Value – and this does not mean cheapest, it means understanding the benefits paid for
- The right chemistry. Everyone and every organisation has a profile. The trick is to fit yours to theirs

Using the list as a guide, in general or specific terms where possible, please use the following page to list the benefits you see your client receives.

BENEFITS LIST FOR [FIRM'S NAME]

Please return your benefits list to [*name*] by [*date*].

List the benefits of consulting a solicitor.

List the benefits of instructing [*firm's name*].

List the benefits of buying a particular service from your department.

List the benefits offered to a client by your department.

AN EXAMPLE FOR A WILLS, PROBATE AND TRUSTS DEPARTMENT

- List the benefits of consulting a solicitor.

  The changing legal position means that solicitors are the best placed professional to deal with wills, LPAs, trusts and inheritance tax planning. The training and experience ensure that a will is drafted and executed correctly and the client has peace of mind that their affairs are in order.
- List the benefits of instructing [*firm's name*].

  Our firm has over 50 years of experience dealing discreetly and promptly with changes in both the law and family circumstances.

  Our firm offers a range of legal services to cover all personal circumstances ensuring your affairs are kept in order.

  Alternatively:

  Our firm focuses on providing up-to-date specialist legal advice that is easily accessible and clearly delivered without jargon. The client can feel confident that there'll be no legal 'surprises' in the future.
- List the benefits of buying a particular service from your department.

  Our service provides wills, trusts, LPAs and inheritance tax planning to combine those elements into a comprehensive and secure future for clients and their relations.

- List the benefits offered to a client by your department.

  Our experience of wills, trusts and estates prevents future problems and provides peace of mind for the client.

  We will maintain the will by contacting the client for periodic revisions, suggesting new ideas in changed circumstances.

  We present a range of options of the client to show the value in preparing a will.

The partnership and departmental heads must recognise the role of marketing in every aspect of the firm's activities.

With the guidance of the marketing partner, each departmental head should undertake a review of their department and its activities in line with the 6Ps. The marketing partner should then collate that to provide a firm-wide overview. This and the other analysis undertaken should form the basis of the firm's 'official' strategic marketing plan.

The partners should introduce a benefit analysis via questionnaire to each member of staff. This can be used:

(a) for promotion;
(b) as training needs analysis;
(c) as a prelude to the task of presenting benefits.

By the end of this chapter, the firm will have undertaken a serious marketing review of its operation, its strategic planning, management and objectives. We will now move on to organisation of this information prior to implementation of the expansion and promotional planning.

6

Databases

In this chapter we will explain the importance of your database to the development and value of your business. We will show you how to overcome the fears of database development and how to face up to the fact that, in truth, you possibly have only a mailing list. We will demonstrate that creation of a true database is the cheapest and easiest way towards business growth and increased profitability. We will introduce you to a simple process we call the 'one minute marketing solution' to facilitate your growth.

We will discuss the need to separate private and commercial clients and then how to subdivide further for maximum performance benefit. We will also introduce you to a new and vital database which we call the 'professional contacts register' and show you how to measure it against potential in your area or chosen market prior to building it up and, perhaps most importantly, we will discuss how to use these databases automatically, regularly and monitor the benefit that databases can bring both to your profits and to the firm's intrinsic value.

You can make new friends, but you can't make old friends. – Martin Amis

This quotation, like so many apt sayings, old or new, is simple, obvious (once it has been said), profound and useful.

If, in fact, it read 'You can make new clients but you can't make old clients', it could be the most important piece of information you have ever received relating to the development of your practice. For a legal practice, your 'old friends' are your past satisfied clients, and yet in our experience, few practices make any consistent attempt to develop that relationship, that friendship.

It is worth considering that The New Competition approach the relationship with their customers on a future profits view. They ask what revenue and therefore profit can we expect to make from each of our customer records in the next one, two or three years? What products and services do they require that allow us to make increased profits?

The answer to these questions comes directly from the detailed databases of the current and past customers. Without that information, it is impossible to assess the future potential. There are two consequences for solicitors' firms. First, to compete in the future ABS environment (see **Chapter 8**) a firm needs to consistently collect, analyse and use client information. Second, if your firm is looking to attract outside investment under the ABS structure, a potential investor will be looking for this type of analysis and its incorporation in the business plan they will be investing in.

It's an unpleasant fact that the value of an established solicitors' practice is now minimal in the harsh commercial realities of the changing professional services sector. Several factors such as increased professional indemnity insurance costs and the lack of client relationship management systems (CRM) means that firms have little hard evidence of where their profits will come from in the future. Past performance is no indicator of value as The New Competition could 'cherry pick' key sections of the legal services market.

Established firms do have a significant advantage in the market: past satisfied clients. Almost all the consumer and SME research indicates that buyers trust solicitors and want to use their service but there is an information gap between solicitors and their past clients. In a 2010 YouGov survey consumers indicated that they would like to have easy-access telephone advice similar to the NHS Direct service (presumably, free of charge) and local 'drop-in' centres where they could discuss their legal services requirements. Using different language, these services already exist. Firms will take calls or visitor enquiries about a particular issue and in most areas people live within two or three miles of a solicitors' office. What is missing is the consumers' understanding of how easy it is to talk to a solicitor and solicitors' inability to use their databases of past clients to communicate their openness to talk to clients.

The purpose of this brief review of the market is to highlight the value, importance and necessity of good client information usage and, therefore, a well-managed database of accurate client records. To effectively and efficiently bridge the communication gap, your firm needs to know who your future clients are, what services you can provide profitably and how you can contact them in a way that is suitable for them. To do that, you must have accurate client details to provide them with timely and useful information and the ability to aggregate your firm's client database to provide management and marketing information to develop the firm.

The importance of a database

Every computer system we have seen in a legal practice includes the facility for the collation, development and use of a database. To date, we have seen few firms who use the database facility fully, and many who do not use it at all. Why is this?

We feel it is a result of a 'production' bias in the firm's management (computerisation is used in all areas of production of work from precedents to standard paragraphs) and, because deregulation is still in any real sense a recent occurrence, the full marketing benefit of IT is not always appreciated.

The purpose of the questionnaire at the end of this chapter (and on the CD-Rom) is to ascertain where the firm currently stands with regard to databases and to assist you to define the best and most practical way forward for your individual firm. This will also build on the results of the work outlined in previous chapters.

But before that, some background thoughts on why marketing information databases are needed and why they are important to the development of your practice.

In many ways, the legal profession is in the middle of two extremes. Not that long ago, the profession was prevented by custom and Law Society rules from doing much more than putting up a brass plaque. It is no wonder that they referred to their client base as 'dead files' because they had no need to be proactive with their past satisfied clients. First, they were in a non-competitive market which, if not strictly a monopoly, was so regulated that no solicitor could compare his/her quality of work with another or even claim to be a specialist. What actual practice development work did take place was almost exclusively on the social circuit where professional contacts, recommenders and potential clients could be met, although even then it was sometimes 'infra dig' to discuss business. Solicitors and their services had to be sought out and most solicitors were happy with that situation.

Second, lawyers could rely on clients' loyalty. The legal profession was, perhaps, 'family solicitor syndrome' and a lawyer truly was a 'man of affairs' to whom it was the client's second nature to refer for advice when any matter occurred. 'My solicitor' was as common a term as 'my doctor' or 'my bank'.

Third, lawyers in those days knew (and many firms today claim) that the majority of their work came as a result of recommendation from existing clients. Therefore, by doing quality, timely legal work, the practice's development would follow automatically. Of course, quality work will always be of prime importance, but in light of The New Competition, this can no longer be the only facet.

This, of course, all raises the question: how did the firm start in the first place? It would, however, be impertinent to point out to the second or third generation of lawyers that they are, in fact, still living on the entrepreneurial skills of the firm's founders.

It is the prime principle behind this book that your firm should develop and expand by underpinning its existing client base, replacing the old 'loyalties' with positive communications, seek to promote a wider range of services to existing clients and actively seek recommendation.

These actions, which in marketing jargon are referred to as vertical and horizontal development (see **Chapter 7**), should be the first priority of your firm and are the quickest, easiest and cheapest ways to promote the firm and grow it. However, it all depends upon looking inside the firm first, at the existing satisfied client base. This is the firm's seed corn. This is why an up-to-date, accurate and easily accessible database is needed.

The SRA's move to 'outcome focused regulation' (OFR) adds another dimension to client records. To show your firm has reliable and regular communications plans to maintain contact with past clients will certainly help towards satisfying the new set of practice principles.

Data-gathering opportunities: 'the one minute marketing solution'

The obvious time when marketing data is collected by fee earners and support staff is at the opening and closing of a matter. Your IT system should be configured to allow easy data entry without interrupting the fee earner's work for the client. These two opportunities to capture the data need to have different approaches, formal procedures and measurable records. It is also worth encouraging fee earners and support staff to update client's records throughout the matter. In the same way that interim billing is encouraged, fee earners should look at interim satisfaction measures and opportunities to offer other services. This will catch complaints earlier, giving an opportunity to deal with them quickly. It will also help provide the evidence needed to satisfy the SRA's OFR approach.

It is possible that if fee earners can see an immediate reason for this data inputting, they will be more inclined to do it. By 'interim satisfaction' we are proposing that the clients should have pointed out to them, as we go along, good things that have happened or dangers that have been avoided making them pleased with their solicitor as the matter progresses and, as a by-product, less likely to query a bill later. These positives can be entered in the client records.

What must be recorded is interim opportunity recognition. When a fee earner sees a current client need, or defines a future one, it should be recorded and, of course, then passed on to the appropriate department.

Matter opening

At this point, there needs to be a balance between getting the information you want, while giving the client the attention they need for their immediate requirements and not overburdening them or the fee earner with a lot of what might be seen as peripheral questions. However, since the client will have to impart the details of their requirements, they may also be able to provide useful additional information that the fee earner should record. Each firm will have its own ways to record a new client or open a new matter, and there will be differences between private and commercial clients. These procedures can easily, with a little thought and training, be adapted to capture all that is available by a standard paper form or IT system entry application.

It is worth avoiding having too many compulsory information requirements on an IT client database. Basic contact details are enough initially for the fee earner to obtain the usual client or matter number they require to get started. If the details are handwritten and then added later, that is acceptable as long as it is done and the system is set up to report where information has been missed.

Most consumer research shows that past clients appreciate being remembered by 'their' firm. Therefore, those people that take incoming enquiries need to have quick access to client records together with the training and procedures in place to use the records appropriately.

Matter closing

This opportunity to collect data involves two steps:

1. Review the contact details and the additional marketing information held for the client.
2. Consider the question: what does this client want next?

As part of the closing procedure and before billing, the fee earner needs to take a few minutes to consider what they have just done and what they feel the firm can offer their client in the future. Reviewing the client's contact details using a paper or IT system form will increase the usable information for that client. It is usually a simple process of going through a few basic questions.

It cannot be overestimated how important this procedure is to the future success of your firm. Perhaps this is the pivotal point in this book! It is simple and takes little time away from fee earning, but is the most efficient and powerful way of increasing profits and developing your firm. As mentioned above, we call this process the 'one minute marketing solution'; it brings together the elements of marketing a fee earner can do and makes an explicit and measurable process that puts clients and their information at the heart of a firm.

When a fee earner has finished a matter for a client, or at a suitable point during the matter, he or she should become responsible for recording the answers to the question: what does this client want next? This takes little time but is the most valuable bit of selling a fee earner can do. The response must be recorded and will take different forms for each firm, mostly depending on what services your firm offers. On all occasions, a future review date must be set to revise the client's information to assess if their requirements have changed (with the exception of the 'no further contact' list).

Again, incentives and procedures can help achieve the desired results. Where fee earners are targeted on billing, ensure that completion of the marketing database form is a compulsory step before a matter can be billed. It is possible to add incentives that encourage the recording and rewarding of internal and external referrals along with the percentage of complete records, and ultimately the additional matters, and therefore revenue and profit from that client.

Ultimately, a solicitor is responsible for acting in the best interests of the client. Since most solicitors specialise, this system allows them to confidently fulfil their professional duty to the client. Once the information is in the database, other fee earners or departments can pick up the requirements and act on those future needs.

Database management: quality control

In a number of practices, we have introduced what can be described as a non-technical database manager. Along with the work of setting up the distinct databases (see below), their main purpose has been to monitor the quality and quantity of data held on each client. Using the IT system's database reporting tools, a database manager can see how many client records there are and how many data points each record has completed. This analysis can be done by fee earner or department and gives the partners a management view of their database's value.

Individuals and departments that have a lower percentage of complete records can have additional training and help to understand the value of this information to the firm. Ultimately, a fee earner who does not keep full records needs to be assessed for their suitability in the job they do. Using small incentives, or even just the competitive nature between different departments, can increase the number of complete records when the figures are produced regularly and used in management meetings. Whatever, this record keeping now needs to become mandatory.

A complete record is usually a set number of fields (text fields in the IT application) that need to be completed. (Below is a list of suggested fields.) You will need to define what a complete record is and let everyone know the details. What you are aiming for is a monthly ranked table of each fee earner's complete records for each client they have dealt with in a set period of time (see Table 6.2 below). Each fee earner will have a percentage of complete records and the last month's number as a comparison. You are creating standards of performance criteria.

Table 6.1 Example fee earners' percentage table

Database records quality report – May 2010		
Overall	**32.8%**	**29%**
Fee Earner	**to May 2010**	**to April 2010**
JL	89%	76%
KE	76%	71%
SO	73%	69%
CHS	67%	75%
CP	63%	50%
NP	59%	54%
CLS	44%	40%
ACP	41%	41%
GG	37%	25%
JVB	28%	1%
GC	24%	29%
JR (W)	16%	15%
BP	12%	9%
CG	10%	5%
SH	9%	4%
AW	6%	4%
RJT	2%	2%
SAH	2%	11%
GIW	0%	0%
PH	0%	0%
MLD	0%	0%

[shaded] denotes an increase on the previous month

The percentage figures for each fee earner are based on the number of client records with a attribute/interest recorded against the total number of clients that fee earner has closed matters for since 1st January 2009

When looking at your current database, complete records can initially be as low as 30–40 per cent, representing just basic contact details like post-codes. As the percentage increases as fee earners become responsible for updating client records, the database manager can revise the definition of a complete record to include more relevant data. While this decreases each fee earner's percentage of complete records, it does increase the value of the database and keeps the challenge of good client information in the minds of fee earners.

For example, when domestic client records reach the 90 per cent complete mark, you can change the definition of a complete record to include the date of birth (+ date of death) as a requirement. For commercial client records the business's accountant or bank manager details can be added. This can also help with the professional contacts register outlined later in this chapter.

A note of caution: 'Dot fields' can be a problem when competitive people want to improve their percentage of complete records or find themselves falling behind. These are fields where a '.' (full stop) has been inserted to fool the IT system into thinking there is data there when there is not. Some IT systems can automatically stop this but it is worth keeping in mind, and should be banned.

Strangely, even in firms that do have a better-than-average client database, there is often little evidence that it is used for either analysis or promotion. It is necessary therefore to ascertain exactly what can be done with the database and what is corrupting it (e.g. poor fee earner updating). We have heard a wide variety of excuses ranging from inappropriate equipment to an apparent unwillingness between partners to share their hard-won contacts. Hopefully, these comments are only excuses with the real truth being pressure of work. Whatever the position, it is a ridiculous situation to have the equipment and the information but not the ability to use it.

Fee earners or departments that have particularly close relationships with their clients often have concerns that they will lose the primary contact role with their clients. They are concerned that others will bombard the client with inappropriate promotional material that will be an embarrassment to the fee earner. However, these high-value clients are possibly your firm's most valuable asset and that value is at risk if the particular fee earner leaves the firm.

To deal with this issue there needs to be clear promotional policies that ensure the fee earners are confident that their special clients will remain just that, in a special category. We have described these as 'high-value clients' and marked them in the database so that they will not receive any promotional material unless their fee earner agrees.

Your firm's database of potential future clients is the most valuable asset in your firm. With your ability to use it to improve clients' interaction with the firm provides measurable management information that is vital for your future success.

When discussing the firm's database, we are, in fact, referring to three distinct databases, each of which needs a distinct approach:

1. The private client database
2. The commercial client database
3. The professional contacts register

Private client database

Much will depend upon how much information about past clients you currently hold within your practice. You may consider that you have enough historical information to complete the inputting without reference to the client, and develop it from there with all future clients. There is, for example, no reason why an existing client should not be asked to complete the questionnaire when coming into the office for a new matter. Certainly, all new clients should complete, or have completed for them by the fee earner, the firm's inputting information sheet.

If it is decided that you will refer back to past clients for the information, great care needs to be taken when distributing the questionnaire, which can be as fraught with dangers as with other types of satisfaction survey. Ideally, you need to demonstrate to the client or contact that there is a benefit to them of completing the questionnaire, which is why we have devised the 'client registration scheme', detailed in **Chapter 11**.

How you go about requesting information from clients is a matter to be discussed and decided individually within the firm. It is most certainly worth considering what you are going to do with the information, prior to asking the question – but, that said, you should be building a database for the future, which may require more information than you feel you currently need. Another observation is that clients are conditioned to answer questions from their solicitor in the same way as they do from their doctor. Therefore, questions that may seem to you a little impertinent may not strike the client as being so.

As mentioned above, a very reasonable marketing objective is to get to the position where your clients consider you to be their solicitor and refer to you as 'my solicitor' in the same way as they would refer to 'my doctor'.

Some solicitors' firms, especially those with a large legal aid or criminal practice, may wish to record certain sections of their work in a separate client database. But, whatever, it is essential that those types of clients can be sorted in or out. In essence, this database needs to hold all essential demographic data on each client of the firm.

To avoid double inputting, firms should use their current systems of practice or case management and use the 'marketing module' if it is available or at least link the marketing database to the IT system. This, presumably, will provide each client with a unique reference number and we would suggest that the same number be used for identifying the client on the marketing database.

One area that causes concern is 'double' clients or multiple entries. With matrimonial matters, the client is almost always a single individual and therefore no complication is found in recording the data. Sometimes, however, married couples are the 'client', for example, in conveyancing and the joint ownership of property. It is conceivable that the firm may wish to subsequently write to or target the husband or wife separately. In some instances a single person may appear several times. A real example is of a local accountant. He is a referrer of work to the firm, is finance director for several businesses that instruct the firm and is a private client of the firm with a large extended family who also use the firm. With a name similar to John Smith you will appreciate that using a unique reference number for individuals will help distinguish this very valuable John Smith from the several others in the database that are past domestic conveyancing clients.

A persistent problem that frequently arises in the conveyancing department is that the client file has been opened with the address the client currently occupies. It is essential that this is updated when you convey the client to their new home; it is surprising how often this does not happen.

The practice management system will undoubtedly capture work by matter type, so that the firm can analyse how much of each of its products it is selling. However, we also need to be able to analyse the evolution of each client relationship and, over time, be able to study how much we have done for them, what we have done for them and, indeed, what we have not yet done for them. Therefore, matter type analysis needs to be collated not only en masse and per fee earner, but also on the client database.

Most firms have a matter type code in the practice management system for accounting purposes. Sometimes, these are too broad. For example, frequently, conveyancing is recorded whereas, from a marketing point of view, it would be more useful to analyse the work under the following headings:

- Sale of property
- Purchase of property
- Sale and purchase of property
- Re-mortgaging a property

There are two other private client and commercial client categories that are worthy of consideration:

- 'Nearly' clients
- Prospects

Nearly clients

Nearly clients are 'clients' who come to the firm, but whose matters do not proceed to completion, or at least not to a point where a bill is raised. Clearly, there is potential here and a need for these individuals to be captured on the database.

We would suggest that they are captured in the same way as real clients (i.e. so far as is possible the same database information obtained), the only difference being that there will be no corresponding real matter(s).

If the client database is incorporated into the practice management system (accounting application), as opposed to a separate computer (termed by some Marketlaw clients as the 'marketing machine'), it may be necessary for reasons of system design to create a dummy matter type for nearly clients. Provided that this can be sorted in and out of the database, it would cause no problem. This logically could be the matter discussed but which did not materialise.

Prospects

It is a similar process for 'prospects', although, in this case, a specific matter is unlikely to have been discussed.

It can be argued that every adult is a prospective client for legal services and therefore the recording of 'prospects' on your database needs to be clearly defined. In the broadest sense, a prospect is a person or commercial entity that the firm, or individual fee earner, believes will place business with the firm at some time in the near future, and with whom the firm should maintain contact.

With private clients, this knowledge will probably be acquired as a result of personal contact, the prospect being a friend or associate of an individual fee earner. Some firms, in our experience, have drawn up a friends and associates contact list, similar to the professional contacts register, to ensure that the firm maintains a professional contact with the individual in addition to the social contact by the staff member.

With commercial prospects, apart from the social contact referred to above, the association is likely to occur when a manager, director or other member of staff leaves an existing commercial client for a new job with another company.

Non-IT information systems

We recognise that we have assumed your firm has a computer-based IT system. If this is not the case, we would strongly recommend you take the plunge, buy a computer and software, then get the training required to operate it successfully. However, paper-based systems can be used, and many firms still rely on paper records. Paper records have the difficulty of being slow to process. With the rise of The New Competition, whose organisations extensively use IT to react to and develop their markets, paper systems will require too much time and resources to manage and use effectively if your firm has more than a handful of clients.

Private client database/questionnaire inputting form

A version of this inputting form is included on the CD-Rom.

In designing the database or modifying your current system and the inputting questionnaire process, it is necessary to try and look forward and anticipate future requirements. We would suggest the following data fields should be included. Clearly, our list is not exhaustive, nor is it obligatory. Individual firms will decide what is appropriate for them.

- Client number
- Client name + title
- Client address (including full postcode – vital for geographical sorting)
- Salutation(s)
- Occupation
- Marital status
- Age
- Sex (important if their 'title' is Dr or Prof.)
- Number of children
- Accommodation, e.g. owner occupier, freeholder, leaseholder, tenant, others
- Mortgage: type/size
- Will: date made, date of last codicil or update
- Is firm executor, yes/no, names of other executors/have executors been contacted
- Introduced by
- Partner in charge
- Newsletter recipient (yes/no)
- Mailshot recipient (yes/no)
- Christmas card recipient (yes/no)
- Client matters: matter number, matter designation, matter type code, date opened, date closed, destroy option date, estimated value, actual value, fee earner code/name, partner in charge (of this specific matter), comments
- Is this client in a position to influence the placing of commercial work?

Estimated/actual values are included in this list because we would recommend that anticipated values should be calculated by the fee earner on the date that the file is opened. The actual value must be entered when it is known. This will enable the firm to:

- estimate at any time the approximate amount of work in progress from the anticipated value of open files;

- calculate, from the value of closed files, the average value of different work types for the purposes of analysis, future budgeting, fee earner comparison and targeting.

The question regarding the placing of commercial work is extremely useful. Is the client a director of a local company, does he run his own business, perhaps he is a shopkeeper or a self-employed artisan? Any such client, and many others, could welcome a discussion (at the appropriate time) totally unrelated to the current matter in hand, but concerning their business, and illustrating the fee earner's attention to detail and continuing, genuine, client care.

Executors are a perfect example of an opportunity to build a prospect list. It is simple to write and inform the executor of their inclusion in your client's will, with a brief outline of their responsibilities, and, of course, a promotion of the firm. They can then be included on all general mailing lists. The same applies to many other areas of legal work where third party names are required.

Commercial client database

Self-evidently, the private client database is a people-driven record. Sadly, many firms record their commercial client database by company name rather than individual contact. While this is understandable from a production point of view – it is, after all, the company or partnership that is the firm's client – it is, nevertheless, somewhat unhelpful from a marketing point of view.

Clearly, what you want to record here, in addition to the important details of the company itself, are the contacts you have in the firm. It is here that things become complicated. First, it is very possible that more than one partner/fee earner works for the company client. Second, it is almost certain that the practice as a whole has several contacts within the client's company. Third, many of those contacts may be, or could become, private clients of your firm. This is a usual practice in the accountancy profession where the private tax affairs of directors, etc. are generally handled by the company's accountant.

Understandably, people, and particularly solicitors, are rightly concerned about appearing inefficient or upsetting people. For example, you don't want to find you have sent several copies of a particular mailing to an individual and to the firm. There is a school of thought that says in the overall scheme of things that this is an acceptable risk, and one that could be avoided by cross-referencing. Whatever the truth, the fear of upsetting people has often caused a commercial client database to be neglected, out of date, underused and therefore next to useless from a marketing viewpoint. The marketing partner needs to show leadership here.

Commercial client database/inputting questionnaire form

A version of this inputting form is included on the CD-Rom.

The level of information required by each firm varies. The list below is purely indicative, and will inevitably need modification to suit your own particular needs. As a minimum the commercial inputting questionnaire must include the following:

- Company name
- Contact name 1
- Position
- Contact name 2
- Position
- Accountant
- Year end date
- No. of employees
- Turnover
- SIC number
- Business type (sole trader, limited liability, plc, etc.)
- Size – number of sites
- Shareholders or owners
- Bank branch
- Main matter type of work
- Estimate of the percentage of the legal work instructed to other firms
- Number of directors or employees already known to firm

Professional contacts register

Within your firm, each fee earner will have professional contacts. We would define a professional contact as someone who, in the course of their work, could say to their customer or client, 'You need to consult a solicitor about this'. When this happens we want at least a proportion of them to say 'You should consult [*your firm's name*] about this'. In short, you want them to recommend your firm. Again, this is probably best developed on a departmental basis, as clearly the professional contacts who can provide work for the commercial market (insurance agents, surveyors, stockbrokers, banks, accountants, etc.) may differ from those who provide a lead to the private client market (estate agents, building societies, Citizens Advice Bureaux, etc.).

Some institutions such as banks may be common to both markets. However, it is likely that the actual contact within the institution will vary (e.g. the mortgage arranger, the small business adviser, etc.).

It should be the responsibility of the marketing partner to bring together all these ad hoc individual contacts into a usable register based on another database. This database will be less difficult to compile than those described for clients but, from a promotional point of view, may be even more valuable. The development of a professional contacts register will structure the activity of maintaining contact on a more formal basis and, it is hoped, will increase these activities within this important promotional area without becoming an additional burden for fee earners.

It is intended that creation of a professional contacts register will ensure that your communication with business associates on the database becomes not just regular but automatic. The marketing department (rather than the fee earner) will get in touch via letter, telephone call, mailshot, etc.; actual personal contact comes from the fee earner. This way the basis of the register can be more widespread and the contact with the register more regular.

Despite its simplicity, this really is a very powerful promotional tool. As noted before, a majority of work comes to any solicitors' practice as a result of recommendation, and what is being suggested here is a formal approach, actively seeking that recommendation. Furthermore, once the register is in place and the campaign of contact agreed and initiated, the actual work of maintaining contact is systematic and therefore far less time-consuming for the fee earner involved.

Once the marketing partner has collated and registered the professional contacts that already exist within the firm, the departmental heads should give consideration to all other categories of people who could in the course of their own work recommend the use of their department. A simple check with the professional contacts register will ensure that at least some representatives of each selected recommender's category are included. If a referrer category is missing or a new one required, telephone and other published directories or the Internet can provide initial details of contacts in that area.

As with commercial clients, it is important to remember that this is a people-driven database. It is easy to lose sight of the fact that a single contact with a bank will not reach all the mortgage advisers and small business advisers. These and probably many other banking categories should be considered individually. Similarly, success in obtaining recommendations from one branch is unlikely to influence work emanating from other branches unless the people within those branches become active professional contacts themselves. A true (though slightly disguised) client story illustrates these facts well.

A successful practice in the south of England opened a new branch in a town with a growing infrastructure, businesses and population. So confident was the firm that it put a partner in charge of developing the branch's conveyancing work. This he had to do from scratch, in the face of considerable competition from other solicitors and licensed conveyancers.

The partners had pitched the branch office's profile exactly in accordance with the young, upwardly mobile, ambitious and dynamic environment and population. Even the office itself, which was at street level, glass fronted, open plan, light and airy, appeared more like an estate agent's office than a traditional solicitor's practice. This was just as well, as it became evident the quickest route to conveyancing was via a close association with estate agents and other allied professional contacts such as mortgage brokers. The firm's premises, people and profile were exactly right and the partner in charge soon became an established member of the increasingly successful 'property sales set'.

This success led to growth based principally on recruiting suitable qualified and experienced staff. Strangely though, the predicted increase in business did not materialise. The partner in charge, perhaps flushed by his early success, failed to see the causes. While his fee earning level had not diminished, the new branch turnover had not increased to meet the substantially increased costs. There was an undoubted element of arrogance ('If I can do it, why can't the others'), but the truth was that his own entrepreneurial spirit and activity were not being repeated by the others, or even to any real extent, by the partner himself. Just like those family firms quoted earlier, who were so dependent upon their founder and the spin-off from his work, so was this branch but without the spin-offs of other matter types to offer.

It took a very simple piece of analysis to find the root cause of the problem and put it right. When asked about his estate agency contacts, the partner in charge would airily state, 'Of course, I know them all'. In fact, this was far from the truth. He knew and diligently maintained contact with just enough negotiators to keep him fully and very profitably employed. Once he had attained this level, and almost without noticing it, he stopped extending his network. Analysis proved that far from knowing 'them all', he had only ever been in contact with just over 50 per cent of the estate agency companies in his town and its growing environs. Of the companies he was in touch with, he knew fewer than half of their branch offices. More importantly, he was only in contact on a regular basis with one in five of the actual negotiators who worked in those branches.

In our opinion, the market was only being skimmed. The branch had an excellent product and profile. All they had to do was talk to people who, in most cases, had colleagues at either the next desk or the next branch who were happily and regularly recommending the services of our friend.

Today, that branch remains the dominant conveyancing practice in its area, and now provides a full range of non-contentious private client services to the ever-increasing client database that it developed through conveyancing and its professional contacts register.

Once your existing contacts have been developed in line with the story above, it is easy to develop further by comparison with published directories such as Yellow Pages and start to look at social media such as LinkedIn and local business groups. Indeed, a useful starting point for deciding who could recommend the firm's services is a departmental study of the business categories in the Yellow Pages and online discussion groups that cover business areas.

We will deal with the regular and systematic use of the professional contacts register in more detail in later chapters. An additional benefit and added refinement to the professional contacts register is that while it is being compiled, the actual people within the contact organisation can be graded in importance, so that those at the lowest level receive a series of regular mailshots, while for those at the highest level personal contact, and perhaps even entertaining, may be in order. It is at that level and with that personal contact that ideas for association or joint promotional ventures may well present themselves.

How to start the database from what you have now

When faced with the database development question, many partners think of their wills and deeds store, and the effort required to use that paper information.

There are three basic approaches to starting the database implementation and these depend on your firm's current IT and filing systems. The approaches are:

1. Convert some or all the paper records into IT system records.
2. Start a new database and convert client records as they come up.
3. Combine paper-based and separate IT system records into one database.

The aim, as already expressed in this chapter, is to get to a position where fee earners and support staff can easily record marketing data alongside their fee-earning work. To get to that position usually requires a considerable amount of work. This should be considered as a specific development project and, in most cases, will require outside resources in the form of your IT vendors and support staff. Using the tasks associated with this chapter will give you an assessment of the effort required and the best method of achieving the desired results in a realistic timescale.

With so few lawyers using databases effectively and efficiently, those firms that take seriously the development and usage of marketing databases can develop a significant competitive advantage over their 'traditional' competitors. This is particularly relevant in the light of The New Competition, made up of organisations like the AA, Saga, Halifax and the Co-op, who are already experts in database marketing and have literally millions of people on their existing systems. All your clients, with only a few exceptions, are almost certainly already on the databases of one or other of your future competitors.

The situation can only get more difficult as additional competitors enter the field. However, given proper care in the set-up, your firm can have a comprehensive database of potential clients, 'nearly' clients and a professional contacts register ready and being used to counter the sales pitches put forward by The New Competition.

Further database developments and communications plans

As the database develops and you have the ability to subdivide the commercial, private client and professional contacts sections, the next step is to devise a communications plan for each section of the database. These communications plans detail how your firm plans to communicate with each subsection of the database. Each plan should be simply defined by each department relating to the services it offers clients and for the firm as a whole. Some examples are given in the tasks section at the end of the chapter.

There may be situations where a single important client has a communications plan of their own, and the converse, where a single client has multiple communications plans attached to their record. These ideas will be developed further in **Chapter 11** covering client registration schemes.

Collating the professional contacts register

The value of recording contacts

Information, in the form of the relationship that fee earners have with related professions who refer work to your firm, is transitory unless recorded. As is mentioned earlier in this book, the main assets of a law firm have two legs and can leave at any point and take their relationships with them. The main aim of the professional contacts register (PCR) is to capture the details of those referral relationships and protect those valuable assets. Although a particular fee earner may leave the firm, the basics of their contact network will remain in the firm and provide the starting point for a replacement person. When a PCR is managed and used properly, the client's relationship becomes with the firm and not the individual. The individual fee earner may feel they are losing control of their personal professional assets, but the advantages of using a PCR to develop a far wider network of contacts outweigh the loss of individual control.

This can be particularly important with commercial work. A well-developed PCR using an IT system can track far more contacts than a group of individual fee earners, and that network benefits all who are part of it. This relies on fee earners recording a wider set of data about matters and transactions where there are multiple parts and professional advisers. As the information grows, the database becomes more valuable in highlighting new areas of development and opportunities to expand your firm's reputation. As The New Competition will be targeting small and medium-sized enterprises (SMEs) with a range of easily accessible services, it will become more important to communicate the benefits of using your firm's services.

The marketing partner should trawl all fee earners so that their professional contacts can be captured in a systematic and standard format for the firm. The draft PCR should then have each contact confirmed. That is, check that you are in contact with each appropriate person in each organisation and with every branch office. Following that, the contacts should be compared with those listed in published directories.

All fee earners will be able to assist and should be involved in the development of the professional contacts register. At the end of this chapter, and on the CD-Rom, you will find a draft letter and staff questionnaire, which may be of assistance. Clearly, this will need to be personalised for your own firm's use but we hope it will be a start.

CHAPTER 6 TASKS **Develop client databases**

Database and OMMS tasks

Implementing a system like the 'one minute marketing solution' (OMMS) can be split into three tasks:

- client record information gathering systems;
- IT system changes; and
- management reporting

Client record information gathering: an example of a matter closing form is included on the CD-Rom. This can be re-worked to fit with your firm's services.

Set your firm's initial 'complete record' definition and organise training sessions around the firm to introduce and explain the principles of the OMMS.

IT system changes – all IT systems that Marketlaw has worked with can be used to record the client data needed. The principle is to make the completion of the OMMS task for each fee earner to take no more than one minute. Therefore, the IT system screens and the process need to be easily accessible.

Management reporting – there are two elements to this: the reporting on the fee earner's individual client record keeping and the handling of the recorded client interests.

The IT system needs to be configured to produce a report for each fee earner that shows their percentage of complete records for all the clients they have dealt with in a defined period of time. Presented as a simple league table with the previous month's percentage to indicate improvement (or not).

The database needs to be configured to report each month's collective future client interests and the report delivered to the person responsible for following up those interests.

While the OMMS is a simple idea, we have come across many excuses as to why it 'can't be done'. However, in every case, there is always a suitable (and not costly) solution. At its most basic, your practice and case management software systems use industry-standard database formats that can be searched using alternative software tools. Don't take 'no' for an answer; it can be done and given the necessity and value of the information we are handling, it must be seen as a priority and a necessity for the firm to have this client information available.

Professional contacts register

Draft professional contacts register collation letter

Dear Colleague

As part of the continuing marketing management development of our firm, we would like you to consider now who in the course of their work could say to their clients or customers, 'You should see a solicitor about this'. These people comprise our professional contacts and we are putting together a register of them so that we can maintain contact with them on an automatic and regular basis. Clearly, each department will have a different group of contacts who could recommend the firm. Perhaps with your colleagues or departmental head you could review the industry categories in the introduction to the Yellow Pages to 'brainstorm' the type of people who could recommend us.

Please remember that this database must be person, not address, driven. It is no good just listing 'The Manager' at a particular address: we need names, and indeed, there will often be more than one name at any given address.

Professional contacts register inputting questionnaire form

Name of contact (salutation, first name, surname):

Name of organisation:

Address (including postcode):

Contact salutation:

Type of introducer (e.g., bank, accountant, surveyor, estate agent, etc.):

Main/principal contact in our firm:

Contact category:

Last contact date:

Action to be taken:

(Please note that all entries on the PCR must be listed by name first, not the organisation)

Questions list for database analysis

Information systems

This section deals with the IT system capabilities and how they are currently set up.

1. Please provide details of:
   - Vendor
   - Version
   - Date of installation
   - Detail of any additional 'software modules' installed
   - Details of any firm-specific alterations to the standard applications
   - Details of any current 'marketing databases' or marketing communications sections of the current applications

   for each of the following:
   - Your case management system
   - Your practice management system
   - Other IT systems
   - Any specialist applications
2. How does the practice management system (or accounts) uniquely identify each client?
3. Is that unique ID used for client identification throughout the firm?
4. Is it/can it be used for marketing purposes?
5. Does your current client database indicate what matters of work have been undertaken for that client?
6. Does your current database system distinguish between commercial and private clients?
7. If you have a criminal defence department, a legal aid franchise or similar, can these clients be distinguished from 'normal' clients?
8. Does the database have the facility to cross-reference single and multiple clients?

9. Does the system allow for an indication that, for example, the MD of a commercial client is/could be a private client in their domestic life?
10. Does the current system indicate those private clients who, in their professional capacity, may have the ability to commission commercial legal work?
11. Is the firm registered within the provisions of the current Data Protection Act?

Information collection

1. How and when is client database information collected and input to the IT system?
2. What client database information is collected? (Please include here a copy of your existing inputting form.)
3. Do you have a facility for capturing and identifying 'enquiry contacts'? (Potential clients described in this module as 'nearly' clients.)
4. How is the nearly clients' information stored on the IT system?
5. Are these clients currently included on any mailing list?
6. Is there a separate system for keeping in contact with these prospects?
7. Does your firm have a collective professional contacts register?

Database management and development

It is important to understand the structure of the databases required.

These are:

- the private client database;
- the subdivided criminal/legal aid database;
- the commercial client database;
- the professional contacts register.

It is hard to over-emphasise the importance of the creation of a usable marketing database. It would be helpful therefore to look at the existing IT systems and that important element of capturing information in the first place and maintaining its quality.

There may also be a need for a training element – not necessarily on the technical side, but to put the IT system at the heart of the organisation so that each partner/member of staff realises the necessity of getting the right information and keeping the records up to date, and the benefit of doing so.

Checklist for a review of your firm's IT systems

1. Review the firm's current database and its ability to record updated information.
2. Review the firm's ability to use a database in communications with its clients, prospects and professional contacts register.
3. Review the current staff's level of ability at maintaining database and client contact.
4. Do staff members' job descriptions cover 'correct recording' of client contact?
5. Do job descriptions need updating to include this?
6. Review the practical point at which it is relevant for the firm to capture all the required data for the practice/case/marketing systems.
7. Review the process of 'finishing' a matter with a client and the process of ensuring that all required data is on the marketing system.
8. Which partner is responsible for ensuring that partners and staff keep the database up to date?
9. How much work do you estimate is required on your current database system?
10. How will the decision between 'starting again' and 'cleaning up the current' be made?
11. If starting again, will the system be integrated or a stand-alone 'marketing machine'?
12. If starting again, how will the firm's existing data be cleansed and input on the new system?
13. Assess the practice management and case management system's ability to integrate with a marketing database.
14. At what point will a training programme for staff be implemented?
15. Who will undertake this training? This needs to include:
    (a) the importance of accurate data capture;
    (b) promotion of the benefits to each department of regular use of a marketing database for communications;
    (c) information for the staff and fee earners across the firm of the benefits of cross-selling and firm-wide promotions.
16. How will the key performance indicators be set for client databases and professional contacts register?

Communications plans

Your firm's database will become more effective as it grows in use around the firm. As the client records increase in complexity, a method of using the power of the database is in the communications plans attached to defined sections within it. Some simple plans might be:

Private client

- Christmas card list only

NO CONTACT beyond:

- Conveyancing
- Will and LPAs updates
- Family law updates

Commercial client

- Employment law updates
- Company law updates
- Entertainment invitations
- General commercial newsletter
- Developing business
- Property acquisition updates

A more detailed outline plan could be:

Beyond conveyancing

Aim: To increase the number of clients buying a will from your firm following a conveyancing matter.

Who: All clients whose conveyancing transaction is for a property of £350,000 or greater and including those completed in the past three years.

Check:

- Has the fee earner asked if the client has a current will not updated in the past three years?
- Does the client have a will with the firm already?
- Which client groups to subtract from the list (remortgage clients?).

How often:

- Series of four will promotion letters over 12 to 18 months.
- Included on general newsletter mailing.

Material to use:

- Pre-prepared will promotion letters.
- Literature kit inserts: promotional, information and procedural.

The definitions above outline what needs to be covered in the plan. The essential element is that you are planning a series of future communications with a distinct group of clients and measuring the responses. The fee earner's part in this is crucial. When a client returns to your firm with any additional enquiries or matters, the fee earner needs to review the communications plans and adjust them according to the client's circumstances. When the client has bought a will, it's obvious they should be removed from the 'beyond conveyancing' communications plans list. At the same time, the fee earner needs to consider what additional services the client may require, and when. In this example the next step is to add the client to the 'Will update and review' communications plan to remind them in three to five years that they should consider reviewing their arrangements.

The successful completion of the recommendations in this chapter will put your firm in a far stronger position than it was before. It will enable your firm not only to compete with The New Competition, but also to stand out from the traditional providers of legal services. Remember, the client base – database – is the firm's seed corn: nurture it.

The recommendations will potentially lead to a number of projects designed to use your firm's IT to maximum effect or identify areas where further investment is needed.

From this chapter you will have a clear idea of the importance and value of databases and the correct integration and use within a firm. The ideas from this chapter may take some time to implement but they are a vital element of the future success of your firm.

7

Practice development

In this chapter we look at various strategies for growth:.

We look at the role of the managing partner, specifically in relation to the marketing discipline.

We explain the simple theories behind vertical and horizontal development, and how they can be adapted to serve your firm's own growth aspirations. We emphasise again that growth need not be numeric, but may well be measured in terms of profitability.

We look at the important area of underpinning the existing client base, to ensure that it does not disappear while we are busy making other plans.

We discuss the difficulties of organising growth in two separate markets (commercial and private client).

We consider staff as a marketing resource and study what it is that clients really want from their solicitor.

We look at presenting advantages and benefits, which will become an increasingly vital task at every area of operation and promotion when facing up to The New Competition.

And we look at cost justification, an important area in a world that increasingly 'knows the cost of everything and the value of nothing'.

> *Days are lost lamenting over lost days. What you can do, or think you can do, begin it.* – Goethe

The majority of firms we met while researching this book and discussing the initiatives needed to face up to The New Competition would say, 'If only we had done this years ago – but we were always far too busy.'

Perhaps the worst example was the firm with which we had worked 10 years ago who, at the partners' 'away day' following the consultancy assignment agreed, and minuted, that a top priority must be the creation of a client database. Ten years later they had still not begun the task. Perhaps our return visit prompted them into action and they have now, at least, got a reasonable mailing list and are embarking on the development of a true database through the client registration scheme (see **Chapter 11**). While extreme, this example is by no means isolated. However, Goethe is right, there is no point lamenting and looking back. The vital decision now must be to develop the practice to enable it to cope with The New Competition.

Almost every practice we have encountered has told us that the majority of their work comes to them as a result of recommendation. Few, however, without being prompted, have ever actively sought these recommendations. Perhaps this is a throwback to the days when all the profession was allowed to do was put up a brass plaque, or maybe there are still some solicitors who believe that it is 'not quite the done thing' and smacks a bit of 'trade'. For those who don't think like that, and hopefully few do nowadays, we have several simple, proven and, in many cases, free methods of becoming proactive.

We have already looked at growth and why it is needed (see **Chapter 3**); we assume, for the reasons stated, that your firm will adopt a growth strategy. In this chapter we consider some of the strategies for growth and enlarge upon the principles of horizontal and vertical development.

Strategies for growth

Frequently, growth objectives are ill-defined and are expressed loosely in phrases such as 'twice the size', '20 partners in three years', 'doubling of profits' and other such general statements. Every growth strategy needs specific quantifiable targets and achievement dates. These targets and dates should be linked to the firm's business plan to provide a complete picture for the future of the firm.

Growth does not necessarily mean a bigger firm with more clients and more fee earners. It is just as valid to plan for more profit, for less work and fewer clients, but it needs to be a clear plan. A growth strategy needs to be realistic in aims and objectives and based upon your firm's current work.

Essentially, there are four possible routes to growth of your firm:

1. Merger
2. Acquisition
3. Organic
4. A combination of the above

Merger

Merger is something that should never be ruled out. Many of today's practices are themselves a result of a successful merger. We believe that more mergers will occur in the near future, in reaction to The New Competition and changes in the market for legal services.

However, some mergers fail and many fall short of the participants' expectations. It is important to note that merger as a response to increased competition is a risky strategy to adopt in a changing market without the commitment of significant resources. Mergers will take the partners' attention away from clients and turn it inwards towards the business at a time when focusing on clients and the changing market is more important.

It would appear from an (unscientific) observation, that mergers succeed best where there is a dominant party (although whether this is strictly speaking a merger in anything other than name is debatable) or where there is an appropriate jigsaw-like fit – each party bringing to the merger an element that is missing in the other. The merger of a strong criminal practice with a non-contentious firm is an actual (although unusual) example. The merger of a private client non-contentious firm with another having a strong litigation base and legal aid franchises, is another. And the merger between a strong commercial practice and a large private client firm is almost the 'Holy Grail' that everyone seeks. It does work well in our own experience, but there are as many partnerships considering splitting up to divide commercial and private client work, as there are firms actively seeking merger.

And this is the inherent risk of merger. What you see is not always what you actually get.

Table 7.1 Advantages and disadvantages of a merger

Merger advantages	Merger disadvantages
• Small financial resource required	• The most risky strategy
• Immediate economies of scale	• Surrender of 'sovereignty'
• Increased range of 'products'	• Possible culture clash
• Potential new skills	• Different methods of work, IT systems and administration to be reconciled
• Higher profile	• Package probably contains 'warts'
• Potential promotional opportunities	• Some divestment may be necessary

Acquisition

With the continued pressure on the smaller practice, the acquisition route to expansion becomes an increasingly realistic growth option for the established and financially successful firm.

We have interviewed several firms recently (in different parts of the country) that have gone on the acquisition trail. One particularly active firm in the north specifically targeted sole practitioners and firms where one or more of the partners were reaching retirement age. This firm initially used its own local knowledge, but as its strategy included development into an additional town, desk research played an important part. The whole exercise produced a very interesting case study. To date, five acquisitions have been made, one failed to be completed and at the time of writing there are two further negotiations going on. Of the completed five acquisitions, the acquiring partnership believes that two were adequate and acceptable, two have proved to be of more value to the acquirer than anticipated and one has proved an expensive mistake. Therefore, of the five, only two have resulted in the partners buying what they thought they were acquiring. The lessons are obvious. Don't be rushed, take time for due diligence, recognise this as an area where natural scepticism is an advantage and ensure a full contract-based acquisition including, if appropriate, penalty charges for misinformation.

Table 7.2 Advantages and disadvantages of an acquisition

Acquisition advantages	Acquisition disadvantages
• Fast growth • Medium risk • Purchaser dictates terms • Methods/management can be imposed • Immediate economies of scale	• Relatively large financial resource required • Large management resource required • Package probably contains 'warts' • Security of investment (exactly what is it that is being purchased?)

Organic growth

In many cases, this is seen as the least attractive of growth options, because of its slowness, and the difficulties of recruitment. However, it has few of the disadvantages or dangers associated with the first two options, and above all ensures that management time and concentration are spent fully on the firm, and not wasted chasing dreams with wishful thinking.

We believe that the majority of problems associated with the disadvantages can be overcome if the firm adopts the marketing management philosophy and puts into practice the recommendations outlined earlier in this book. By doing this, the firm will be managing its practice more effectively and efficiently, which includes consideration of, and planning for, its future strategy. In short, your firm should prove attractive to young, qualified people who seek association with a well-organised, dynamic practice that has planned for and is in charge of its own destiny, operating in growth areas, from both marketing and matter type points of view. It is worth remembering that recruitment is, at least in part, a selling process, ensuring that the ideal applicant understands fully the benefits of joining your firm.

A few years ago, when every practice was seeking expansion in the commercial market, established, qualified, experienced and high profile commercial lawyers were in great demand (this, of course, remains true today). In our own experience, one of the best qualified young commercial lawyers eventually took up a partnership with one of the least obvious (from the outside) firms seeking his services. We asked this lawyer why he had joined this firm. 'I joined the firm that was planning its destiny' was the short reply. That firm continues to be a major success story. Apart from putting marketing at the heart of its management philosophy, it put resources behind developing the commercial client base and capitalised upon its success by developing its private client base through the offer of legal services to its commercial clients' workforce and their families.

Of course, not all firms can follow this example. A strategic growth plan has to be based on the firm's actual and current position but it should be a full plan. You should be planning the destiny of your firm, not it planning yours.

Table 7.3 Advantages and disadvantages of organic growth

Organic growth advantages	Organic growth disadvantages
• Least risky • Relatively small financial resource required • Pace of growth is controllable • New personnel easily assimilated • Personality/ethos of the firm is not threatened • Direction of growth is wholly controllable	• Potential recruitment difficulties • Relatively slow

A combination of the above

It is probably wise not to close any options, and a growth policy when adopted should consider all options on a continual basis and, indeed, may adopt this fourth option. It is fair to say that merger and organic growth can work together, as can acquisition and organic growth. However, the literal combination of the first three options could prove very distracting to the management of the firm.

Most of the firms we discussed this subject with seemed to have come to the conclusion that they would 'adopt an organic growth strategy, while looking for acquisition opportunities, and not closing their mind to merger'.

At first glance, this would appear to be a 'cop out'. But it is a sound strategy with one proviso. The strategic plan and the tactics for organic growth must be implemented against an agreed timescale and must be monitored before consideration is given to either of the other options. Do what our successful acquirer did. Draw up a hit list and allocate the responsibility for exploring it to one partner, against a specific timetable. Then rigorously cull that list upon the first report back and reduce it to a really manageable number that can be pursued on the basis that acquisition would be desired for these, but would not affect the organic growth strategy. Do not allow wishful thinking to creep in. Similarly, if you are considering merger, decide first whether you are going to be the initiator of talks; if so, with whom; and again draw up a timetable that does not interfere with organic growth plans. Note that if you are planning to wait for someone to approach you, you are probably not serious about merger anyway and should dismiss it from your plans until you are ready. That is, don't use the prospect of a merger or acquisition as a spur to sort out the rest of your firm's strategy.

Quantifying growth

Once the strategy for growth has been agreed and the policy finalised by the partnership, there is an urgent need to quantify it.

We believe and have seen proof of the fact that this will be an important part of the growth planning stage. Clearly, a growth plan should only be a first draft and will need constant review by the partnership. It will, however, be a start and enable the firm's objectives to be defined more succinctly, and targeting to become more meaningful, being expressed in terms of matter type and fee earner rather than just total billings.

At this stage therefore, we would seek to define realistic growth targets for the next three years, initially office by office (if appropriate), certainly department by department, ideally by matter type and ultimately by fee earner. This last is important. If a fee earner can see that his/her target is part of an overall growth strategy, they are more likely to adopt and own the target as it is more meaningful than the usual percentage increase on last year.

The involvement of staff in partnership plans is an area that almost always needs attention. The 'them and us' syndrome is alive and kicking in the legal profession and is often an inhibitor to growth. Involve your staff, seek their opinions, explain your decisions and thinking, be open about your strategy and ensure that each member of your staff at every level knows where they fit into the overall plan. Management advice books will tell you that this improves productivity – and it does, provided that you are not just paying lip service to it.

Your growth objectives will illustrate, perhaps graphically, where resources will need to be applied. You will have to consider: how much capital will be involved in the development; at what stage will additional fee earners need to be recruited; in which disciplines will they be required first; what skills will be lacking and need reinforcing; how will this growth pattern affect premises and equipment; and who will be in charge and have overall responsibility for the successful implementation of your strategic plan.

A managing partner

Perhaps you already have a managing partner, if not in name: a partner who has, by seniority or accident, taken on the management responsibilities. If not, we believe that your partnership must appoint one to take executive responsibility for implementing the growth strategy and plans.

In many practices, the managing partner and the marketing partner may well be the same person, although this position can develop into the equivalent of a full-time, i.e. non-fee earning, job. Clearly, this is a matter for individual partner debate. Most solicitors of our acquaintance want to be lawyers and do not wish to give up the practice of law entirely to run a business – even if that business is a legal practice.

For this reason, these two essential roles may have to be divided between two willing partners. But we would stress again that the most successful firms we have encountered have been led by marketing-minded managing partners.

The point of the emphasis at this stage is to flag up the need for the firm (and essentially the partnership) to recognise that management, especially marketing management, is crucial to the firm's growth and has to be paid for. Resources, in the form of time and money, have to be allocated. In other words, the partners charged with definable, quantifiable management tasks must be allocated the time to perform those tasks and have those tasks recognised as a valuable contribution to the firm.

In our experience, the most successful firms have a dedicated managing partner. In some cases, they have no fee-earning responsibility at all. Clearly, firms will vary between that extreme and the other, where management is done at weekends and in the evenings after the fee-earning target has been achieved. The successful firms, however, will be moving towards the situations where partners are rewarded, at least in part, for their management efforts as well as their billing.

A delicate point to be raised here is that there is a vast difference between managing partner and practice manager. Many firms employ extremely competent people as practice managers. Generally, these are administrative and organisational experts and perhaps 'office manager' would be a more accurate, though less flattering, title. We have seen some highly skilled people with military, building society or bank backgrounds being employed, and then not allowed to realise their full potential because they have 10 bosses (in a 10-partner firm) and no managerial/shareholder authority. There are exceptions, but we have seldom seen this work. Competent people are often reduced to the level of IT trouble-shooter and organiser of the firm's social activities.

It is our belief that the partners should manage their business. They are, after all, the owners of it. Ultimately, the partnership should have the courage to allocate the most appropriate person or persons to these vital tasks and should seek outside professional assistance, if appropriate.

The non-managerial partners then need to recognise that as part-owners of the business, and senior fee earners or heads of department, it is probably in their best interests to leave the business management responsibilities to a managing partner and his/her team. This releases them from the committee-style, part-management position to concentrate on their legal work while still retaining the ability to influence management initiatives in their roles as department heads and part-owners. Essentially, they leave the management team to implement the partners' approved plan and do not interfere until it either succeeds or fails to deliver against the agreed key performance indicators.

Developing vertically and horizontally

This area, expressed in marketing jargon, was touched upon in the context of the need for a firm-wide client database (see **Chapter 6**). The database was described as the firm's 'seed corn' from which at least initial growth and development would spring. Vertical development is described as selling more products or services to existing clients. Horizontal development means widening the client base by actively seeking recommendations from existing clients and professional contacts.

You may recall that we encouraged you to think of actively seeking recommendation, rather than waiting for recommended prospects to come to you. We also emphasised that this is the first stage of underpinning the existing client base. In its simplest form, it is all to do with communications and the development of communication plans. What we mean by that is communicating with the client in words they understand to promote the benefits of using your firm or recommending it on a regular basis.

Vertical development

As we said above, vertical development means selling more products to existing clients. The first key to this is observation and opportunity recognition. Most fee earners, including partners, are often too busy looking at the matter in hand to recognise other requirements or opportunities the client might present. By listening more closely to the client or asking a series of questions, they may discover that there is a wealth of need within that client. The more we know about our client the better able we are to identify their needs and demonstrate how we can serve them. When this information is stored with client records, a firm can look after the future needs of their client by anticipating requirements and communicating those ideas to the client in a way that is perceived as excellent service. Is this not, in fact, providing a client with improved client care and best advice?

Opportunity recognition is really the key and each member of the fee-earning staff should develop skills in this area. For example:

- Surely that person making a will also needs a lasting power of attorney?
- How can you allow two people purchasing a house together to enter into this transaction without a trust deed?
- If an elderly person is selling a house, what other advice, assistance and support are they going to require?
- Is the business executive buying a house that is going to stretch his resources going to need further advice and additional services from you?
- Does this private client have the opportunity to influence the placing of commercial work?
- Is the managing director of a firm buying a factory building expanding the business and in need of employment law advice?

The marketing partner must understand opportunity recognition and discuss it in detail first with all departmental heads and subsequently through them with each fee earner. Only then can the need for cross-selling between departments and disciplines be fully understood by the staff who will have to do that cross-selling.

Apart from the fee earner, there are many other means whereby the firm, and specifically the marketing partner, can enhance the activity under 'vertical development'.

A full understanding of benefits and benefit presentation can enhance the presentation of the firm's services both in a literature kit (see **Chapter 9**) and on the firm's website (see **Chapter 10**).

A firm's newsletter (see **Chapter 11**) is an ideal opportunity to promote new and existing products to current and past clients. A newsletter is particularly effective in areas where a direct approach could be embarrassing. For example, nobody would want to suggest to a client or prospect that their marriage was in trouble and they may need the services of the matrimonial department. However, the successes and benefits of the matrimonial or family department can be easily expressed anecdotally in a carefully written firm's newsletter.

Mailshots, special offers, seminars, advertising, clinics, publicity and press releases are all other methods of developing the firm vertically which will be discussed in later chapters.

The vertical development of a satisfied client base is the simplest, quickest and cheapest form of practice development available.

Horizontal development

As defined earlier, this is the method of finding new clients of a type similar to existing groups, or finding new groups of clients with requirements similar to the services already offered by the firm.

This, again, is largely a matter of observation and opportunity recognition by fee earners and client-facing staff. People often talk to their solicitors about unrelated matters such as their daughter's impending divorce, husband's problem with a potential industrial tribunal, the fact that Mum is 'going doolally', or that Dad hasn't made a will. With one simple question, such as 'Can I help?' this throw-away line can be turned into an instruction or a recommendation. Formalising the fee earner's approach to such opportunities through training and IT system developments provides the firm with the structure to respond to client and prospect opportunities.

It doesn't happen in part because of divisionalisation, and often because individual fee earners have simply not been instructed or trained in the arts of recognising opportunities and seeking recommendation. It is the marketing partner's responsibility to discuss this with individual fee earners and to ensure that departmentalisation does not lead to compartmentalisation.

A study of the types of client groups identified in the firm's database will assist in horizontal development and, indeed, vertical development. A review of niche market services offered by a firm, or geographic analysis of clients by matter type, will also assist in identifying areas of horizontal development. But as noted above, one of the most powerful tools for seeking recommendation is the professional contacts register. Here, the active communication of benefits to referring professional groups can quickly show areas of expansion. If a firm has contact with several local independent financial advisers (IFAs), why not find the contact details for all the IFAs in your area? This form of networking is very efficient for communicating the benefits of using your firm's services. When it is done well, the professional referrers can then take those benefits and present them to all their clients far more cost-effectively than can be achieved through any other form of promotion.

There are many marketing activities that will help in both horizontal and vertical development. The marketing partner's responsibility is to ensure that these activities are implemented and that the maximum gain is achieved, both horizontally and vertically.

Underpinning the existing client base

You may have noticed that we have not yet spoken of spending any money on advertising or other traditional promotional methods, or indeed, looking outside the firm for new business. (OK! The professional contacts register is outside the business, but you know what we mean.)

Of all preliminary activities, i.e. those prior to looking outside the firm, the most important is underpinning the existing client base. We have previously talked a lot about the historic attitude of the profession, its extreme regulation, its brass plaque and dead files, but while none of this was the fault of practitioners at that time, those times have gone and new circumstances apply. A good starting point for the marketing partner is to assume that even the most satisfied client will be disloyal, has adopted a consumerist approach when placing future business with anyone, including the solicitor and will therefore seek out the best deal. Fortunately, the best deal often includes previous satisfactory dealings and familiarity – 'the devil you know'. It could also be argued that there is a sense of belonging, which is why a receptionist greeting a client by his name may seem trivial, but can, in fact, be extremely important.

Then, to the legal profession's great advantage in the face of The New Competition, there is client apathy and the understandable desire to keep things as they are. It is easier for your past client to contact you than to seek out your competitor if that client is satisfied (which includes a feeling of value for money); if he has your name and telephone number on the tip of his tongue because you have communicated with him regularly; and if he knows that you will be able to take his call virtually immediately (or at least your staff will). And this will apply even more strongly with The New Competition. Clients surely prefer to deal with a known, established professional who has performed satisfactorily, above buying legal services from a supermarket, a building society or a breakdown service.

However, this can only happen if your firm makes it easy for the client. Ease of action is the first satisfaction reinforcer. Your task is to maintain contact, to make it easy for clients to contact you when they need to and for your firm to respond positively in a friendly and professional manner. To do this, you must use every means available to you to communicate with your past satisfied client base, to ensure that you have underpinned, if not their (non-existent) loyalty, then at least their awareness of the simplicity of contact, and the promise of a friendly welcome. Without that, you may not get the chance to prove your professional skill, expertise and timeliness.

An example from a recent client satisfaction survey: a businessman, following the death of his father, had tried to contact the firm that held his will. This had been the firm his father had chosen, and although the businessman had established relationships with a solicitor in his local area, he decided initially to use his father's preferred firm for the probate. The businessman reported in the survey that the firm his father had used took too long to answer the phone or call him back after several attempts to discuss the matter. After a short time, the businessman rang his own solicitor from the stored number in his mobile phone and had the matter started immediately by a firm several hundred miles away, 'because they had had their chance, but it was easier to call the person I knew could deal with it quickly, and would be pleased to help'.

Growth in two separate markets

There is a distinct difference in the needs and requirements of the two basic markets (private client and commercial) that the majority of legal practices seek to serve. Recognition of the different benefits required by the two markets should mean a different presentation of what may be similar legal services.

The departmental heads and their staff may serve both markets, for example, both private client and commercial in the conveyancing department. But, from a marketing point of view, the marketing partner needs to consider the difference in the requirements of the two markets, rather than the similarities in production methods.

For the purposes of this section, we will assume that your practice has an established private client base, and a smaller commercial client portfolio. Working on this premise, the majority of the development and promotional matters to be discussed in later chapters will apply first to the private client market, and secondly will need to be adapted for the commercial client market. But we would like to make the following comments at this stage.

Essentially, we are recommending that the marketing partner begins to divisionalise the firm into private client and company/commercial sections. As this suggests, we would also recommend that the marketing of each of these two divisions be considered separately. There will be some overlap between departments, but the essential strategy and policy making should be divided in line with the view different clients will take of the firm.

What we are specifically not recommending is a marketing partner for each of the divisions. As we have already stated, your marketing partner must coordinate activity, especially growth and promotional activity, to ensure that the actions of one division do not damage the image of another. But they are separate markets and need dealing with in different ways.

Commercial market sectors

The potential commercial market may become increasingly more important to even the smaller private client practice, in the light of The New Competition. We frequently find ourselves persuading what is normally a predominantly domestic or private client firm to create the perception of a commercial department before a promotional approach to the commercial market.

For example, by creating separate promotional material for the commercial department (and the literature kit referred to in **Chapter 9** assists here), a firm is able to promote the commercial conveyancing expert, without having to refer to the majority of domestic conveyancing that he undertakes. Similarly, there is no need to acknowledge that your specialist in commercial contract law also undertakes matrimonial work.

With the accelerating development of law surrounding customs and excise, health and safety, and EU law, a business manager or company director can quickly face exposure to potential criminal prosecution. The fact that the head of your criminal department spends much time dealing with domestic crime does not need to be emphasised when outlining his/her expertise in the criminal side of directors' responsibilities (though it may do no harm to acknowledge their considerable experience in defending motoring offences).

The potential criminal liabilities of company directors or business managers are of particular interest, as they are generally unknown and raise obvious alarm bells, which may well encourage your clients, or potential clients, to seek a 'legal health check'.

In essence, if the firm has a small but developing commercial department, it should be presented to clients as a valuable complete service, even if, inside the firm, it is only a small department. Clients are interested in solutions to their problems, not the internal structure of your firm. As with horizontal and vertical expansion, these smaller departments can often provide useful routes to new groups of clients.

Staff as a marketing resource

If the marketing concept and management philosophy are truly adopted, and the emphasis of the firm is placed upon the satisfaction of client needs rather than the production of work, it becomes evident that the firm's effort and resources must be geared towards this end, and will therefore demand the full involvement of all staff.

It is well known that a large proportion of work comes into the legal profession in the form of personal or professional recommendation; it is estimated that anything up to 80 per cent of work is obtained as a result of personal recommendation.

The public, as potential clients, judge solicitors largely on how they 'feel' they are treated, and handled. Generally, however, we have found that there is little guidance or training in the genuine area of client care (not Rule 2 issues). We deal with this subject further in **Chapter 9**.

Clearly, some people in the firm are better suited than others to an involvement in marketing or promotion; an analysis and discussion of the forms returned during the skills and interests audit recommended in **Chapter 2** will assist in this area. Not many enter the legal profession to become salesmen. It is likely that the completed skills audit will illustrate who are (to use an unpleasant but useful American phrase) the 'finders, minders, and grinders'.

Hopefully, perhaps with the assistance of an outside training agency, the marketing partner will be able to encourage through advice and training those who have the ability to assist in your practice development. Once the people, the enthusiasm and the training are in place, consideration can be given to a new client introductory bonus/commission scheme. We are not proposing that the firm is ready for this yet, and would point out that the introduction of such a scheme needs careful planning as it can be fraught with dangers. However, it is something we have seen work with considerable success for some of our clients, and most certainly it provides a focal point for staff (or at least some of them) to feel part of the firm's expansion plans.

What do clients want from a solicitor?

Regrettably, the answer is many things. The client wants, as a minimum, the following:

- help in solving problems (getting out of trouble);
- help in preventing problems;
- money – ways to save it, keep it or make it;
- background – experience of, or even expertise in, a particular matter;
- background – experience of, or even expertise in, the client's industry or field (in the case of commercial clients);
- attention and respect;
- availability;
- new ideas;
- timeliness;
- confidence that provides the client with peace of mind;
- a 'big name' in the area or a recognised expert in their field;
- to be kept informed throughout;
- follow-up;
- general business counsel (in the case of commercial clients);

- general personal counsel (in the case of private clients) – as it was in the days of the family solicitor or the 'man of affairs';
- value – and this does not mean cheapest, it means understanding the benefits paid for;
- the right chemistry; everyone and every organisation has a profile; the trick is to fit yours to theirs.

This checklist is reproduced on the CD-Rom (document 7.03), allowing you to consider and note the extent to which your firm meets these ideal requirements. Please also bear in mind the benefit analysis recommended in **Chapter 5**.

Presenting advantages and benefits

There are many occasions when dealings with clients will call for you to make recommendations, present a proposal or suggest a course of action. The objective is to persuade the client to take a positive view of your proposals and therefore accept the advice, and continue to instruct your firm.

There are numerous examples of when such skills will be an advantage. There may have been a delay in dealing with a complaint, or a letter may not have been answered in time. Through no fault of our own, your firm was unable to do as it had promised, or a person originally dealing with the client has had to pass the file over to a colleague. Perhaps someone has failed to call a client back.

Sometimes, our powers of persuasion are needed in our relationships with our colleagues. We may have to interest a colleague in an idea, or persuade someone to undertake certain work. In these examples, and many more you will come across in your day-to-day work, you are faced with the problem of persuading others to accept an idea, or agree to a course of action. This is exactly the problem that is experienced in a practice when gaining or trying to gain new business. You have to persuade the client to use your services for their benefit in the face of their own lethargy and the alternatives available. In fact, what you are doing is selling: persuading another party to one point of view, to ensure that they buy your product or service. But whether the selling involves persuading clients to part with money, or persuading clients to a course of action, a knowledge of some of the techniques of salesmanship can assist.

A successful firm in the north east, with both private client and commercial departments, wanted to develop its presentation of benefits to clients, but was very concerned about the 'sales' title in the proposed training project. The senior partner's problem was the attitude towards sales within the firm. Colleagues and staff thought of salesmen as people in sharp suits trying to con you out of money for a product you don't really want – certainly not the style of their firm. Staff would resist the sales training as something that would annoy their clients, and as a legal services professional, it wasn't their job to sell things to people. The firm had tried various methods in the past but found that the staff considered 'sales' as someone else's responsibility. To help the firm, we removed all reference to 'sales' and used terms such as 'extending client service', 'ensuring the client gets the benefits from all areas of the firm' and 'providing solutions to all our clients' needs'. This built on their benefits analysis work and, although using the sales techniques outlined in this chapter, capitalised on the enthusiasm of the fee earners and staff to achieve significant increases in cross-selling and unsolicited enquiries from clients.

In everyday life, we are selling when we present our ideas, plans, aspirations or whatever to friends, family or colleagues. In this sense, 'selling' is not something to be fearful of. It is, to be honest, just a fact of life in a basic form of communication. A salesman establishes the needs of his client and creates a desire in the client to satisfy these needs. Then he puts forward the relevant advantages or benefits of his product or service, which will satisfy, demonstrably, the client's needs. Finally, the salesman will attempt to gain the commitment of the client to purchase, and if successful, will have made a sale. What you have to do in presenting benefits and persuading people to a course of action is essentially the same thing.

For now, we would like to introduce a simple technique for explaining your firm's benefits, which should help you to enjoy a better success rate both in actual selling, if that is an intrinsic part of your job, or in persuading people (clients or colleagues) to your point of view.

The technique is quite simple to understand. It has three steps:

1. State your idea, proposal or advantage.
2. Emphasise the meaning or significance of your proposal in terms of the advantage it will give the client.
3. Ask a question to make sure that the client understands and accepts the advantage, as an advantage, or benefit to them.

As a simple example, let us assume that you have been asked to explain that there has been a delay in receiving information, and therefore an agreed deadline is going to be missed. You can see that a bland statement of facts could well upset, or even anger, the client. 'We haven't got all the information yet, so I'm afraid we are going to be late.' While true, this is not going to impress the client with your interest in him/her, or the efficiency of the practice. How much more effectively the same information can be imparted using the three steps discussed above:

1. State your idea, proposal or advantage.

   'I'm afraid we don't have sufficient detail to give you an answer yet so we would like to keep the papers a little longer.'

2. Emphasise the meaning or significance of your proposal in terms of the advantage and benefits it will give the client.

   'That way we will be able to give a more complete answer to all your queries and sort out your problem.'

3. Ask a question to make sure the client understands and accepts the advantage.

   'I think that is the best course of action, don't you?'

Using this technique ensures that you explain the significance of your proposal, in terms of advantages to the client, and that the client accepts their significance by his answer to the question. In accepting your proposal and answering 'Yes', the client is acting in a team formation with you, rather than against you (or, worse, feeling that you may be working against him). In an actual sales situation, the process of building up a series of yes answers leads almost inevitably to a successful transaction.

There will be many examples in your day-to-day working activity where the use of these techniques would be of significant advantage to you. With practice, it will simplify your day, make your relationship with clients and colleagues smoother and therefore easier and, in many cases, provide the client with a clearer understanding of what you are doing, and therefore a greater appreciation of the firm.

It is therefore worthwhile thinking about the three-step technique discussed above and practising it. Without doubt, you will be using some aspects of the technique already, perhaps without even realising it. Adapting the use of the whole technique should not prove too difficult. In most cases, the bit that is missed is the reinforcing question and this is, in fact, the most important element.

As we have already mentioned, the techniques described above are very similar to those used in the process of actually selling a product or service. Most of us are involved, from time to time, with actual selling, i.e. presenting ideas, talking to clients, colleagues and other professionals. It is therefore worth considering the slight change of emphasis that the sales technique demands.

The difference is in the first part of the technique. Instead of presenting an idea or a proposal, what the salesman does is to present a particular advantage or benefit that the product or service offers. To use the most ubiquitous example, a car salesman might well say: 'This car has fully reclining and adjustable seats. That means whichever one of your family is driving the car, there will be a seating position which is ideally suited to them. That is an important safety advantage to you, isn't it?'

What he has done is state one of the car's benefits ('This car has fully reclining and adjustable seats') and has then gone on to explain the meaning and the significance of the benefits to the customer ('That means whichever one of your family is driving the car, there will be a seating position which is ideally suited to them'). Most important of all, he has asked a question in order to gain the agreement of the potential customer that the benefit is an important one to them. 'That is an important safety advantage to you, isn't it?'

It is important to realise that a salesman is unlikely to make a sale of something as complicated as a car simply by stating one benefit. As illustrated above, he will go on to state other benefits and, by using the technique, will gain a series of yes answers.

However, people buy things for different reasons. It is worth remembering that even something like conveyancing will be bought from the practice by different people for varying reasons. It may be speed, security or convenience (there are, of course, many other reasons). There will be little point in emphasising the speed of your service to someone not in a hurry, and whose prime concern is that every document relating to the purchase is scrutinised by an experienced expert. Clearly, therefore, the benefit being expressed must be appropriate and the experienced salesman will understand the need to find out more about his potential client before launching into a sales patter. There is no room for a sales patter. You are not timeshare salesmen.

So, therefore, the benefits offered must be those you judge will satisfy the needs of an individual client that you are dealing with. The rule for stating benefits in a selling situation is simple and can be remembered by the mnemonic BMQ:

- State the Benefit.
- Explain the Meaning (or significance of the benefit).
- Ask a Question at the end to gain commitment.

Benefit, Meaning, Question = BMQ. For example:

- *Benefit*: 'Your instructions will be handled only by legally qualified, experienced people.'
- *Meaning*: 'This means that you can be secure in the knowledge that the whole job can be handled professionally and comprehensively.'
- *Question*: 'With a purchase as important as a house, we feel that this is far better than entrusting the process to one of these new computerised services, wouldn't you agree?'

This and other examples have been used very successfully by firms as the basis of a staff meeting to encourage members of the fee-earning and support staff to understand that presenting ideas and benefits to clients not only enhances the firm's future and its growth plans, but also secures their own employment.

It is also a principle that can be used in letter writing, in the development of literature kits, websites and newsletters. It is absolutely vital to remember than in all spheres of life, including the legal world, people buy benefits, not features or procedures of the production unit. There are available numerous staff training courses that might best be described as 'sales techniques for non-sales people'. The marketing partner would do well to investigate these and consider their introduction into your firm.

Cost justification

A format similar to the BMQ technique can be used in overcoming objections. Quite often, objections are voiced in price concerns and as a sign that the client is interested but requires to be reassured of the benefits of using your firm and that service. For example, 'Haven't you overcharged me?' is clearly an objection raised at the end of a transaction. 'Why are you more expensive than other solicitors?' is most probably an objection raised prior to the transaction, when a prospective client is making a choice of solicitor (or even potentially a DIY approach to law). Both these objections are, in fact, invitations to present, or re-present, cost justification.

The technique used is much the same as for overcoming any other objection. Most certainly it demands the use of the 'yes, but . . .' technique.

'Yes, I can see that it may seem expensive, but . . .' the empathetic approach: '. . . we should perhaps look together at what you are getting for your money and the dangers of not having the work done properly'. The 'but' part is inviting a reappraisal of the benefits, an opportunity to reassess the client's requirements and present your firm's benefits to match them. It can be worthwhile to ask a question to effectively gain the prospect's permission to run through the presentation of benefits again: 'That would help you make an informed decision, which I am sure is what you want, isn't it?' As in all 'selling' situations, when the number of benefits recognised and acknowledged by the prospect as beneficial to him outweighs the perceived cost, a sale results and your prospect becomes a client.

There are two points to note. First, there is often an assumption that the client understands and has knowledge of what he is getting for his money. Second, without good information about what it is the client does want, presentation of benefits that are not important to the client sound like 'sales patter'.

An understanding of what the client is really buying from a solicitor is dealt with above: the recognition that it is not your services (themselves a derived need) that the client purchases but the benefits to him (e.g. conveyancing is simply a tick along the path of a client's true objective which is a new home).

'Haven't you overcharged me?' is an indication that the client did not clearly understand your quotation or cost indication at the outset: better promotion of the benefits of the service may be required. The BMQ technique will be to outline the benefits derived and the risks avoided and perhaps an additional cost comparison might be justified. The fees for a probate matter may well be compared with the costs that would have been incurred had a bank or other institution undertaken the work. A clear statement of the taxation saved will further justify the fees, while reference to the tax paid may well provide a cost comparison. In conveyancing, a comparison with estate agent's fees, removal firms and the cost of advertising is very pertinent.

Remember, all these examples must be accompanied by a benefit presentation as well as a cost comparison.

Finally, perhaps it is hardest to justify costs that are higher than those of other firms. Solicitors are still prevented by professional rules from making quality comparisons. Therefore, the public are led to believe that the standard of work and service is identical anywhere, and anyway all lawyers must carry indemnity insurance to cover them if something goes wrong. In these (perceived) circumstances why should a prospect do anything but choose the cheapest?

Again, your justification will derive from an understanding of the client's needs, what they are actually buying and the benefits, unique or otherwise, your firm has to offer. Where a firm has a well-developed and maintained database of current and past clients, those clients' needs may already be well understood and easily available.

Cost justification: discussion points

In **Chapter 5** we proposed that a benefit analysis was undertaken throughout your firm to prompt discussion with all fee earners and partners regarding the benefits clients can gain from using your firm. Using the collated results and analysis of benefits identified, the following may assist you to apply the techniques from this chapter, or suggest that a further review of benefits would be worthwhile. It is worth remembering that benefits change, and a regular review of the firm's benefits to its clients can help keep the ideas fresh with fee earners and clients.

The benefits of consulting a solicitor

This basic issue illustrates the point at which a firm should start to communicate with clients. For example, what are the advantages of a solicitor dealing with a complex will when an accountant and a will writing service can do the job and could be better at the tax implications? What could a growing company save or avoid by having regular discussions with your firm? Why can a solicitor help me? This list of benefits tackles the basic sales message.

The benefits of instructing your firm

Here, the position of the client has potentially moved on to a choice between solicitors' firms. Bearing in mind the above checklist of what clients are looking for, how does your firm provide specific benefits? The firm might (accurately) be described as 'long-established in [region], with several comfortable and discreet offices, offering multiple practice areas with experienced partners, assistant solicitors and support staff'. These are all nice features and assets to have, but what benefit is that to the client?

As an alternative description, consider 'a successful firm in [region], supplying accessible legal advice covering all areas of law, having many satisfied clients in 30 years of service to the community'. Turn the assets into the benefits they provide for the client.

The benefits offered to a client by your department

This is similar to the benefits of instructing the firm but focuses on product, specific benefits. If, for instance, your firm has a comprehensive IT case management system for conveyancing, how does that benefit the client? Again, a nice asset, but how does that translate into a demonstrable benefit to the client?

The benefits of buying a particular service from your department

A further breakdown of services within a department achieves the level of detailed benefits analysis that will provide the client with the answers they are looking for. 'What is it your firm does to satisfy the needs and wants of the clients?' Product packaging as mentioned previously forms a more advanced approach to clients and the marketplace. Cross-selling between departments, commercial to private client, PI or conveyancing to wills and probate, can produce a wider range of benefits to a client. 'Our firm provides a complete legal service' is a good start, leading back to answering many of the requirements listed under 'The benefits of instructing your firm'.

CHAPTER 7 TASKS **Develop your business**

Mergers, acquisitions and organic growth questions

Mergers

Consider the firms in your area and draw up a list of the firms you would hypothetically consider a merger with in the future. Rank that list using a 1 to 5 scale where 1 is a good fit of services and 5 is a firm that offers all the same types of services to clients. Also consider any relevant local information that is known about the willingness of that firm's partners to agree to a merger.

Acquisitions

Again, consider the firms in your area and draw up a list of the firms you would hypothetically consider as an acquisition target. Use a similar ranking scale (1 to 5) where 1 is a good fit of services and 5 is a firm which offers all the same types of services to clients. Also consider any relevant local information that is known about the partners' individual positions towards being taken over or selling their firm.

Questions to consider for assessing horizontal and vertical practice development

- How would you define your firm's growth objectives in quantifiable terms over the next three or five years? If you have a quantified business plan, that should include the details required.
- What is the route to that growth? Include details of issues such as: who, when, where, with what, how.
- Who is your firm's managing partner? Is that person credited with the time he spends on the firm's management task? Is that arrangement ad hoc or formalised as part of the partnership agreement?
- Having initiated the development of your firm's client and professional contact database, what tactics do you intend to apply to actively seek recommendations?
- How will you introduce the concepts of vertical and horizontal strategies to your fee-earning staff?
- What actions do you currently take to underpin your client base?
- Do the different departments or divisions in your firm currently operate together or separately in promotions? What percentage of the promotional budget is spent on joint promotions and individual promotions?
- Following the skills audit, what action has been taken to encourage and assist the staff in becoming a marketing resource? What sales training is proposed?

Practice exercises in using BMQ

To assist your firm in developing and practising the BMQ technique with fee earners and staff, below are discussion points that may help you improve interaction with clients. Use each set of questions and ask the fee earners to say how they would deal with that situation.

1. Persuade the client to your point of view from the following negative positions:
    - It will be several days before you can give the client an answer.
    - You need more information.
    - You can't tell how long the process is going to take.
    - A client's file has been passed to a colleague.

2. Discuss the following courses of action you want to take with a client, and how best to persuade the client to take the time to participate and help you:
   - To record a potential client's details for the firm's database.
   - To understand the benefits of your firm employing specialists in each department.
   - To appreciate the benefit of the fact that yours is a long-established firm and the leading firm in the area.
   - To emphasise the benefit of the staff all having local experience and knowledge in comparison with alternative service providers.
3. Consider how to present the client with the 'bad news' in the following situations:
   - A decision (court/tribunal/legal) has gone against the client.
   - You are late ringing a client back.
   - You need to advise the client not to proceed.
4. List three circumstances in which you may have to present a proposal or course of action to a client.
5. What are the three steps to go through when presenting a proposal to a client? Think of a recent proposal you have had to present to a client or colleague and illustrate it by use of the three-step technique.
6. Why is it important to emphasise the meaning and significance of your proposal in terms of the advantage it will give to the client? How do you ensure that the client has understood and accepted this advantage?
7. Why is it important to select from a full range of benefits? List three benefits to a prospective client of using your firm. Present those benefits via the three-step technique.
8. Why is it relevant in a solicitor's non-selling job to understand sales techniques?

From this chapter your firm should now have an understanding of:

(a) the marketing implications of strategies for growth through mergers and acquisitions;

(b) a framework of the horizontal and vertical development of your firm's clients and services;

(c) methods for understanding and delivering clear benefits to clients; and

(d) ways to present cost justification to clients that will enhance your firm's profitability.

8

Business structures and alternative business structures

In this chapter we look, from a marketing point of view, at the business structure of the average legal practice and some of the issues that arise given the changing regulation and competitive landscape.

Alternative business structures (ABSs) need careful consideration because of their significant effects on the legal services market. Well before their full introduction, ABSs have influenced many businesses and firms active in this sector. In this chapter we look at ABS as a management process and, more importantly for firms, what to do about it and its effects.

We also consider departmentalisation and divisionalisation, which while obviously providing centres of excellence, can also introduce problems that need to be addressed or avoided.

Finally, we consider the role of personnel succession planning within the overall business and marketing plans of the firm.

The best way to predict the future is to invent it. – Alan Kay, computer programming pioneer

ABS and business structures

You may think this is getting a little outside the remit of marketing. The ABS regulations cover (amongst other things) the ownership of, and investment in, firms that provide reserved legal activities. So what has it got to do with marketing?

Marketing is defined by the Chartered Institute of Marketing as 'the management process responsible for identifying, anticipating, and satisfying customers' requirements profitably'. First, you need to have a sustainable and solvent firm for that management process to act within. Marketing is a management view of your firm and a set of methods, tools and techniques used to deliver profit. Therefore, the structure of the business is part of that remit equally alongside the finance and production functions. Your firm could be:

- LDP (until ABS)
- ABS
- Limited company
- LLP
- Partnership

The ABS regulations now offer alternative ways to structure a firm that will affect the management and therefore almost all aspects of how the firm is run. However, to bring profitable services and products to a market is essentially a marketing issue and the vehicle used needs to confer some competitive advantage. Whichever structure you choose, it needs to be sufficient to maintain that competitive advantage over a long period or over the period the investors plan to gain the best investment returns. Those investors could be equity partners, non-lawyers or anyone who passes the 'fitness to own' criteria. It now does not matter who they are but how much added value (as well as cash) they bring to the firm for its future prosperity.

For some firms ABS has become a strategic destination typified by the phrase, 'we want to be an ABS by 2012'. However, this is mistaking the purpose of ABS: it is not an end in itself but a business structure that a successful firm can use to manage investment and profits (or losses). A profitable and successful firm may look at the opportunity to increase investment in their business through the ABS regulations. Weighing the 'pros and cons' of bringing in additional but external investors to provide funds to develop the business profits from a particular market position is a continuous business management decision process. To have that confidence in returns from a set of client services on a purely commercial level means having a clear marketing management approach that will deliver the profits.

Rather than a destination to aim at, ABS or the alternatives needs to be the appropriate administrative vehicle that moves the firm forward in a planned direction.

Where is the client in ABS?

The ABS regulations that govern the provision of reserved legal activities are already having many far-reaching consequences. ABS affects the commercial environment that a firm works in, markets are fractured along consumer demand lines and what had been distinct solicitor legal services are being absorbed into other consumer and business offerings.

While the ABS changes are being driven by the supply side of the legal services industry for the intended benefit of the consumer, little or nothing has yet changed in the buying behaviour of clients. Consumer research from the SRA, YouGov and other reputable organisations has yet to show any significant change in the buying habits of clients, other than the rise of the web as an information resource, at the expense of the traditional telephone directories. Inspired to create a more competitive market, Clementi and the Legal Services Act 2007 have done their bit to alter the provision of legal services but this does not change the demand side. So where is the future client in all of this change?

Before we look more closely at firms' internal organisation from a marketing management view we need to look at what effect the changing regulatory environment in the legal services sector has already brought.

The changes that the prospect of ABS has brought

The mere threat of change in the traditional solicitors' market has brought several reactions that need to be studied. Learning from the impetus of these ideas will help your firm identify its strength, weaknesses, opportunities and threats (see SWOT) in your area of work.

Solicitors' groups

There have been solicitors' groups for many years. Their type and structure has varied and some have remained successful where others have come and gone. LawNet is a good example of a successful solicitors' group. It serves the needs of its members although it is not overtly a consumer-facing group. Others, like Quality Solicitors and High Street Lawyer, are more recent launches that look to establish a recognisable consumer brand alongside serving their members' business needs. More groups will follow and their approach to the legal services market will vary, as will their offering and benefits to solicitors' firms.

Legal enquiry handlers

Although not directly in response to the ABS regulations but rather the consumer and small and medium-sized enterprises' (SMEs) lack of knowledge of the legal services market, there are many businesses set up to put people in touch with legal services that can help them. These new entrants fall into a number of categories and in **Chapter 10**, which covers websites and the Internet, we consider them further to help you understand their services.

- Comparison sites: companies that compare lawyers against certain criteria including price and provide the user with the results.
- Referral sites: companies attracting legal enquiries and referring them on to solicitors for a fee.
- Find-a-lawyer sites: sites that provide a list of lawyers and charge a fee for basic or enhanced listings.

- Legal brands: companies endeavouring to establish a brand from a network of legal firms, e.g. Quality Solicitors, High Street Lawyer, and claims management brands.
- Legal networking sites: companies that facilitate solicitors and/or clients to 'talk' online or solicitors to talk to each other.
- Legal information sites: companies providing some type of information on legal companies or legal issues.
- Legal companies: companies offering a legal service, e.g. Co-op, Halifax, traditional solicitors.

Your firm may already be using some of these services and be a member of several solicitors' groups. Each has their own merits and, in the context of business structures, needs to be assessed on their contribution towards achieving the firms' business targets set against the costs.

Consumer and SME market divergence

A further feature of the changes the prospect of ABS has brought is the continuing divergence of the market for legal services. This has already been seen in the market for personal injury litigation enquiries. But ABS will bring a greater split in identified market groups and the services offered to them. While these distinctions already exist, we will see them more actively exploited. A good example is the Co-op's legal services division and its links with their funeral business. In effect, it offers a complete 'life to death' service selling in a neat package: wills, funeral and probate. Banks offer SMEs employment law advice and a choice of other direct legal solution services. The benefit to the client is an easy-to-understand single service point that is offered by a business they use regularly for other services. Market segmentation is dealt with in **Chapters 5** and **7** and is increasingly important in future markets. We can see areas of legal service that will be taken up by non-solicitor run ABS business, characterised by the synergies with their other offers. These will include:

- PI claims;
- probate or estate management;
- conveyancing and moving home;
- corporate and commercial advice;
- SME business services;
- private client services.

What is important to consider is that the clients are primarily looking for a suitable solution to their perceived legal services needs. Expertise, availability and convenience, alongside price and recommendation, are the determining factors. While solicitors' firms are trusted to deliver the best advice and solutions, they are seen as expensive (YouGov research) and often difficult to contact. If the ABS businesses can achieve a similar level of trust and benefits with potential clients, their ability to better promote and deliver the legal services alongside their core business will result in satisfied customers who will use their services again.

Current thinking is that ABS investors, outside the big city firms, will concentrate their interests in the high-volume, commoditised work where they can deliver a fixed-price service for a fixed outcome. Where the consumers' requirements fall outside their systems, they may have a bespoke service department or a panel of solicitors to pass the work on for a referral fee.

Alternative business structures

The first thing to set down is an outline of ABS and how it relates to marketing management given the details above and throughout this book. In the end we need to look at how ABS will affect or improve each fee earner's daily interaction with current and future clients.

To put it into context, ABS is one part of the system of regulations for the provision of legal services to clients. What we want to deal with here is its effects on the marketing management in your firm. ABS, like the term 'marketing', has been used widely and misunderstood in the short time it has been introduced. As mentioned previously, some firms have taken up the idea of becoming an ABS firm as a strategic goal. This is a potential error in management planning because it seeks to use a capital structure as a target. The decision of whether to become an ABS should come from an analysis of the best route to exploit the emerging market opportunities.

Having the goal of becoming an ABS potential misses the important stage of building a profitable firm with a set of services clients will need in the future. That goal may distract attention away from a focus on innovation and development of services to clients. As outlined previously, without a clearly planned approach to the changing legal services market, the choice of ABS could be said to be a case of the proverbial 'fiddling while Rome burns' or, to use another analogy, 'putting the cart before the horse'.

While striving to become regulated as an ABS may induce the necessary development of services to clients, it should be the other way round. A successful and profitable firm should ask itself if the ABS regulations would help it deliver new and innovative services to clients more profitably or quickly.

ABS investor expectations

It is worth considering what an investor is looking for in the businesses they analyse. Return on capital employed (ROCE) over a set period of time is a key performance indicator (KPI). However, as you would expect, there's a lot more to consider than that analysis. In other commercial markets the business idea is not the only consideration and often it is the least important. More often it's the management team behind the idea that gets the financial backing. Venture capital or private equity investors need to have confidence in the team with the right mix of skills that will deliver the return on investment. For example, in mid-market commercial investments (£3m to £8m) one in four investment deals needs a new finance director in the business to guide its development. Accurate management reporting, information and statistics become increasingly important, as the business is under pressure to deliver on its potential. In many of the firms we have dealt with, this 'now and future' mind-set of the firm is not part of the current management thinking. Most firms have a 'past to now' perspective with few actionable business plans and objectives.

A clear business plan can only be part of the story. Given that the traditional model of legal services is now not a good indicator of the future, firms that want to attract external investment will need to show how they will address the future market for legal services. Innovation in services and a credible marketing and promotional plan are just two of the elements needed. A traditional firm that has high fixed costs and retiring partner liabilities is unlikely to present an attractive investment opportunity.

For a traditional multi-practice firm the view of a potential investor is from the future profits position. A firm will be judged on the quality of its database.

- How many client contacts does the firm have?
- How much does the firm know about each contact's future needs?
- How much profit does the firm plan to make out of each client contact in the next three to five years?

In short, the marketing plan is absolutely integral to the future value of the business.

Having dealt with the choices of structure, ABS threats and the other issues raised by the changing legal services regulations, what is most important is how this changes the way you organise your firm to adapt to this change.

New competition unleashed by the regulation changes that allow non-solicitor owned businesses to offer a full range of legal services need not be seen as the end of the traditional solicitors' business. All the tools and techniques those organisations will use are available to solicitors. Use them and take an open view of how to deliver valuable service to your clients and your firm is just as likely to win the business as any other. The big brands have no secret tricks or magic formulae to win business, they just use marketing management methods to promote the benefits of the services they offer in a more effective way than others. Properly funded ABS practices may create bigger budgets to explain the benefits of their services.

The collective firm

The practical implications of a firm's structure need to be translated into systems and procedures that help fee earners deliver services to clients and profits to the business. Planning the future structure of your firm will benefit from the current divisional or departmental structure but, importantly, with a change to a client-focused service.

Having looked at a firm's structure from the top down in terms of ABS, LLP partnership and others, we would suggest you need to now look at where you want to be and plan back from there. How should you organise the fee earners to maximise their ability to deliver value to their clients? This bottom-up approach allows you to organise the firm to speak directly to the people who have an interest in your work. You can become a centre of excellence, not only in the production of legal work, but also in the understanding of your clients and their needs: demonstrating to potential clients the benefits your department has to offer, and will deliver, to satisfy their needs.

The collection of departments is an internal structure to help administer the business and it is worth remembering that the clients are less interested in which department they deal with and more interested in how to achieve a solution to their needs. The client focus is on how you can help them and not on which department they need. This is often a point that training needs to address and we look at that later in this chapter.

Your departmental staff will also need to learn more about their clients and be able to speak their language more easily when they use a well-managed database system (see **Chapter 6**). In other words, they can become experts in solving their problems, as well as producing the legal goods, and at selling the department's services to prospects.

While the marketing partner must coordinate the efforts made in publicity, promotion and selling throughout the firm, it is usual that the ideas, initiatives and even actions will stem from the departments. And this is how it should be. The marketing partner needs to encourage this and report on progress to the management structure and around the firm.

Publicity, promotion and selling should always be on the standing agenda of departmental meetings, in recognition of the fact that they are as important to the department as production of legal work and an important part of the job for everyone in the department. The marketing partner should attend at least one in three of these departmental meetings to add a marketing impetus, to provide a marketing service and to assist in the production of marketing support material, to coordinate the firm's activity, to incorporate this department's activity and to provide information about, and perhaps even ideas from, other departments.

Perhaps one of the most difficult tasks facing the marketing partner is to encourage divisionalisation as a centre of excellence in production and client handling while avoiding the 'compartmentalisation' that can so easily lead to a failure even to understand the need to cross-sell between departments, let alone developing the enthusiasm to do so. One of the main rationales behind the literature kit proposed in **Chapter 9**, as opposed to a firm's brochure, is to ensure that the contents are relevant to the recipient. However, even a highly targeted folder on one subject should include a menu insert to ensure that all services provided by the firm are at least acknowledged.

It is the same with departmental personnel. Of course, they will concentrate on their own specialism, but must be encouraged to look up from the file and consider what else the client may need from the firm, and then make it easy for the client to make contact with the appropriate department or fee earner. (See **Chapter 6** on the 'one minute marketing solution'.)

Departmentalisation versus compartmentalisation

Consider the case of the recently widowed 'Mrs Jones'. She is a model example of someone who needs far more than the simple provision of probate services. She needs sympathy, she needs time, and she needs understanding. Perhaps she needs a friend, but most importantly, she needs to have the faith that she can entrust all her matters to people who will take care of her and not just tie up the legal necessities, but also appreciate her emotions. This is an actual case, and the probate department concerned looked after her perfectly. She would not have felt the same if greeted by a conveyancer just returned from entertaining an estate agent for lunch, or felt important enough to the firm if she was met by someone who had just completed a major commercial purchase. This illustrates the best of divisionalisation, and yet the kind and gentle probate practitioner needed to advise her on selling the family home and, indeed, the commercial implications of her late husband's share portfolio. The observation and awareness of the probate practitioner and her willingness to cross-sell between departments led to new business in three departments of the firm and, of equal importance, a first-class service for the client provided by specialist departments, introduced to her by someone she trusted.

Each division or compartment may claim that life would be easier for them if they could be kept away from other department's clients. We have all heard stories of undesirable clients in conveyancing or the intolerant businessman upset by the behaviour of children waiting with a parent to see a family practitioner. Not all firms have the luxury of being able to separate clients by department, but there are actions that can be taken. The businessman can be met at the reception door and whisked swiftly through to an office or interview room. Security doors may encourage the more disreputable to wait outside, if the smoking ban has not already achieved that.

One firm that we worked for some years ago had the physical ability to set their departments up to suit their clients. The firm was a full-service private client practice with a substantial commercial department. It was located in an area with a strong, but reducing, military presence, which led to a major increase in commercial work because of the redevelopment of released MOD land and a noticeable increase in matrimonial work, possibly because personnel were being moved around the country. The family department was housed in a separate, though adjoining, building. The conveyancing department had its own car park and entrance, and an entirely appropriate feel – similar to that of an estate agent. As the firm did not undertake criminal work, all other clients used the 'main entrance'. This was luxurious although not opulent, and well suited to the type of business client that the firm increasingly attracted. It had the feeling of the reception of a corporate office. In contrast, the reception area of the matrimonial and family department was open plan, informal, with the receptionist in T-shirt and jeans and a radio playing music (quietly). There was a large supply of toys which clients' children were encouraged to play with. In short, parents returning from a supermarket shopping trip did not feel out of place and were made welcome. Office hours were flexible to allow meetings up to 8 pm. The department was geared to their needs, as indeed were the commercial and conveyancing divisions.

Of course, not all firms have these physical opportunities, but the principle behind servicing the client and the client's needs is clear. This could have been the perfect set up for compartmentalisation; however, because the partners had instilled in everyone the need for cross-selling and the promotion of the firm's full service range, this did not happen. Indeed, each member of the fee-earning staff recognised it was part of their job to seek opportunities for other departments, and was monitored and rewarded for success.

The obligation to cross-sell

The firm referred to above made cross-selling between departments an obligation. It made it part of the job of all employees, and monitored it in the same way as it did every other part of performance.

But it was not imposed, it was explained. Much of this book is to do with growth, and development of the existing client base. We have referred throughout to vertical and horizontal development, and to the client database: past satisfied clients or newly won clients. This is the 'seed corn' of your firm and your staff must not be permitted to squander it.

We know that there are entrenched attitudes in the profession, but also that the people coming into the profession now, and over the past few years, are more commercially aware. They are commercially aware because they have to be. And this is before The New Competition has launched large-scale promotions of their services. Now, it is essential for everyone to understand that their job is far more than the satisfactory production of legal work. They must nurture the client and encourage additional and repeat usage of the firm's services. They must actively seek recommendation and there is no better time than when a case has been satisfactorily concluded.

Divisionalisation works against this need. The marketing partner must establish an obligation to cross-sell between departments by using systems like the suggested 'one minute marketing solution' discussed in **Chapter 6**.

The conduit for cross-selling

You must ensure that you do not give staff an excuse for not cross-selling because it is too complicated. Or for poor production performance, because 'we were busy selling other products'. The solution is to establish a conduit for cross-selling.

The marketing partner should have individual meetings with each departmental head. At these meetings, a list should be drawn up of all the cross-selling situations or scenarios that are likely to arise, opportunities for each department to promote another. Get this down on paper so that it can be used to support the one minute marketing solution.

Each department head should appoint one person who does not necessarily need to be a fee earner, so long as they are methodical, reliable and accepted by their departmental colleagues as such. This person (often a senior secretary) will be responsible for fielding all referrals from other departments. This referral should be form-based (see the form at the end of this chapter, and on the CD-Rom). It should be simple to complete, but carry all the relevant information, including a comments section. The form should be standard throughout the firm and, obviously, you can send it by email if appropriate. Some case management software systems provide a system for referrals. However, they usually rely on the fact that the system is fully implemented and used by all parties. If this is the situation, a manual or email system must be used as a firm-wide alternative.

The person receiving the referral will have the responsibility of informing the referred what action has been taken within 72 hours of receipt of the form. Therefore, the person charged with this responsibility must have the gravitas and authority (and the backing of the partnership) to compel even the departmental head into action.

This system has been used by many firms of our experience, and it works. It is dependent, however, on monitoring. People who are operating the system should be encouraged. Reward is an emotive subject, and often subject to abuse. That is why it is important to establish it as part of the existing job and not an addition to it. In any case, reward can often be a simple 'thank you', a monthly bottle of wine to the best performer and a note on the annual appraisal review.

Those who do not perform should be encouraged to do better. There will be excuses – you will be amazed at how many excuses there are for not doing this – but that is all they are, excuses, for not putting an instruction into action. If this is the case, the instruction needs to be continually repeated, along with explanation and encouragement. An ongoing refusal to participate is either an indication of an irrevocably entrenched attitude or a genuine inability. We have said before that not all people are cut out to be 'salesmen' and you may have to live with lack of performance in this area providing, of course, performance in other areas is outstanding to compensate.

'It's not my job'

Oh yes it is! As we have said elsewhere, everyone is responsible for presenting the firm in the best light. Everyone is responsible for promoting the benefits of the firm, for client care, and actively seeking recommendations. All of you! It is this, perhaps more than anything else, that will differentiate your firm from The New Competition. They can only work at arm's length. You, and your staff, must get closer to your clients. It is this approach that will enhance the service that you provide.

EXAMPLE **Focus**

A firm we have helped had a problem in the busy conveyancing department. Their success was built around two very efficient and effective conveyancers who processed matters quickly, accurately and professionally. However, neither was interested in, or saw, the value of doing anything other than producing top quality work. After several failed attempts to introduce cross-selling procedures, the senior partner was becoming concerned at their ability to contribute to the future plans for the firm. On balance, the senior partner did not want to lose the conveyancers because of their excellent work, but needed a solution that fitted the situation. The answer lay in the focus on their work. Their attitude was competitive, and anything that got in the way of their quality, complexity and speed duel was ignored. This caused difficulties with file opening and closing procedures, and contact with clients. To solve this, the senior partner appointed an existing and trusted secretary to relieve them of any administrative work. The secretary's focus was to ensure they had a clear flow of matters, with all the administration dealt with, which allowed them to process the matters more quickly. Once they had completed their work, the secretary then ensured all cross-selling opportunities and client details were up to date. The increased cost of that secretary's time was more than recovered by the increase in the conveyancers' productivity, and the business passed to other departments.

Centres of excellence for departmental promotion

In **Chapter 9** we refer to 'the three tiers of promotion'. The first – corporate image – is not a matter for the departments. However, product promotion and, to a certain extent, market promotion are departmental responsibilities. And they are also an area for the development of centres of excellence.

Market promotion

We deal with market promotion first, because this provides a range of services to a specific market group. It is likely that those services will be packaged together from different departments within the firm. However, it is also likely that they will be led by one department that provides the majority of the package.

Why is this an advantage? As noted earlier, departments are likely to have a deeper understanding of their clients than does the firm in general, and that understanding should extend to the recognition of the problems faced by the clients. In turn, this leads to a presentation of how these problems can be overcome. This, essentially, is benefit presentation. It is benefit presentation in a form of words appropriate to, and understood by, the client from a particular market segment.

There is also an added opportunity to demonstrate how associated products, perhaps from other departments, enhance the first main product and improve the likely resolution of clients' overall problems.

Each department will have its own section of the firm's professional contacts register. The obvious examples of this are conveyancing dealing with estate agents, commercial with accountants and family with Citizens Advice Bureaux, etc. Therefore, part of the promotion being undertaken by a department towards a specific market can, in part, be directed at the appropriate professional recommenders.

Product promotion

Clearly, product promotion is a departmental responsibility. The involvement in the creation of the literature kit by the department, the development of articles for the newsletter, the departmental website content and the development of each department's own section of the PCR will all have led to the department being able to mount a sustained promotional campaign for their product range.

Generally speaking, provided the cross-selling conduit is in place, it is better to promote one single product rather than a range from individual departments. A seminar on inheritance tax planning should concentrate purely on that issue, although the interested parties may later be introduced to all sorts of other ancillary services including conveyancing and perhaps commercial services. But in the first case, stick with the subject in hand.

Focusing promotional campaigns

The department or division is the ideal place to focus a promotional campaign, and to gain support for it. Senior management will be strongly motivated to succeed if they have declared their objectives to their staff. Involve your staff and you will be amazed at the level of feedback and innovative ideas you receive in return. Where there is criticism, there are two responses. First, listen and respond, restating the need for this specific campaign; second, ask them for their alternative contribution.

The pitfalls of divisionalisation

In many ways, all the pitfalls of divisionalisation stem from the danger of compartmentalisation. This can lead not only to the failure to understand marketing in its wider context, and the disregarding of the cross-selling needs of the firm, but also to a damaging 'them and us' attitude between different sections of staff. This can only be detrimental to the firm and create additional problems for personnel management from retention and recruitment through to development and attitude.

If, as we hope is accepted, the firm understands that marketing involves everything that isn't pure production or accounts, then personnel play a major part in marketing, if predominantly an internal role. The marketing partner, perhaps with the support of departmental heads and other partners, must ensure that all members of staff understand that they may be in a department, but they are primarily part of the firm. As such, it is important that they understand everything that the firm does, and the benefits it has to offer. That is one of the main reasons why the benefit analysis that was proposed in **Chapter 5** should be applied firm-wide to every member of the staff at whatever level, discussed with them and used as a basis for explaining the firm's growth objectives, its marketing tactics and their role within it. To illustrate that non-legal staff need to understand the firm, and the wider legal profession, to ensure they do their jobs well, then:

- The post-room staff must ensure files and communications are received and arrive promptly.
- IT support staff must be able to provide knowledgeable help.
- Maintenance and cleaning staff need to be able to differentiate between important papers and rubbish.

A minor additional point covered in earlier chapters: when all staff are included and made to feel valued, they are more likely to recommend their firm to family, friends and contacts. Inclusion does not take much effort and the rewards to your firm's morale can be significant.

Departmental attitudes

If there is a 'them and us' attitude evident between partners and staff, note that it may also exist between departments, often rather obviously between the 'glitterati' of the commercial department and 'the others' in domestic or high-volume legal work.

Indeed, it has not been uncommon in the past few years to see commercial firms separating from their private client departments and concentrating on the lower-volume, high-margin commercial areas. Without doubt, these firms are the most protected from The New Competition, but also the least likely to be reading this book. For those that remain together, the 'them and us' attitude, be it between partners and staff or departments, needs to be addressed.

The firms that succeed will require strong management and open leadership, and need to be able to demonstrate it. Strong management is defined by clear strategy, detailed planning and the involvement in those plans of each person who is a stakeholder. Conversely, weak management is often the product of unclear strategy and a fear of being found out by the staff.

The adoption of a growth strategy and the development of a vertical and horizontal organic growth approach are the basics in establishing strong management. Developing a market understanding with a promotional plan and communicating all these in detail to staff, division by division, will ensure that they know where they fit in, and that everybody knows that their contribution is important.

Departmental competition is inevitable and often a good spur for innovation within a firm, but it is beholden upon the senior management to ensure that there is no 'them and us' syndrome, and that everybody understands their position in the firm and their worth to it. This is not woolly, 'touchy-feely' niceness, it is about making profit more easily: using teams, where previously individuals worked alone and often in conflict; creating a business that is focused on the outside world and the potential customers; and using the collective resources of a firm to add up to more than the sum of its parts.

Developing niche markets

The department is essential to the understanding and development of niche markets. If it has not already been done, a departmental review of the client base, with the specific intention of identifying and subsequently developing niches, should be undertaken.

For all the reasons outlined earlier, a niche market can be one of the strongest ways forward for the independent firm, and one of the least likely avenues to be adopted by The New Competition. A niche may be geographic around one town with full service or a collection of services aimed at a particular group of clients.

Conflicting images

Let us return, again, to our friend in the 'Will Power' suit (see **Chapter 4**). In fact, it did not damage his commercial standing, but this was totally down to his own personality, and the support, perhaps even respect, of his client base. But think again of widow Jones and the businessman, the junkie and the home purchaser, the brat and the recently bereaved. Service your department, promote your firm, but do not let your activities produce a conflicting image.

Succession planning

Finally, a sensitive subject that some firms prefer to ignore!

We worked with a senior partner for many years and for whom we have a huge respect. He was extremely successful as was his firm. He did an enormous amount of charity work and alongside all this had time to learn Japanese 'as a hobby'. He also declared that he was keeping Italian until he retired. He was exceptional in many areas but took on board what we had said, was not offended and applied it.

When, eventually, he did retire – at 72 – he learned Italian within a year and his firm flourished. His firm flourished because he had laid down the foundations to enable it to do so. In short, he had a detailed succession plan, and despite his exceptional qualities, never considered himself irreplaceable.

Recruitment plays a part in succession planning but it is the timing of recruitment within the long-term development of a firm that is crucial. The ideal succession plan allows for people to grow into new jobs, usually from lower levels, while being mentored by the current incumbent. Leaving the recruitment process too late will risk a rush into a situation that will almost inevitably result in the recruitment of someone who will bring an entirely different ethos to the firm or be a short-term 'fix'.

Not everyone can be a partner in their firm. Indeed, there are an increasing number of people coming into the profession who do not wish to become partners. There are numerous reasons for this, but the most evident is the recognition that not everybody can become a member of the board of directors or a shareholder of the company for which they work in the normal commercial world. In essence, that is what partnership is, and it should not be seen as the be all and end all of a career.

Nevertheless, partnership succession needs to be addressed and the existing partners need to plan well ahead the size and shape of partnership required for the future. For example, what are the roles of consultants, associates and salaried partners? Similarly, there is a need to plan ahead for management succession and to take into account the changes to the legal services market. How much management of the firm, including marketing management, is going to be undertaken by the partner, and how much will be delegated to other fee earners, or recruited from outside either through full-time (non-fee earning) employees or outsourced? It is arguable that management succession planning is actually more important than partnership succession planning.

Succession planning should be natural. Like everything else, ideally, it should be a declared policy and transparently open to all. We have seen some real horror stories where people are reluctant to retire, consider themselves irreplaceable, have been workaholics with no outside interests and have, on occasions, been damaging to their own firm. It amazes us how often we find firms that have relied upon an inadequate partnership deed – or none at all. Perhaps the first step in succession planning is to get the deed right, have it approved, and include within it retirement ages and the programme leading up to retirement. Since this is a central issue to the owners of the firm, we strongly recommend getting professional help, starting with the Law Society. It is often a difficult issue with many vested interests and attempting to deal with it in-house often leads to stagnation or dispute.

Similarly, the firm should consider what happens if people, even senior partners, leave; you need to recognise that, without care, the number of non-partners can lead to a higher turnover of senior people. Above all, we would recommend that your firm recognises the future requirements of your business and does not allow itself to become tied by tradition.

As an example, we would offer what we have known within Marketlaw for some years, as the 'Oli syndrome'.

EXAMPLE **'Oli syndrome'**

Oli was a hugely successful practitioner and had the largest billing in the firm. He was a man who understood marketing and client care in its true form, and as such, was the best member of the firm when it came to cross-selling, to encouraging subordinates and to actively seeking recommendations from past satisfied clients or his wide range of professional contacts.

Oli was a very intelligent man, a very experienced man and would undoubtedly have been a success in any area of business endeavour that he chose to undertake. Oli was very well paid. And so he deserved to be. But he had the wrong qualifications. Oli had never become a solicitor. As such, of course, he could not become a partner. Because he was not a partner, he was excluded from partnership meetings and any formal management role within the firm. It was obvious to us, as outside consultants, that he should be co-opted into the management of the firm and be treated, effectively, as a partner. But the partners would not have this.

Oli left the firm! He didn't want to leave but really had no option. Within a year, the firm had lost more than a third of his business. Within two years, it had lost two-thirds of his clients. Oli never became a solicitor although he continued to practise law very successfully. What Oli did become was practice manager of a very important local firm that treated him as a partner in everything but name. He flourished, and so did his new firm.

Oli did not want to leave his original firm where he was happy and successful. He was forced to do so by the intransigence of the partnership. Do not let that happen to you. Build non-solicitors into your succession planning. The Legal Services Act 2007 allows non-solicitor partners, which will provide a solution to many firms that want to attract and retain key managerial staff.

CHAPTER 8 TASKS **ABS tasks**

1. A successful and profitable firm should ask itself if the ABS regulations offer a better value structure that would help it deliver new and innovative services to clients more profitably or quickly than the alternatives. A potential investor in your firm asks, 'What is it that makes your firm different for clients compared to your competitors?' List five elements of your firm's competitive advantage.
2. Marketing is a management approach that looks at the firm from the clients' perspective. Looking at your firm's past client database, can you answer these questions from a potential investor in your firm?

   How many accurate client contacts does the firm have?

   How much does the firm know about each contact and their future needs?

   How much profit does the firm plan to make out of each client contact in the next three to five years?
3. Explain to a person as a potential investor how the departmental structure of your firm is an environment that supports innovation and development of your firm's services to clients?
4. Cross-selling management.

In conjunction with the OMMS ideas in **Chapter 6**, now review how your firm manages cross-selling opportunities.

The list below is for use in developing a system for cross-selling between departments. It should provide the basis for your firm's form and be amended to suit your current systems.

Form: cross-selling

Referring department:

Name of referring person (fee earner or support staff contact):

Target department:

Name of person receiving the referral:

Client reference:

Nature of service required by client:

Notes on client's requirements:

The implementation of the suggestions contained in this chapter will ensure that the personnel structure and production resources of the firm are in a good position to grow, implement marketing plans and face up to The New Competition.

9

Underlying promotional matters

In this chapter we consider the first impressions made by your firm.

We introduce the concept of the three tiers of promotion, and explain them while looking at the measurement of promotional activity.

We discuss a firm's brochure and introduce the idea of a 'literature kit' that has so much more to offer for the same price as a brochure.

As the first step into the area of promotional activity, we look at presenting your firm to the outside world, but start with presentation to your existing clients.

> *Any activity becomes creative when the doer cares about doing it right or doing it better.* – John Updike

Many people believe that human beings are naturally creative, but frequently lack an outlet. If Updike is right, then caring and doing better will produce creativity in people that will make them more satisfied with their working environment, and more productive for their employer.

Certainly, understanding and being involved in promotion is a creative process that can be both rewarding and enjoyable. The key, as so often before, is ensuring that everyone understands why something is being done, and what their role is in it. And once a task has been successfully completed, a 'thank you' is one of the strongest motivational tools.

In this chapter, you will be asked to consider matters that might affect the outside world's perception of you. What do clients, prospects and fellow professionals think of you at first sight? Increasingly, these days, this first contact may be by letter, email, fax and the telephone. Even before that, many will have looked at your website – see **Chapter 10**.

What impression do you give? Effectively, any form of communication and all promotion are primarily geared to persuade people to talk to your firm. We consider staff, at all levels, and staff training to be of paramount importance as an underlying promotional matter. We deal with this in some detail.

Within the staff training element of this chapter we will look at the concerns, fears and needs of clients, and how best to handle them. First, we will look at a structure for understanding promotional activities.

The three tiers of promotion

'The three tiers of promotion' is a concept that outlines the different roles and, indeed, purpose of promotion, and may assist in the selection of specific campaigns and the allocation of appropriate resources to them. Broadly speaking, there are three types of promotion. Some are firm-wide, being for the benefit of the whole practice; some are departmental, in promoting, as they do, a specific product; and a further area of activity is aimed at a specific market or market niche.

Corporate promotion

This activity is organised to ensure that all past clients, existing clients and professional contacts know where your firm is, what it does, how to contact it and, wherever possible, have an indication of the firm's profile or ethos. This last is of particular importance, especially when corporate promotion is used to expand into new territory, be that matter type, geographical or industry category.

In essence, we are suggesting that like attracts like, but also in this area consideration must be given to the damage the activity of one department can do to the promotional aspirations of another.

Product-specific promotion

This is where the firm, or a department within the firm, takes a specific product, service or package of services and promotes the benefits of them to prospective or existing clients. This relates to the horizontal practice development outlined in **Chapter 7**.

Each department has a range of products including some 'prime products' and a resource capacity for increasing the volume of work in this area. These are the products that should be promoted and should be defined by the departmental head or the marketing partner.

Market-specific promotion

This is an activity where a specific market niche has been defined and a full range of appropriate services can be offered to the client. Again, this is an element of horizontal practice development. This might be as wide-ranging as, for example, the licenced trade on the one hand, to welfare seekers on the other, with everything in between. The most obvious market at the moment is the high-profile, relatively wealthy and continually growing 'elderly market', and it should be noted that the recent association between the AA and Saga is, at least in part, a deliberate process of offering legal services to this vital marketplace and one that undoubtedly provides a significant proportion of all legal practices' bread-and-butter work. Saga, it should be noted, has redefined 'elderly' on a regular downward trend, to now include everybody over the age of 50.

An approach to 'industry' is probably too general to succeed, or even perhaps describe as a market. An approach to an industry category (in which the firm has experience) in a clearly defined appropriate geographical area is a better tactic for a market-specific promotion.

Some campaigns and promotions operate across more than one area of activity. For example, the literature kit that we propose later in this chapter, or your current brochure, will help to underpin your client base and cross-sell while assisting in geographical expansion. An approach to the elderly market may start with existing clients via a newsletter, perhaps, but continue with new clients in your existing catchment area and then form part of a geographical expansion.

At the end of this chapter, we ask you to consider the firm's current promotional activity and see which of the three tiers it most easily fits into. We will also ask you to check and highlight any conflicting messages and, perhaps most importantly, list the areas where there is no significant promotion at all.

Measuring promotion

There is a simple key to this. Define the objective of the promotional activity and measure the results against it. This should, of course, include quantification based probably upon cost and anticipated return. Unfortunately, this seldom seems to happen in the legal profession, with the exception of larger, marketing-minded firms.

First, there will be what we have termed the 'blackmail budget'. Few firms acknowledge this, but it is there in spirit to provide the money for the promotional activity and advertising to which members of the firm and partnership have been unable to say 'No'. This could include mostly pointless (from a new business point of view) advertisements with local sports clubs, entries in local church magazines, sponsorship of a programme for local amateur dramatics group, a prize at the local flower show, etc. All this is perfectly justifiable and will undoubtedly demonstrate goodwill. But the essence of the 'blackmail budget' is that the damage suffered by saying no will be greater than the relatively small cost of participation in something that everybody knows (or should know) will result in little or no new business.

Second, there are the mistakes: the rushed purchase of advertising against a deadline that was not considered fully because the person responsible for placing the order was too busy; the over-zealous advertising salesmen who, frankly, are often paid by commission only, whose income depends entirely upon underplaying the negative and overplaying the positives of the proposition. These mistakes often get ignored as nobody likes to admit they have been sold a 'pup'. We have come across an extraordinary number of examples of firms who have signed a standing order for directories, etc. and have completely forgotten about it for some years.

Then there is expenditure on particular interests of partners or partners' spouses: golf days, boxes at Wimbledon, sponsorship of a racehorse, dedicated art gallery days. It is almost the same as the 'blackmail budget'.

So, before a single penny is spent, think – is this blackmail or is it getting business? If it is blackmail, and understood as such – fine. If it's a personal interest – OK. But, if it is supposed to be getting business, what are the objectives? A clinic held at a commercial client's premises for his employees should have a specific objective. A late-night opening initiative should have a quantifiable target. Even a golf day should at least include the aspiration of entertaining a satisfied client who will introduce you to a new prospect with a glowing reference.

In hard business terms, no promotional activity, and specifically promotional expenditure (either time or money), should be undertaken without a declared return or objective. Of course, it has to be accepted that sometimes targets are missed, objectives are not achieved, but too often the profession's promotional activities are ill-conceived, badly prepared and are undertaken 'because we said we'd do it'. Stop! These are at best junkets, and possibly actually damage the reputation of a legal practice from whom we (the clients) seek planning, professionalism and attention to detail.

A literature kit versus the firm's brochure

The three tiers of promotion have one common end point. When you have approached, pitched, talked to or entertained a possible client or professional contact, that person is usually expecting either to take something away from the meeting or to receive a follow-up letter or call. To back up that personal contact your firm must have good quality print materials (and a compatible website, see **Chapter 10**) that complement and enhance the potential client's view of the firm. Brochures, leaflets and letters need to be relevant, timely and useful to the recipient and this is an area where firms often fall short of the standards of other commercial organisations. The hard work of fee earners needs to be supported by the firm, enabling them to communicate effectively and efficiently the benefits to potential clients of using your firm. The literature kit (a folder with loose-leaf inserts) is a simple way to achieve this and controls how the firm presents itself to the outside world.

It may appear initially to be a considerable amount of work; however, this should be balanced against the alternatives and the common mistakes made by many firms in the past. It is important to put the brochure issue into context with a brief history that will explain the significance of printed material, how it can be a focus for the firm both internally and externally, and the likely significant returns on the costs of its production.

When the legal profession was first deregulated, it was seen by many advertising agencies (and even some consultancies) as an exciting new market. Indeed, it was. Unfortunately, the advertising world did not understand the uniqueness of the legal profession, and the profession that had until very recently been forbidden to advertise certainly did not understand the world of promotion (let alone marketing).

As a result, much money was wasted on the ubiquitous 'firm's brochure'. In general, no commercial organisation should try to serve so many different people (markets) of differing requirements with a single brochure. The wide range of legal products offered, each one a derived need, cannot be well presented in one piece of print that costs a fortune and quickly goes out of date.

One can overlook the inevitable pictures of partners and other staff in the brochure but the failure to point out relevant benefits is a waste of recipients' time and your firm's money. There is a better, cheaper and more flexible way, which we deal with in this chapter. It is a literature kit and a literature kit is not a brochure. It is what it says: a kit, and ideally will become a sales kit.

Rationale

In truth, all the firms interviewed for this book have proved themselves to be commercially aware and intent on improving their own marketing abilities. Without exception, they are practices noted for their quality of work with clients. Most have taken a great deal of time and trouble over their staff training and development, some even winning awards in this area. Others have won awards or accolades in different areas of the business world, or have had members of staff who have done so. In short, they care about their clients and strive to do a first-class job for them.

However, few of them are good at communicating with clients, and equally important, potential clients. Why is this?

First, it is true to say that in almost all firms, all fee earners are very busy, with some support staff genuinely stretched. Very few firms are regularly communicating with clients or potential clients, other than about the matter in hand. Most fee earners understand there are future work opportunities but often do not have the tools available to communicate the benefits of another department's services.

Second, all legal firms are production-based organisations. Fee earners go into the legal profession to produce legal work. They were educated and trained in the production of legal advice; they are targeted and monitored by their employers, by the amount and quality of their production; and they are judged similarly by their peers. Their own personal business objectives are likely to be production-orientated, and it is on this basis that they are paid and promoted. Many fee earners consider 'selling' to their clients and prospects as 'not their job', not of importance for the firm or anything more than an interruption to their work.

Third, most firms nowadays are departmentalised for the production of work. This is obviously highly appropriate, as it creates centres of excellence and eases communications. However, it does have the effect of compartmentalising the firm where everyone, including partners, considers their department first rather than the well-being and growth of the firm as a whole.

If you consider the typical firm's brochure, it is evident that this single piece of print tried to be all things to all men (clients). It had to cover or refer to all disciplines or matter types. It often attempted both to promote and to explain on one page and frequently assumed the reader understood what they needed to buy. It then began to go out of date, and eventually out of use.

These documents were often hugely expensive pieces of print and produced in glossy format similar to a multinational company report. They usually contained confusing details of information about the wide range of services offered with portrait photographs of all the partners. If you remember that some of the larger firms were the first to take this approach and that they could have as many as 60 partners, you get the impression of what these picture galleries must have looked like. As can be seen, the firm's brochure was, in fact, showing up a major problem for the profession. It demonstrated graphically not only the vast range of services that even the smallest practice usually offered, but also illustrated the wide diversity of markets that a legal firm of any size sought to serve.

It is at about this time that phrases such as 'junk mail' spring to mind. Not only were they junk, but as already noted, the brochures quickly went out of date. A glossy brochure with a retired partner pasted out is not impressive. Removing pages and adding typed amendment sheets quickly make the expensive printing look cheap and untidy.

Material does not have to be cheaply produced to be seen as junk, it simply has to be irrelevant to the recipient to be considered 'junk' by them. By definition, these brochures had to be mostly irrelevant to almost all of its recipients. Apart from the size and areas covered by the brochure, there were two main reasons for the 'junk' label:

1. The legal profession was not good at presenting benefits. It was excellent at explaining what it did, but not the benefit derived. Generally,

the profession failed to realise that they provided satisfaction to a derived service need.
2. In their justifiable attempt to maintain dignity and professionalism, most of these brochures were extremely aloof and off-putting.

Above all, these firms' brochures failed to recognise that a potential new client such as a managing director wishing to purchase and develop a new factory was no more interested in residential conveyancing than domestic clients were concerned with commercial conveyancing. The brochures did not address the different needs of their different market sectors and the different benefits derived by those clients from what the firm collectively referred to as 'conveyancing'. A real danger with the firm's brochure was that it made, or potentially made, a firm look too big and important to the private client, and at the same time, too domestically focused to carry out serious corporate work.

A further example is where a firm has a criminal defence department. Commercial and private clients can be put off by the thought of sharing a reception area with criminal defendants.

Of course, these are extreme examples, and the profession did begin to realise these problems for itself, but at about this time, firms began to divisionalise. These specialist departments had detailed knowledge of their markets and products and served the specific needs of a limited part of a firm's clients. The problem, as noted before, was that with departmentalisation came compartmentalisation and a separation of aims and objectives. Frequently, departments started producing their own promotional material and activities with little or no coordination between departments.

The result was promotional activity of one department that potentially damaged the stance of another. A classic, and actual, example was a firm that had set itself out as being 'upmarket' with its fee structure, to discover that there was a high-profile conveyancing department promotional campaign indicating that they, the conveyancing department, had joined the discount race and had become a cut-price 'bucket shop' operation.

Another example is one we mentioned in **Chapter 4**: a serious commercial and private client practice found that their probate partner had dressed as 'Will Power' (the Batman-type character dreamed up by the Law Society to promote will writing) and had been featured on the front cover of the local paper leaping about in the shopping centre. Although an apparent success for the probate department, the stunt would confuse both client groups with an unclear message about the firm's services.

The underlying problem of divisionalisation is that people work in tight legal departments. While excellent from a production management point of view, this presents barriers to cross-selling around the firm and the coordination of promotional effort. Taken to its logical conclusion, it can mean that people within a department rarely think about the client at all, but rather the matter in hand, simply because they are not encouraged to do so and departmentalisation virtually prevented it.

Clearly, these are extreme cases. But the fact still remains that departmentalisation does not allow for an easy cross-sell, and it certainly doesn't promote the idea of opportunity recognition (actually looking at the client and thinking 'yes, this client ought to be advised on this particular aspect of our service').

If clients fully understand the benefits to them of what they are purchasing (rather than the process by which it is delivered), they will be more willing to part with their money in exchange for that service. That creates a satisfied client, a recommender of your services, and with any luck, a regularly returning customer.

A literature kit will be an important tool to fee earners and partners in their ambitions for the firm. It gives fee earners the ability to communicate the benefits of using all your firm's services without having specifically to 'sell' other departments' benefits. In conjunction with a well-maintained database, this provides a powerful marketing resource, generating profitable future work at low cost.

What must be realised with a literature kit is that unless it is fully understood by staff and training given, it may be used in the same way as the firm's old brochure. This is not, and never was, the intention. The main rationale behind the kit is that it will be made up individually for each recipient (or group of recipients). In this way, it will be pertinent and useful to the recipient and will not fall into the category of junk mail.

The kit concept

So what is the literature kit? Although we will continue to avoid using the description, the kit is effectively a 'sales kit'. Physically, it is a designed folder with a range of loose-leaf inserts. The folder can incorporate graphic design material that you may already have within the firm (e.g. the firm's logo and house style), together with any wording you may already be using and existing leaflets that reflect your firm's ethos. Nothing that is worth inclusion will be thrown away, and while taking a new approach, we certainly appreciate that there is no point in 'reinventing the wheel'.

What the literature kit is not is a standard brochure in another format. It is extremely unlikely, except for illustrative purposes, that a kit will ever go out including all the available inserts. The key thinking behind the literature kit is that the folder can be made up correctly from a range of individual inserts so that it is tailored to the interests or needs of the particular recipient or group of recipients. This will ensure that the information included is relevant, current and specific to them. In this way, you can avoid giving the client so much information that the bit you want them to have is lost, and you can avoid frightening off the commercial client by being too domestic, or the domestic client by being too corporate.

You can also separate aspects of a criminal department so that, for example, inserts referring to corporate criminal responsibility, or criminal liability for non-compliance with requirements of the Health and Safety Executive and HM Revenue and Customs are kept separate from inserts relating to offences such as theft or burglary. This gets across the benefits to the client of a firm with a criminal defence department without suggesting that a commercial client may have criminal issues. Conversely, you can talk to the appropriate people about the duty solicitor scheme and legal aid without making you appear too 'corporate' for that potential client group.

You are also able to provide information to the exact level of detail that is required by the individual client or prospect.

This is achieved by having three types of insert:

(a) promotional;
(b) informational;
(c) procedural.

These are fairly self-explanatory.

The promotional leaflet deals with what the service is, why the client or prospect needs it, the benefits to the client of having it, and why it should be purchased from your firm. (See **Chapter 5** on benefit analysis; **Chapter 7** on benefit presentation.) Other promotional leaflets will talk about the firm, its ethos, how to make contacts and (where relevant) details of the partnership. Again, all these inserts should be expressed in terms of benefit to the recipient.

Informational inserts go that bit further. They provide the detail that is not required by the casual considerer of the service, who might well miss the important sales point if there is too much detail on the services. For example, consider lasting powers of attorney. A promotional leaflet would explain what an LPA is and why the client should have one, but the informational leaflet would go further in explaining the full detail of an LPA, how it operates and what you can get out of it.

Finally, there are procedural inserts, which are probably most appropriate to people who have already become clients, in that they explain exactly what is required of them, what preparation they should make, and what actions will be taken on their behalf. An example of a procedural insert would be 'What to do when you are buying or selling your house' or 'Material to prepare prior to seeing your solicitor about your will'.

There is a fourth type of insert, which might be termed a 'menu' insert. Strictly speaking, of course, this is a promotional insert, but is worthy of discussion separately. For conveyancing, a menu of services insert allows there to be a competitively priced headline rate with clear information on additional costs in particular circumstances.

While you do not wish to distract a commercial client with details of private client services, you need to acknowledge that he or she is also potentially a private client in their own right. Therefore, the inclusion of a single insert such as 'Services for the private client' should be included with commercial client literature kits when appropriate.

Similarly, some of your private clients will be in a position to influence the placing of commercial work. Therefore, an insert such as 'The departments of our firm' can ensure that private clients are fully aware of all your services, but because they know you are departmentalised, will not be overawed by your glamorous and prestigious corporate activity.

In every case, a promotional leaflet should have a 'call to action'. Clearly, one of the main aims of this approach is to begin to engage a client or prospect in some form of dialogue. The idea is that once somebody has seen the promotional inserts, they will be encouraged to ask for more information, and because you haven't just sent a brochure, you are able to give them much more additional information by sending them informational or appropriate procedural inserts. The literature kit provides the opportunity to give each prospect or client sufficient information, while maintaining the option to develop both the 'conversation' and the relationship.

There is one final point regarding the physical kit that should be touched on here. The folder should be printed in bulk by a reputable local printer. It is then perfectly practical to develop a 'library' of inserts held on your firm's IT system or a CD-Rom. Each insert can then be printed on your own equipment as it is needed.

Graphic design is an important element of any printed material and we would strongly recommend using the services of a professional graphic designer to generate presentation ideas and layouts for each insert. This will save time, money and effort in producing each insert and will provide an overall look for your literature kit. You should also be able to use much of these materials for your website – not only saving time and money but also producing a cohesive brand for your firm.

Literature kit usage

There are five main areas where the use of the literature kit can be of real assistance to the firm and its clients:

(a) promotion;
(b) explanation;
(c) cross-selling;
(d) client contact; and
(e) seeking recommendations.

Promotion

The literature kit is useful for all three tiers of promotion and can be made up appropriately for corporate, product or niche market purposes.

Corporate promotion

When it is the firm itself that is being promoted (corporate promotion), the background, profile, ethos and client charter, etc. are the most important inserts, along with a list of services, maps and methods of contacting the firm, and perhaps an indication of how to enter your website for further information.

Market-specific promotion

When a specific market is being tackled (e.g. people arranging their parents' LPA), less of the firm's background will be needed, but a demonstration of the firm's understanding and experience of that market would be required, together with a selection of inserts explaining the benefits of the services that are being offered, and why they are appropriate to that specific market. The kit will allow this approach to be taken one stage further. By putting together a kit from the standard inserts, with perhaps a personalised covering letter, one could approach a very specific niche market, for example, care homes in your geographical area.

Product–specific promotion

When a specific matter type such as conveyancing is being promoted, clearly, the details of that product and its benefits need to be included in the kit, together with perhaps more elaborate explanation of the procedure, and of the danger of having the work done inadequately. Associated products (product extension and differentiation) such as wills or inheritance tax planning might also be included with the package. It is worth noting here that if you are targeting the elderly market, an insert relating to the pitfalls of buying sheltered accommodation might also be appropriate.

Explanation

When a literature kit is being sent or given to an existing client or related to an existing matter type, there is a great opportunity for simplifying the explanation about the matter by the production and inclusion of additional inserts. These inserts would include explanations based upon 'things you need to know' and also procedural matters 'things you/we must do'.

This might be particularly important in conveyancing and matrimonial, but no doubt departmental heads will assess their own procedural matters individually. Another area for consideration is mediation and alternative dispute resolution services.

Cross-selling

As noted above, despite the need to make the kit specific to a particular market or matter type, there is, of course, ample opportunity for cross-selling. This may be by means of simply including the 'Services we offer' or 'Departments of the firm' inserts or by including more detailed inserts relating to associated products, e.g. will making with conveyancing.

Client contact

The use of a personalised letter within the pack should not be ignored. It may take the form of an encouragement for the client to keep papers relating to the case in the folder, or to point out that while it is a 'conveyancing matter', you, the lawyer, thought they should have details about the firm's will writing service. It might be appropriate to include an insert relating to, and promoting, the website. Imaginative use of the literature kit can really enhance and simplify regular client contact, and make it pre-prepared and systematic.

Seeking recommendations

The literature kit should also be used in conjunction with the professional contacts register. Once again, consideration needs to be given to selecting the most appropriate inserts. In this case, the kit will need to include a covering letter and can, in conjunction with a client newsletter, for example, form the basis of a series of mailings to the PCR. As you will remember from earlier chapters, we have emphasised that regular client and PCR contact is essential. This is an easy and inexpensive way of achieving that.

There is scope, although care needs to be taken here, to use the kit for actively seeking recommendations from clients. The financial services industry is very adept at asking, 'Who else do you think I should see?' and there is much you can learn from them.

A précis version of the copy used in promotional inserts might usefully be put into a booklet for distribution to the staff, to encourage them (following training) to promote the firm and take more value from a possible new client introduction scheme.

Example kits

Although we have suggestions, we must emphasise that the literature kit is entirely your own: no two practices are the same, and as we have repeatedly asserted, individuality and firm's profile are essential. The benefits analysis in **Chapter 5** will have helped identify your firm's uniqueness. We are not seeking to impose any ideas on you and, indeed, your own corporate image, logos, wording style, layouts and existing copy may be included.

Of course, there is no point producing a long list of several hundred inserts, many of which will be of no interest to you (surely, if nothing else, the literature kit is about avoiding boring your reader). However, the headings listed at the end of this chapter in the tasks section are common (see Table 9.2). There are, in fact, many more niche-geared inserts and a large number of specific procedural inserts.

Similarly, we have produced a wide range of specific individual kits for clients. However, as a starting point, we usually sort a client's literature kit library into the following individual kits:

- All inserts produced at one time
- All inserts produced – individually
- Promotional kits – general
- Promotional kits – commercial
- Promotional kits – private client
- Promotional kits – litigation
- Promotional kits – criminal
- Promotional kits – for the professional contacts register
- Private client general user kit (informative)
- Commercial client general user kit (informative)
- Litigation client general user kit (informative)
- Criminal client general user kit (informative)
- Welfare kit
- Conveyancing kit
- Property kit
- Planning ahead
- Family law kit
- The young professionals kit
- Wills, trusts and probate kit

It would be fair to say that no two firms have the same approach or the same kit structure. We hope that the above, and completion of the tasks attached to this chapter, will be of assistance to you in developing your own literature kit.

Literature kit training

To get a return on the investment of time and effort developing a literature kit, it is essential to train the staff and fee earners in its correct use. If you think the above looks complicated, you can imagine how your staff, who actually use and produce the kits, will feel. In fact, with organisation, forethought, clearly stated 'rules' and careful copywriting, the kit is both simpler to use and far more effective than a brochure, but it does depend upon training.

The firm's database should record which inserts any particular client or professional contact has received. Repeatedly sending the same information means you are back with the junk mail problem. Planning the staff training and the explanation of the literature kit's usage must go hand in hand with its development.

It is worth repeating that training will help fee earners and staff use the literature kit efficiently and effectively. The training also helps with the client records on your firm's IT system by informing fee earners of the relevant inserts to include and recording the inserts they have already received.

Getting the basics right

The majority, if not all, firms have polite staff and tidy offices, providing good quality services that people require. There may occasionally be exceptions but when compared to other commercial organisations dealing with the public and commercial clients, solicitors' firms present a professional persona that their clients expect. The basics of human interaction are rarely questioned; however, there is a need for a benchmark that can be used to judge all the firm's staff and help ensure the basics are not overlooked.

Some of the following sections may appear too obvious or simplistic but it is worth reviewing these issues to ensure that you can manage, implement and check on each element. All training, staff development and the image or ethos of your firm require these areas to be dealt with and managed. Please take the time to check your firm has all these matters under control.

First impressions count

It is an old trick, but sometimes it really is worth looking at your firm as if you were a complete stranger or even getting a complete stranger to do so on your behalf.

- What does your building look like as clients approach it?
- How good is the external signage?

- How tidy and efficient is the reception area?
- Are the front-of-house staff well dressed?
- How well are telephone calls really handled?
- How well are telephone callers handled once they get beyond your professional receptionist?
- What system is in place to ensure that telephone calls are returned, where necessary, on time?
- Do your emails and faxes look cluttered to the recipient?
- Are your letters to clients positive and jargon free?
- Does the firm have a system for spot review of external communications?
- How well are personal callers to the firm handled?
- What training has been undertaken to assist fee-earning staff to understand the fears, concerns and, occasionally, trepidation of your clients?
- Are your interview rooms friendly and private?
- How good are you at maintaining day-to-day contact with other professionals?
- How good are you at keeping clients, associates and other interested parties up to date on their cases?

There are, of course, many other questions that the 'stranger to your firm' may like to ask. This, as ever, is only a starting point.

Some of the above obviously leads to the difficult question of staff development. Not all training is for all staff. Some need to know and understand the application of marketing matters, without necessarily taking part. Others will need to understand true 'client care' and client handling (well beyond the 2007 Code, Rule 2).

While there will be some business getters who will benefit enormously from what we term 'sales training for non-sales people', we do realise that few came into the profession to become salesmen.

Presenting your firm to the outside world

All firms have to present themselves to the outside world in general, and to prospective clients specifically.

In the previous section, we questioned the initial impression that your firm may intentionally or accidentally give to people. It is important also to realise that your firm must maintain contact with its existing clients and wherever possible remind them of the satisfactory service that they have received, and the other services the firm can provide.

Some firms are particularly skilled at this. A few are noted within the profession and by other professions as high-profile firms. This did not come about by chance. It is usually a deliberate policy, and often incorporates a firm's excellent and growing literature kit, its regular publication of client newsletters, its website, the various seminars that the firm may hold on different subjects to both clients and prospects, and also its relationship with its own professional contacts and recommenders. Indeed, many firms make a great deal of effort to develop, grow and use this professional contacts register. Others have realised the value of a client registration scheme, and all these subjects are dealt with in other chapters of this book.

Modern desktop technology has enabled the assembly and delivery of professionally produced presentations at very little cost. Indeed, slick Microsoft PowerPoint presentations are now so ubiquitous that it is said over a million are given every day around the world. Used correctly and judiciously, such software programs can become an effective tool in presenting the firm, a department or product.

It would be a useful exercise in preparing the practice's corporate image and benefits of the firm particularly to commercial clients. Department heads should be able to assemble and deliver a specific presentation from a practice-wide agreed template featuring the firm's current branding. PowerPoint and similar programs also make a great medium for staff communication and communication.

Some progressive firms have introduced them in reception on a rolling loop or via touch screen. If that is not too intrusive, it may well be appropriate.

However, beware of pitfalls. Try to keep presentations simple, clear and not too long. Focus on the key messages and put them across in bullet points without being too wordy. Above all, avoid doing the fancy graphic tricks available just because you know how to do them!

All this activity is geared towards encouraging people to come to, or return to, your firm. And, all this effort can be wasted if the impression the client or prospect gains, having eventually contacted the firm, is not reflected in how they are handled by fee earners and staff. Everyone acknowledges that a satisfied client is the most important promotional asset a firm can have and, indeed, an asset in terms of both profit and the development of a firm. Yet few firms consider this when presenting themselves to the outside world.

The successful firm adopts a strategy of vertical and horizontal expansion (see **Chapter 7**) and realises that to achieve either, the firm needs to take care of its 'seed corn' which, of course, is the client database (see **Chapter 6** on databases). The nurturing of this seed corn is a major part of the exercises we have recommended in underpinning the existing client base.

The role of staff in presenting the firm

Essentially, all marketing and promotional activity undertaken by your firm is to present its services and benefits to the outside world, to encourage them to use your services. This activity demands a considerable resource investment (time, money, people). It is rarely understood how easily this expensive activity can be damaged (often inadvertently) by staff and the long-term effect that this damage can have.

A colleague of ours was visiting his elderly mother in Windsor and needed to purchase a new pair of business shoes for a seminar he was attending the following week. At the time, the high street near his mother was full of shoe shops, and – not being an ardent shopper – our colleague simply approached the first one. 'No, not that one dear,' said his mother 'they are not nice people in there.' Of course, our colleague responded to this maternal advice and purchased his shoes at the shop further along the street.

However, as a marketing man, he was curious and questioned his mother about her attitude to the first shop. It turned out that a Saturday morning sales assistant (probably part-time) had been rude to her – 15 years ago. So, for 15 years, this lady had been telling her story and actively steering people away from those premises because of a single ill-conceived remark, or maybe a lack of sales training. It is too easy to say, 'What does one customer/client matter?' but, it is not just one client. In this case, it was 15 years' worth of people being told the story who then retold the story, etc., potentially cutting the retailer out of a small but significant percentage of its total market. And what if that same salesperson behaved in the same way to just one person every week – for 15 years?

This is a true story, and serves to illustrate just how every member of staff can affect the success or otherwise of the firm's marketing and promotional activity, and its growth aspirations. Of course, all members of staff should handle clients in all circumstances in a professional and friendly manner. We know that client care is needed to maintain the satisfaction level of your clients, which is the key to profit and development of the firm.

We have already used the phrase 'vertical and horizontal development'. Put simply, this means selling more services to existing clients (vertical expansion) and seeking recommendations from these clients and finding similar groups (horizontal expansion). All legal firms know that a majority of their work comes as a result of recommendation. However, few actively seek recommendation. Those firms that do actively seek recommendation will do so through a variety of methods such as cross-selling via websites, seminars, newsletters, literature kits and by a variety of other promotional methods, but the key to the success of it all is staff training and attitude.

The importance of good client contact

Successful interaction with people requires a set of minimum standards. All partners, fee earners and staff in any firm have contact with, or deal with, clients, even if this is incidental to their main job. All therefore need to be aware of the importance of handling clients in a friendly and professional manner, which factors sometimes make that difficult, and the different needs people have that influence their behaviour.

Generally, most staff in legal firms are good at looking after clients. Our task is to help them understand the process, and to assist you and them in gaining the results we all seek. It may appear a little odd to discuss and plan such basic human skills; however, there are two reasons this is important. First, it may have never been considered as an issue or only raised as one when problems have occurred in the past. Second, if you set minimum standards for all in the firm, you can easily manage and communicate those standards around the firm and not have to rely on people's innate politeness.

Getting the basics of client and interpersonal contact right helps a firm in several different areas:

1. Clients' impression of the firm will be partly formed by their impression of you as individuals.
2. The reputation of the firm, and therefore its future viability, is largely dependent on what clients think of you as individuals.
3. Your own job satisfaction will be greater if you are more successful in handling clients.
4. Your job will in many ways be easier if you can overcome the problems sometimes associated with handling clients.
5. Your relationship with your colleagues will improve, leading to a better working environment (better understanding of each other's jobs and all pulling together in the common cause).

For client handling to succeed and be managed constructively, there are several elements that need to be addressed. Each looks at what a client needs or why they are seeking the services of a solicitor. Human behaviour plays a large part in this and, while we are certainly not psychology experts, we have drawn together some of the theory to illustrate what is required. The partner responsible for marketing will need to discuss these issues with the partner responsible for staff and your personnel or office manager. Most firms have some sort of training and development programme and these contact issues may already be dealt with in initial training. For the purposes of this book in developing marketing management techniques, it is important to lay out the issues in this area and ensure that your firm's hard work is not lost by misunderstanding or unintentional rudeness to clients. In this respect, here are a couple of points worth remembering.

The 'negative' start point

People come to solicitors initially when they have a problem. Often, they come reluctantly. New clients especially can be wary of solicitors. Even on occasions to the point of mistrust. The profession continues to get 'bad press' and this is only increased by the 'friendly' stance taken by The New Competition.

Clients, especially new clients, are concerned about how they will be treated, how much the solicitor will cost, whether they are going to be made to look foolish and whether or not the visit will actually solve their problem.

This is a negative start point and one from which it is hard to recover if an arrogant approach is taken.

The truth is, nobody wants to go to a solicitor. They want something else and may even start by seeing you as a hindrance rather than a help.

Understanding clients' behaviour

If a client is feeling in a traumatic situation it may well manifest itself in the appearance of being rude to a solicitor or his staff.

Clients come from all walks of life and social and economic classes and have different capacities. When they first walk in we have no idea whether they are a house purchaser or the victim of a criminal accusation. So while we will probably claim to be courteous and friendly, there is still a tendency to react 'in kind' if somebody is rude or aggressive with us. Every member of a solicitor's staff must clothe themselves in a professionalism that will prevent them from rising to this 'bait'.

Moreover, as noted in **Chapter 6**, these face-to-face meetings are the perfect opportunity to gain information about clients for recording on the client database. When this is used, excellent client contact can be maintained on a regular basis through methods other than face-to-face meetings and without putting an additional promotional obligation onto fee earners. This must be seen as part of the fee earner's job. Get the information right and the firm can benefit for a very long time afterwards.

CHAPTER 9 TASKS Develop your promotion

Assessing and monitoring your firm's promotions using the three tiers of promotion

Draw up a list of all the promotional activities your firm undertakes. Include all advertising, mailings, public relations (PR) events and consider the costs of the time taken by fee earners and staff to organise these activities.

For each promotional activity, assign it to one of the three categories of promotion:

1. Corporate (whole firm)
2. Departmental
3. Product specific

Using the information gathered, consider whether any promotional activities present a conflicting message to the potential client. Use the box below (Table 9.1) to plot (roughly) how each department or service is presented and would be perceived by a potential purchaser. Please note, we understand 'quality' is a subjective measure and most solicitors produce good quality work. Here, we want you to consider how a potential client will compare your services to others that are available when they are making a purchase choice. See **Chapter 5** on how to view the quality proposition your firm presents.

The aim is to identify where there are conflicting promotional messages.

Table 9.1 Promotional message conflict analysis table

High quality (Services that focus on partner lead and high-value services)		
Low quality (Services that focus on price to client or high volume)		
	Low price	**High price**

For each promotional activity proposed, you should ask the following questions:

1. What is the activity and why are you doing it?
2. Who is going to participate and what do you anticipate the benefits will be?
3. What is the cost, and how will you justify this to your partners?
4. Are you prepared to declare the benefits achieved to your partners (or, ideally, your staff) in six months' time?

You might say, 'Can't answer any of the above – but it will be great fun and that is why I'm self-employed!' – which is perfectly acceptable, perfectly understandable, perfectly justifiable, and one of the reasons it is fun being a lawyer – but it is not marketing.

Use these questions to assess how cost-effective an event or promotion will be. Consider how that budget could be spent on alternatives that may deliver greater returns and increased profits. See **Chapters 12** and **13** for details of other promotional ideas or how to turn a loss leader event into a profitable result.

Developing your firm's literature kit

The literature kit is designed to be specific to each department and put together for each individual client and their needs. Therefore, it requires the staff and fee earners to have asked the right questions of the client to be able to put a kit together. It is occasionally not possible to get all the details required; however, using a paper or onscreen enquiry form can help and provides a record of the enquiry. As outlined in this and other chapters, with training, the right questioning techniques can assist staff and fee earners to gain the information they require easily and without the fear of feeling they are pressurising or selling to the client. Developments from earlier chapters, particularly the database development ideas, should be used to capture this information for nearly or prospect clients.

Your firm may already have a literature kit style brochure or a similar arrangement. This can provide the starting point for the wording required alongside the benefits analysis work from **Chapter 5**.

As a first step, circulate to each department head the list of possible inserts (see Table 9.2) with the attached instruction in the draft memo (below). The aim is for each department head to choose for their department the insert headings they feel they will need. If there is not a suitable heading, please ask for suggestions.

We would also suggest that each department head outline briefly what benefits each promotional insert should highlight, using the lists already completed regarding benefits to clients. What we would like you to achieve at the end of this process is a list of insert headings and brief outline wording required by each department.

Having gathered this information from each department, and using your firm's current brochure material (and/or website copy) along with the benefits to clients' lists, go through and separate the wordings for use in the three insert types:

1. Promotional inserts – focus on the benefits of the service to the client and exclude anything that is informational and not directly linked to a benefit or procedural.
2. Informational inserts – repeat the benefits but add the additional services and product information.
3. Procedural inserts – use these as a 'how to' guide or a 'what's required to complete a . . .' list.

We would recommend using an advertising copywriter, PR agent or marketing services company to review the wording for the inserts. Often, it is difficult to take an objective view of your firm's services and an external review will be well worth the expense.

Print production and graphic design

As noted earlier, the folder will require the services of a graphic designer and professional printer. The inserts should tie in with the firm's graphic design/house style (new or existing) as applied e.g. to the firm's website. If your firm does not have a graphic designer, your letterhead printer or website provider will be able to recommend one.

Training

Once the kit has been finalised, an instruction manual for each member of staff should be produced, with an example of each insert fronted with specific instruction on its uses. Each department will implement the kit in different ways, either support staff or fee earner putting the kits together for each enquiry. The important element is that each member of staff has received, read and understood each insert. You need to avoid, where possible, kits being made up in bulk. The underlying idea is that each kit fits each client's enquiry and the fee earner has considered the client's wider needs and not just the matter in hand. For example, in residential conveyancing, is the client a first-time buyer, family buyer or last-time buyer? Each type of client will require different additional inserts. First-time buyers may only want wills, while family and last-time buyers want a mixture of wills/probate, LPAs and inheritance tax planning.

The wider benefit to your firm is the dissemination of common information across all departments. This can encourage cross-selling by providing an easily accessible library of the services of each department. New and revised inserts repeat the importance of using the literature kit correctly and, when use is monitored across the firm, can provide useful management information on service enquiry levels and the ratio of enquiries to new instructions.

As outlined in earlier chapters, all promotional activity must have a plan that reflects the return on the investment. Time and costs put into a literature kit can only be realised when it is fully implemented, monitored, managed and maintained. If not, all the work done will just produce another old-fashioned brochure that is a cost to the firm.

Draft memo wording for department heads

Below is a list of headings as a guide to the inserts required for the firm's new literature kit. Along with the general inserts listed first, please indicate which heading may be suitable for your department. Please add your own heading(s) at the end if you feel a topic is not covered.

Table 9.2 Literature kit inserts

Introduction	
About the firm(s)	
About the partners	
How to contact us	
About our support staff	
The services we offer	
Services for the private client	
The client registration scheme	
Introduction to the welcome pack of the client registration scheme	
Conveyancing	
Our conveyancing services	
Property sales	
Purchases of property	
Leases	
Commercial property	
Residential property	
Buying your home	
Selling your home	
A voluntary 'seller pack'	
Title defects	
Rights to buy	
Remortgages	
Properties abroad	
Probate	
Services for the older client	
Planning ahead for a more secure future	
Family homes and the elderly	
Caring for the elderly	
Ordering your affairs	
A free affairs assessment	
Management of financial matters	
Probate and the administration of estates	
Making a will	
Lasting powers of attorney	
Settling a person's affairs after death	
Preparation of wills, enduring power of attorney, and living wills	
Deeds of gift	
Formation and management of trusts and settlements	

Inheritance tax planning	
Contested probate	
Family and social welfare	
Matrimonial and family law	
Family law	
Marriage problems	
Matrimonial and mediation	
Relationship problems and domestic violence	
Divorce	
A divorce helpline	
Matrimonial transfer	
Separation agreements	
Financial settlements	
Maintenance	
Child protection and care	
Court of Protection	
Child Support Agency agreements	
Child care	
Child residency	
Child contact	
Adoption	
Cohabitation	
Company and commercial	
The commercial department	
Services to business	
Directors' responsibilities	
Company formation	
Business structure and management	
Trade practice and development	
Company taxation	
Terms and conditions of trading	
Insolvency	
Insolvency	
Personal and corporate insolvency	
Public Guardianship Offices work, e.g. appointment of receivers	
Debt collection	
Employment	
Employment contracts	
Employment law and the employee	

Employment law and the employer	
Unfair/constructive dismissal claims	
Redundancy	
Discrimination on wage claims	
Compliance and Transfer of Undertakings (Protection of Employment) Regulations on transfer of business	
Employment law changes	
Contract review	
Preparing and conducting Employment Tribunal cases on unfair dismissal, constructive dismissal and discrimination cases	
Mergers and acquisitions	
Sale and purchase of businesses	
Mergers	
Acquisitions	
Management buyouts	
Partnership agreements	
Partnership dissolution	
Partnership and corporate disputes	
Personal injury	
Personal injury compensation	
Motoring cases	
Road traffic accidents	
Motor Insurance Bureau disputes	
Criminal Injuries Compensation claims	
Industrial injury and disease	
Tripping accidents	
Private client litigation	
Civil litigation	
Contract disputes	
Domestic and commercial property disputes	
Commercial litigation	
Alternative dispute resolution	
Agency and distribution agreements	
Other	
Construction law	
Welfare and immigration	
European law	

CHECKLIST

- List of inserts required from each department or service.
- List of additional firm-wide inserts.
- Consider which inserts to produce in-house or to have pre-printed.
- What printer or systems technology is required to print colour pages in-house?
- Consider what is the best use of the literature kit approach per department.
- Gather wording and research the copy required for each insert with the heads of each department. Use the benefits lists generated in earlier chapters.
- Brief graphic designer.
- Get quotes from printers for the folders and supply of pre-printed inserts.
- Discuss and plan the training and implementation of the literature kits per department.
- Establish the monitoring process required to ensure the kit is used correctly.

Chapter 9 is a far-reaching chapter. At the end of it, the firm should have a literature kit that is far more than a brochure, but is in itself, effectively, a sales aid.

The firm should understand how best this sales aid (the literature kit) can be used.

10

Websites and the Internet

In this chapter we look at websites and the Internet. Perhaps no area has changed more, or increased in importance more, between this book and the first edition. Three years is not a long time, but much has happened between 2008 and 2011.

What was 'The New Competition' is now simply COMPETITION. They are well-established, known increasingly to the public, respected and here to stay. And, they all have extremely good websites. Websites that are easy to navigate, clear, interactive in many cases and providing legal advice and access to solicitors at all times, commonly referred to as 24/7.

They have set the standard of providing information about legal services in terms of benefits derived by the client, rather than procedures and rules, and almost always speak in the language of the client rather than the profession.

New readers would be advised to review their own website in comparison with these others. Hopefully, readers of the first edition of this book have already done so and, as a result of what they have seen, have websites that are better than the general standard for the profession. These readers will still need to constantly review their own website and those of their competitors.

Another development is the advent of the legal work-seeking website, the comparison site and the apparent advisers. These now go much further than the old 'big shed claims farmers' as they were called, and in a recent survey (May 2011), we found no fewer than 50 separate sites, standing between you and your prospective clients.

Of course, many of these sites provide a valuable service to individual practices, and in part because of this, they are unlikely to diminish in number. But, too often, they are seen as an alternative for a firm's own marketing. At best, they should be an addition to it.

Lastly, we look at the recent phenomenon of social media and what role they might play in promoting your practice.

The future is here already – it's just not evenly distributed. – William Gibson, science fiction author

Introduction

There are already great examples of innovations in IT and client services that show the way forward in some sectors of the legal services market. Prof. Richard Susskind's 2nd edition of *The End of Lawyers?* has several detailed descriptions and analyses of these new ways of working. However, for the purposes of this chapter, we need to look at the Internet from your firm's perspective, look at how best to use it now before we look at the future.

Cyberspace novelist William Gibson's quote is a useful starting point because there are many good ideas already in use and it's easy in many situations to apply it to your firm's systems. However, there is much confusion and misunderstanding about the Internet that is not helped by enthusiastic, and often pushy, salespeople constantly approaching solicitors' firms with a 'complete solution' that will 'do everything you need'.

This chapter will help you understand the taxonomy of the Internet and provide a guide to minimising cost while maximising the return to your firm without having to become an Internet expert.

Your firm's website has one primary purpose that should be the basis for all decisions on content, interactivity, design and promotion: it is to capture client enquiries. That is how its success should be measured and all efforts, investments and tools employed for the website should be reflected in the website's improved ability to connect clients and their matters to your firm's services.

Internet taxonomy

The Internet and the web are often terms used interchangeably but it's worth knowing the difference. The Internet is the basic underlying infrastructure that allows different systems to communicate. Systems like email have been around on the Internet since almost the beginning. Email has changed the nature of the relationship and speed of communications with clients and produced great improvements in productivity.

The web is a system that sits alongside email on the Internet. It consists of a varying set of standards that shifts text, pictures, video and lots of other information around so that your web browsers can display the pieces as the sender intended. More recently, the Internet is providing the conduit for other devices to access content and the use of the web has shifted to version 2.0, as it is often described. Mobile devices, smart phones, iPads and netbooks all use various elements of the Internet and the web to present content to their users. Social media has developed a further aspect of the web in closed communities offering security and easy to use tools that can be confusing to find on the open 'wild' web.

For marketing management and promotional purposes, it is already acknowledged that the web is having a significant impact on legal services.

Clients have almost instant access to your firm's promotional information through the web and your competitors are just a few clicks away. This is so dramatically different from the way consumers and SME businesses were used to accessing solicitors' firms that both the solicitors (on the supply side) and consumers (on the demand side) are still unsure about how best to use this interactive communications medium. We can be sure that consumers will take the easiest option available to the services they perceive as valuable, therefore the challenge is to convert the visitors to your information into profitable client matters.

Describing the benefits of your firm's services requires close management and a lot of thought. As we move on to the practical management of websites and other Internet tools, we will need to keep in mind work completed for previous chapters:

- Competitive advantage of your firm – **Chapter 4**
- Strategy of vertical and horizontal growth – **Chapter 7**
- Database development and clients' records – **Chapter 6**
- Professional contacts register – **Chapter 6**
- Literature kit – **Chapter 9**

Essentially, what we are beginning here is a formal promotional campaign. Promotion has many facets beyond websites and newsletters, and many objectives – ranging from a general desire to raise the profile of the firm, to a wish to carry out a highly targeted individual campaign offering a specific legal 'product' to a small group of clients (known as a market niche).

Websites can be used in all promotional endeavours and they have additional, valuable potential. Used properly and regularly, they will enhance client loyalty, usage of, and recommendations to, your firm. They can be invaluable in cross-selling, and are in many ways the strongest tools for actively seeking recommendations from past satisfied clients and your professional contacts register (PCR). In fact, handled properly, they can make the passing of recommendations and dealing with enquiries (from any source) both easier and far more efficient.

But there is a downside. Your own website with blogs, newsletters and twitter feeds, LinkedIn groups and discussion forums are time-consuming so, without care, can quickly consume large amounts of time for little visible return. And if you get them wrong, they can actually damage the image and reputation of your firm. These perceived dangers have been used throughout the profession as excuses either to do nothing or to pay lip service to the subject.

Unfortunately, The New Competition will make us all look to our laurels, but in this, as in everything else, you must remember that you are taking them on not by emulating them, but by seeking to become a big fish in your own smaller pond. Your own firm's name and its image (your brand) should be recognised with as much ease and understanding by your clients, prospects and professional contacts as, for example, Halifax Legal Solutions.

In fact, you need more clarity. Is Halifax a bank, a building society, an estate agent, an insurance provider or a legal firm? Doesn't The Co-op Legal sell beans? Doesn't the AA collect broken-down cars (and, it would seem, run a mail-order company)? Why should they deal with personal injury matters? Doesn't Saga organise holidays for old folk? Brand extension and expansion from these companies can often conflict with other areas of their business. Trusted brands they may be, but how far that trust will extend is yet to be seen. A recent banking problem can illustrate the point (albeit hypothetically). Northern Rock is primarily a savings and mortgage company. If they had started to offer general legal services at that point in 2007 when they experienced the first run on a high street bank in over 100 years, would potential clients have trusted that brand to handle such services?

As discussed in **Chapter 9**, there is the possibility of conflicting messages with a solicitor's firm. The Northern Rock example shows that national brands can often overstretch their brand 'equity'. Websites and newsletters (see also **Chapter 11**) are your firm's basic method of communication and promotion, and should be aimed specifically at stating and restating the benefits of using your firm's services. You really are a specialist. If handled correctly, your 'brand image' in your area can be stronger than The New Competition's national brand approach. You are, after all, a long-established, professionally qualified, dedicated provider of legal services that is obliged to put your clients' interests first, and provide best advice. Isn't it time you started telling people that?

These days a website is often the first point of contact with a potential client. First impressions count.

Outside specialists

The legal profession has been held back by the 'enthusiastic amateur dabblers'. They are visible in every area where there is computerisation – especially in setting up and usage of databases. Brochures (or more often than not, the lack of them) are another example but overwhelmingly the dabblers are evident in the creation, development and exploitation of websites.

The trouble is, people think they can do something, and then, after an enormous amount of time, discover (or have discovered for them) that (a) they can't do it as well as they expected; and (b) there are experienced people outside the firm that could have done it for them with greater efficiency and at less cost. Just as few lawyers have ambitions to be salesmen, few come into the legal profession to become experts in either website development or graphic design. When you add to this the need for search engine optimisation (SEO), pay per click (PPC) and service integrations like outsource document creation, the time of the DIY website is over.

However, strong management of the project, an understanding of what is required and its coordination with the firm's overall promotional activity and stance are essential. So, too, are the selection and management of the outside service provider. This starts with the briefing, which must be clear, specific and monitored. These are tasks to be undertaken by the marketing partner.

Your websites

The starting point is your firm's website. Later in this chapter we will deal with other aspects of the web and Internet and how they can help you attract visitors to your site.

Website design

It is difficult for a solicitor's firm not to have a presence on the Internet. Web-listing companies have been around for a number of years in competition with Yellow Pages and its website (yell.com). More recently, specific legal services listing websites have proliferated. To illustrate this, put your firm's name into Google's search service for the UK and look at the results. Your firm's website will appear in the listings somewhere, alongside many other offers of useful 'legal' websites.

Our main concern here is to ensure that the greatest benefit is derived from your website, that it is updated as necessary, in line with your traditional competitors, and that it is ready to be used as part of your marketing armoury in light of The New Competition.

If, however, you do not have a website but would like to develop one, there is some very sound advice in Lucy Adam's *Marketing Your Law Firm* (Law Society, 2002) under Section 3(B) – 'The promotional tools'. In this section, Adam describes what a website is and rightly points out how it can improve client loyalty, help generate new clients, help to promote work from existing clients (cross-selling) and help develop the firm's image or ethos. Most importantly, she states that websites vary enormously, and that is perhaps where we should start.

Analyse the competition

The marketing partner should take time, enlist some help and use the form at the end of this chapter and on the CD-Rom to undertake an analysis of competitive websites. First, look at your immediate geographical area and traditional competitors (other solicitors). Then, look at some of the websites of solicitors' firms in the city/cities nearest to you, and to which you are losing commercial and high-value clients. It may also be useful to review other regional or national high-profile firms you have heard of. Now look outside the legal profession and at those companies offering quasi-legal services and The New Competition. Review how they address their website viewers and the range of services offered.

Once this information has been collated, you will see from the results that you have produced an overview of related websites. Use that overview to compare your own existing site and rate it, truthfully, with those you consider to be the best and the worst. Remember that 'best' and 'worst' are very subjective words: always include why they are and what makes them best or worst. How much detail you go into in your research and comparison is clearly a matter for the individual firm, but it should not be allowed to become too time-consuming.

During this comparative exercise it is obviously worth noting items on specific sites that could be adapted to improve your own, and ideas that are worth considering. Generally speaking, you are not looking to be too elaborate, and certainly 'gimmicks' should be avoided, as should anything that could be construed as reducing the standing of the profession in general or, of course, the image of your firm.

Review your own site

Armed with your comparisons, now review your own site again, specifically looking for the points you like and would like to improve, and those you don't like and would like to see removed. Now list exactly what you want to appear on your site. Do not start producing a sitemap yet.

Consider how your improved website will tie in with your other promotional activity and what links there will be. For example, much of the copy and illustrations produced for your literature kit can be used on your website. Do not, however, fall into the trap of just replicating the literature kit pages. Not only will you have far too much verbiage but you will have destroyed one of the prime purposes of the website, which is to initiate contact and conversation. The easiest way to achieve this is to suggest that the website visitor should ask for more information. You must keep the additional information for the appropriate part of the literature kit that you will send on request.

There is an old marketing adage. To get someone to remember, tell them what you are going to tell them; then tell them; then tell them what you have told them. At least in part, the website should tell visitors what you are going to tell them, the literature kit should tell them and your first face-to-face meeting will reinforce it all.

Design brief

At this stage, some firms would form a website committee. If you want such a committee, it should be managed (by the marketing partner) and used primarily to interpret the results of your analysis (perhaps having helped undertake it), and to put forward suggestions for the improvement of your site and its usage in the future.

Effectively, the marketing partner is now at the beginning of drawing up a website design brief, which will lead to a sitemap. In most cases, the sitemap is a document the website developer should generate for you, having the wider knowledge of the options available and the competing benefits of each design approach.

It is worth noting that unless you are going to be the actual creator of the site (see warning above), you should concern yourself not with the mechanics, which will be discussed later with your designer, but rather with what the website should include. For example, under 'first impressions' you might well write 'friendly'. A good idea; note it, but take no further action at this stage.

It goes without saying that your website should reflect the ethos of your firm and the gravitas of the profession. It should also quite obviously be legal, decent, honest and truthful. But beyond that, what should it be? The following ideas, as with most of the suggestions in this book, are indicative, not exhaustive.

First impressions

- Professional
- Friendly
- Efficient
- Interesting
- Uncluttered
- Easy to navigate
- Benefit-based
- Market specific

Ease of navigation

The visitor needs to be taken from the 'welcoming and friendly' homepage into their area of interest in as few mouse clicks as possible, following an obvious progression of links in one visual area. As you are using the site to encourage contact, it is arguable that ease of navigation is even more important than content. One of the basic facts of websites is that your competitors are just one or two clicks away from your website. Your website developer will be able to advise you on the navigation structure with the intention of keeping clients on your site until they have either contacted you or viewed service-specific pages.

Copy and graphics

- Ensure that your site is uncluttered.
- Ensure that your site is benefit driven by referring to the benefits analysis in **Chapter 5**.

- Use photographs as often as possible, pictures of people, friendly faces are best. These can illustrate pages and anecdotal evidence shows that clients find them more acceptable than abstract designs. It can be difficult to find the right picture but online picture galleries offer a vast range at low cost.
- Do not be afraid of white space. The purpose of your website is to encourage contact with you.
- If you are going to go into a lot of legal detail, put it further into your website, possibly within a password-restricted area. You will, at least, know who is viewing your site if they have to contact you for a password to your 'library of legal information'.

Interactivity

To get an enquiry from a website visitor requires some level of interactivity beyond just clicking around the site. The marketing partner will have to decide just how far your firm wishes to go with interactivity. There are many options available and the future will hold more. However, at this point, we would suggest caution. Many firms have bought expensive interactive 'all singing, all dancing' websites but have gained little from them. This is usually because the firm has not integrated the systems into their businesses well enough to see a suitable return. There are a limited number of suppliers that have invested enough time, money and effort in understanding the needs of solicitors' websites. Those that provide excellent services are where the firms have changed their working practices to accommodate this new ability to capture client matters.

Essentially, the web is being used in two ways for interactivity. Some firms list the type of questions the lawyer will ask when someone visits the firm to make a will, so that the client can be well prepared with their answers. Other firms ask for the information to be emailed to the firm in advance by way of a completed questionnaire. This second approach is one that is already adopted by The New Competition and, in this case, the strategic decision is whether to compete by demonstrating the benefits and cost savings that you have introduced to assist the client, or by emphasising that this is a personal matter that is not suitable for a standard form.

Consider which approach to apply in every department and in each discipline. The New Competition is already using an array of standardisation techniques that allow clients to start the process of getting the advice they need quickly and cost-effectively. At present, these systems are difficult to replicate as many years of work have gone into their development to ensure they are secure and usable. For the purposes of most firms' websites, interactivity should encompass some or all of the following, depending on the volume of enquiries anticipated:

1. Email contact forms: avoid 'mailto:' that uses the viewer's email software. Webpage enquiry forms are just as acceptable; 'mailto:' links encourage spam (talk to your IT manager); where possible, include as many people as possible per department. This can unfortunately become a recruitment consultant's 'contact list'. However, the advantages of direct contact from clients and the benefits of working for your firm should outweigh their offers.
2. Helpful downloads: usually in the form of 'how to' lists and user guides. There needs to be a balance between helping and giving away advice. Keep the documents brief and based on the informational inserts from your literature kit (see **Chapter 9**).
3. Online document assembly systems: this is a powerful client capture device offered by a limited number of suppliers. You can develop simple alternatives using text input fields on your web pages, however, the level of sophistication of the available supplier systems means this is often not a viable choice (see details later in this chapter).
4. Firm's or individual's blogs: regular opinion and informational articles written by fee earners on specific legal services issues. These online commentaries usually allow responses, replies or comments from visitors to the site.
5. Telephone call-back services: where you want to generate enquiries by phone. Adding a call-back service to the website encourages client enquiries, particularly in complex matters.
6. Quotations, automated or manual: usually for domestic conveyancing enquiries and used to capture the potential client's details to be followed up by letter, call or email.
7. Appointment booking: there are automated and control options, which can be used as part of a client registration scheme or additional benefits to clients. However, appointment booking should be closely controlled as misuse can waste a lot of time.
8. Text message (SMS): for online quotes, contact details, matter alerts or appointment reminders.

However far you go with the Internet and interactivity, all services have to be clear, easy, attractive, logical and in keeping with the overall site. It is unlikely, however, that the potential client at this stage takes on board all your benefits, particularly unique or added benefits. You may not have the opportunity, for example, to explain your different approaches to first-time and last-time buyers. Therefore, all of the interactive service on a website must be monitored and managed to ensure all enquiries are followed up and the potential client's details added to the promotional database. This follow-up is essential in gaining the return of thousands of pounds in website costs.

Mobile web

The web is no longer tied to desktop or laptop computers as smart phones and other Internet devices like the iPad become popular. These devices often use web browsers that are not as powerful as those found on PCs so your website may need to be optimised to account for these types of users.

If your firm has a target market group that is more likely to access the Internet and web information from mobile devices, then you will need to discuss how this will work with your planned website.

Look to the competition

Websites have developed the range and scope of products and services sold via the Internet dramatically in the past 10 years. Amazon, eBay, Google and many hundreds of lesser names have shown the way in developing online interactive services. Legal services are developing some elements of web-based delivery. MoreThan insurance has a wide range of domestic legal services available to its policyholders and NatWest and other banks have a suite of services for small businesses. Their email, web and call centre services are able to handle fairly complex legal matters and their abilities are constantly being expanded. This type of service represents a significant threat to the traditional high street solicitors. MoreThan's website presents a service that can be accessed at anytime, easily and quickly, by a section of the domestic market that is of most value to solicitors. This is the 'time poor–cash rich' market: people who are too busy during the day to see a solicitor and find it easier to look at a website in the evening.

This target market must be a priority for traditional solicitors' firms and they must use the Internet to present their service benefits and compete for this valuable sector's attention. Potential clients visiting your firm's website need to see your services are as easily accessible and can deliver suitable solutions in comparison to those available on other branded websites.

Improving your website

Taking the information you have gained from your competitors' site analysis, your review of your own site and the points outlined above, the marketing partner should now be in a position to produce a basic document that will assist in the provision of the following:

- Ideas to the partnership. It is important to take everyone along with you, and to gain approval at each stage, even though the marketing partner may him/herself be charged with the executive tasks.
- An action plan for the marketing partner and team. Actions plans must be quantified and should include who is to do what and by when.

- The basis of a graphically drawn up website sitemap (see example at the end of this chapter, and on the accompanying CD-Rom).
- A preliminary design brief for discussion with your website designers.

As with any outside service, the selection of your website designer is extremely important. Certainly, you should initially interview more than one company, and seek recommendations from earlier users. However, a lot of the success will depend on the empathy between the partnership and the designer, and the clarity of the design brief.

Your firm's information

History and people

Some firms feel that it is necessary to include, often by way of introduction, the history of the firm and a profile of the partners. At revamp time, consider whether to retain these. Of course, people want to know whom they are dealing with, especially potential clients and professional recommenders. However, history and the background of partners do not immediately give potential clients a clear view of why they should use your services.

A slogan such as 'Monk, Moyes and Partners – serving the Sussex community for over 120 years' should be sufficient; the benefits of the firm's services are the primary message to impart. The history of those 120 years can be elsewhere in the site and accessible to interested parties.

Similarly, the photographs and details of partners and staff can be in a separate section. This section should use photographs with names, qualifications and specialisms with a brief profile and a link to the appropriate departmental page. Remember, people really only want to know what is in it for them. How will they benefit? In this context and at this stage, knowing that the senior partner was the Gold Star graduate from law school is irrelevant because it does not confer a specific benefit to the reader.

Services and benefits

The initial page or homepage should include a *menu* of the firm's services. However, it should be simply that – a menu. The idea is to move people quickly to their area of interest, explain the benefits of making contact with the firm about this interest and make it simplicity itself to make that contact through the push of an email button or a telephone call-back service.

Once a visitor to your site has selected the subject they wish to view, the information should be clear, concise and, above all else, expressed in terms of benefits to the client, including the benefit of seeking further information.

However, it is important that at each point, the visitor can be directed to associated products within the department or even in other departments to ensure that despite the clarity of your system, their own navigation is not preventing them from finding what they actually want – possibly by using the wrong name for it. Often firms' websites use the legal names for services: matrimonial, when the client is looking for divorce information; probate and wills, when a client is looking for help with an elderly relative. The navigation should be presented in the terms the client will understand.

One reason for visiting a law firm's website is to gain detailed information about an area of law that is of interest to the visitor. As this information is in the public domain already, and therefore identical, irrespective of which site is visited – except perhaps the copywriting, how can you improve the usage of your site, and the likelihood of maintaining your contact?

Once again, there appear to be two totally opposed opinions. Neither is wrong, so the marketing partner has to make the choice:

1. You provide the information in a succinct and clear form so that the visitor is satisfied with the answer, considers that you 'know your stuff' and is sufficiently impressed to contact you.
2. The alternative is to make the information more detailed and more personal but restrict access to it. The danger is, of course, that you will turn a prospective client off, and they will simply go to another site. However, if the access is through a password-protected section, the viewer can request a password via a web form and you will have captured the name of the person, which you can use to follow up with a benefit-based pitch for your firm and department.

It is essential that every page has contact details that visitors can easily access if they want to register an enquiry, and that any questions raised can be answered at the next contact.

Managing your website

One of the biggest problems with websites is that many areas of content can quickly go out of date. The law changes, your firm changes, the personnel within your firm change. Sometimes, the product range you offer changes and, continually, your operating environment changes. The inheritance tax threshold is revised often; your library of downloadable information needs regular updates. Your latest newsletter, although we would propose that you archive past editions, must be put up on site, on time. And there are, of course, dozens of other changes.

An out-of-date website is unprofessional, inefficient and off-putting. Many sites are launched and maintained for a few months, but then get neglected. When you are researching other sites, check to see how many have news items that are more than three months old.

There are three areas of maintenance to consider:

1. Technical maintenance of the computer hardware and website delivery to the Internet.
2. Content management and maintenance.
3. Editorial access and maintenance of the IT systems to allow you to control the website.

Technical maintenance

The technical maintenance will be the responsibility of the company that hosts the website. That covers the computers the website data is stored on, the connection to the Internet and the delivery of the website to the web. In hosting it, the company should guarantee that the website is available to the Internet 99.9 per cent of any given period, usually a month. That does entitle it to have just over seven hours' outage (i.e. unavailability). However, this is rare as most data centres maintain 99.999 per cent availability. If you are intending to offer interactive and more complex services, this issue becomes much more relevant. If your business is to rely on Internet connectivity, we would advise you to seek professional Internet management.

Content management and maintenance

Content Management Systems (CMS) are readily available and your website developer will be able to advise you on which will suit your purposes. Commonly referred to as 'the back-end' of the website, these editing systems are much like web-based word processors and usually require only brief training to understand and use.

Editorial access and maintenance

More important is the question of who will perform the regular editing, management and the generation of content from fee earners and external sources.

While you are developing or improving your website, the overall management of the process must be the partnership, through the marketing partner. Part of that development and management process must be the development of systems and the delegation of authority for the day-to-day management of the site in two key areas:

- website response management;
- management of updating and maintenance of quality.

Website response management

Ideally, your website will quickly divide from the homepage into commercial and private client sections, and from thereon into department and individual matters. It is logical, therefore, that response should be at departmental or fee-earner level. The problem with this approach is maintaining a consistency of response and monitoring that consistency.

As with database inputting and updating, our observation is that response time and quality will greatly vary throughout the firm unless some rules and disciplines are imposed. It is not unusual to find that this situation is exacerbated by the poor example set by the partners. The Internet is often thought of as a more casual environment with a less serious business attitude. Things have changed, and although it is a less formal communications route, enquiries via email should be dealt with as if the client were on the telephone waiting. Similarly, SMS or text messaging is seen as a business communications tool with examples of conveyancing updates being automatically sent.

If you do not believe you can encourage or impose a system that incorporates speed and consistency throughout your practice, then it may be better to have one person responsible for taking all website responses, passing them on to the appropriate fee earner, and (this is vital) monitoring response time and quality on fee-earner response. Indeed, Lucy Adam (in *Marketing Your Law Firm* (2002)) recommends this approach, but it should surely be a fallback position.

If your firm is truly going to adopt the marketing management philosophy and genuinely put the needs of the client uppermost, every fee earner and member of support staff needs to accept that the presentation of benefits is as important as the timely provision of quality legal work. As an intrinsic part of their job, fee earners and staff need to include the recognition of clients' needs and how that leads to cross-selling; the ancillary service over and above the provision of legal advice; not just what we do, but how we do it and how the client feels about your firm. These new elements of a fee earner's job should be measured as part of an annual assessment process in the same way as their legal work is judged. If your firm truly accepts this and implements it, then direct access to the appropriate fee earner from the website is the logical conclusion.

There are two main types of people who will respond to the website:

1. Visitors that have found you, perhaps by chance, and are curious to know more about your services.
2. People that have already decided to instruct your firm (because of previous satisfactory experience or following a recommendation) and have entered your site initially to learn more, reinforce their decision and to communicate with you.

In either scenario, a quick and efficient response is essential. Too often, the opening of a new website is seen as the end of a long development process. It is not. It is the beginning of a sales process that will only have any point or value if it is handled well, responded to and, indeed, promoted. Essentially, there are five ways a visitor can respond to your website:

1. They can do nothing. Ensure that the reports you get on your website management system record the number of visits that resulted in no action from the visitor – it can be very instructive. Many website reporting systems allow you to see just how far into the site a visitor has gone, and therefore at what point they have been turned off.
2. By email: either direct from your site, or subsequently. This response may be a simple request for contact or further information, or the completion and delivery of one of your questionnaires/forms. In either case, as noted above, the sooner it reaches the correct fee earner, the better.
3. By telephone. With the best will in the world, a computer system can only ask you to fill in predetermined boxes. Many of us do not fit exactly into these boxes; most of us would prefer a conversation with a human being rather than a screen. In the relationship between client and solicitor this is particularly likely. This is also a valuable advantage for a solicitor over The New Competition.
4. Downloading. If you invite people to download material from your site, it is essential that your system can tell you what has been downloaded by whom and when. For this reason, a restricted area, or 'law library', is worthy of serious consideration. Some firms of our acquaintance who have developed a client registration scheme (see **Chapter 11**) have added value to the registration, and differentiated the standard material they are offering, by limiting access to this type of download to registered clients. Of course, they make it very easy for non-registered clients to register and gain access, but this way you know who they are and can follow up this initial response.
5. Document assembly. Using this type of system can turn a person browsing the web into a profitable client in a matter of minutes. It is a valuable client/matter-capturing device that engages clients in solving their legal problem. Having said that, in practical terms, it will generate significant telephone enquiries from people who have got some way into the questionnaire but then want to talk to a 'live' solicitor.

Before you launch your new or improved website, ensure that the response system is in place and that its importance is understood by everybody. In training sessions on client care and handling we start by pointing out to fee earners and staff that very few people approach a solicitor other than in some state of anxiety. This may be extreme – a divorce or bereavement, threats of litigation or a complicated house move. On the commercial side, it is usually to do with the increasing of profit or loss avoidance, and we all know that is pretty stressful.

Therefore, ease of contact is essential. Take a look at The New Competition. All their promotional material, including their websites, promotes their email addresses, freephone telephone numbers and freepost addresses. You have to make it easy for people to contact you or they will contact a competitor.

Management of updating and maintenance of quality

The maintenance of quality and updating is essential. An out-of-date website immediately makes the firm look inefficient.

Where the physical changes and updating are handled will depend on whether you have decided to do this in-house or through your website developer. Either way, the material will need to be collated in-house and an individual needs to be appointed to the task. This person, who should report to the marketing partner, needs to have an understanding of your website and an enthusiasm for its role within your firm. This person also needs to have the authority from the partnership to demand required information on time, even from partners.

The marketing partner should have a monthly or quarterly meeting with the website quality manager to evaluate the site, look at the number of visitors to the site, monitor the response time by the departments, analyse the visitor-to-enquiry ratio and, ultimately, the enquiry-to-work ratio.

Of most importance is to review what has changed in the law or environment (see above), within the firm or elsewhere. In other words, what is it that needs updating and from where will the updated material come? Newsworthy material can come from a variety of sources. Changes in the law, service and price changes from the firm and press release sources can often provide enough items of news to keep the website changing regularly.

There should be one final question at each of these regular meetings: Are you proud of your website?

Website usage reports

An essential part of website management is the reporting of how often it is viewed, what has been seen and done on the site. This is a very complex area and you will need expert advice on the right methods to use. In general, website activity is known as 'traffic'. There are several basics to consider.

- Number of page impressions (not 'hits'). Page impressions are defined as the number of web pages requested and completely delivered to the requesting web browser. 'Hits' is an old technical term that has been misused to describe page impressions. You should only be interested in the number of page impressions delivered from your site as it indicates that a person (with some exceptions) has viewed the page and therefore has read the benefits presented on it.

- Number of downloaded documents. If you have documents that can be downloaded, it is useful to see how often these have been accessed. Commonly, these are in Adobe's PDF format as this allows control of the content of the document.
- Referring domains. In most situations, the domain from which a person is requesting your website can be recorded. This can be useful when viewed in an aggregated summary. Most will be from large known domains such as BT Internet services and other major Internet-service providers. This does indicate that it was a person viewing the site although these numbers cannot be taken as absolute because of the way the Internet handles web pages.
- Website 'cookies'. These are small data files used to identify when a particular web browser has accessed a website. Often, they are used to identify returning registered users and can contain non-attributable data that helps the website provide better access by pre-filling a username field so the viewer just needs to provide their password. At the basic level, cookies are an attempt to count individual users, although the result is often inexact. Your website will probably use cookies at this level.

Other more complex web reports can be produced and are useful in managing more sophisticated websites. If you have document assembly or payment facilities on your website, web activity reporting can track a person from a Google search, through your system to a profitable solution. These are tools developed for retailers of Fast Moving Consumer Goods (FMCG) sales where Google Adwords and tracking become a vital part of their business. However, legal services are not at that point yet so many of these tools will appear over-complicated for your needs.

Website quotes mechanisms will require separate reporting as would SMS messaging and telephone call-back features. There are also many elements that can confuse or distort website statistics. These include Internet service providers' local caches, search engine crawler software and lost 'cookies'. Your website developer will be able to advise you in more detail, and for the purposes of this book, we will not delve any further into this subject. Your requirement is to ensure your website is available and being used and viewed on a regular basis. Once the website stats have been collected for a while, you may use them to assess and improve areas of the site. Services offered by Google Adwords (see below) have website reporting tied into their advertising systems and provide a basic standard for website usage reporting. Again, it is important to seek professional advice on these services and your website developer will be able to advise you.

Promoting your website

Many of us, especially those of a certain age, are still bewildered by the position the Internet has attained so quickly, and the vital part a good website has to play in commerce today. The attitude still often prevails that it is enough to say, 'We have got a good website, we respond to it, and we keep it updated when required.' Regrettably, this is no longer enough when considered against the cost of website development and your firm's requirements on return on investment from all forms of promotion.

Since the Internet first came of age, and the worldwide web became a reality, we have been closely involved with our clients in the legal profession in the design, development, updating and maintenance of websites. But, of equal importance, is the promotion of the site. At the time of writing, more than one million searches a month were for the word 'solicitor' in the UK.

As the number of people using the Internet increases, visits or traffic to your site cannot be left to chance. At the design stage, you'll need to ensure your designer has all the metatags (labels) in place to enable the search engines to recognise your site's attributes (see details below). These will incorporate keyword descriptions of your site's content such as solicitor, conveyancing, commercial contract, divorce, the name of your town, Law Society, and others relating to your firm.

Search engines

Website search engines give rise to a lot of discussion, many myths and much money wasted by firms and organisations. Search engine optimisation (SEO) is, first, a technical matter of setting up your website so that the search engine can easily understand the content of your website. Secondly, it is a service offered by consultants to improve the position of your website on search engine results pages. The degree to which your firm goes into the details of these matters depends on the amount of enquiries you want to generate from your website.

Google is the dominant website search engine in the UK. It has significantly more searches than all the alternatives combined. For your purposes, it is the only search engine to be considered for the foreseeable future. In addition, Google's Adword service is now a dominant rival for Yellow Pages and its website. You should consider Google and Adwords as important as your Yellow Pages entry.

A significant point with Google is its method of ranking pages in its search returns. This system is constantly changing and is the driving force behind all of the search engine optimisation services. Since the rankings change, there is a need for many Internet-dependent businesses to manage how their site is listed to optimise their position. A simplistic description of the ranking systems is a combination of the content of a site and the number of similar content sites that link to it. Therefore, links to your site from the Law Society, other legal groups or associations and other law firms improve your Google ranking more than links from unrelated sites. A small number of related links is better than a larger number of unrelated ones, although any link will improve your position slightly.

If your firm is intending to generate the majority of your enquiries from Internet searches, you will need to have professional advice and a large advertising budget. For many organisations, it is a full-time job managing just their web presence. For the majority of firms reading this book, there are some basics to achieve that will help improve Internet searches for their website.

Metatags

Metatags, or labels on each page, are used by search engines to understand what the website is about. At present, Google's crawlers (the indexing software that looks at your site) use metatag data, the viewable text on a page and the site map. However, the information and the weight Google assign to it changes and it may take into account other elements of the website. Google regularly changes the way it ranks websites and repeatedly re-indexes sites. In 2011, it changed the way it presents business lists on the local business search terms. Google uses a list of business terms that includes 'solicitor' and 'lawyer' so that it can present maps with firms placed on it in addition to the text lists of websites.

With the tags, you should include single word or short phrase descriptions of the page and include locations (area, town, city and county). Do not be tempted to add too much: 10 or 15 words are sufficient.

The most important element is the actual text on the page. Getting that right is a matter of clearly explaining the benefits of the services you offer. Attempts to improve this for the search engine crawlers often lead to odd grammar, and should be avoided. Simple, clear and concise wording and bullet point list are the best methods.

Google's methods are a closely guarded secret. Do not be tempted by businesses offering to use overly complex methods to improve your ranking. While some may work for short periods of time, Google is aware of, and constantly vigilant for, websites and business methods that try to trick its system. In some cases, Google will suppress or disregard a website that attempts to gain an unfair advantage.

Google Adwords system

The Adwords system is now as important as a listing in the telephone book. Google's phenomenal success as a business was mostly due to adding paid-for 'keyword' search services to its system. These sponsored links are the most cost-effective way of getting your firm's ads in front of relevant search terms. There are plenty of advice books and websites that will go into the details of how best to use this system. Below is a brief explanation to help you get started, and at Figure 10.1 there is a picture explaining the different sections of a typical web search results page.

For the technical requirements, the Google Adwords website has all the details you require. Before you start, collect together a set of keywords that reflect your business – the metatag data can help here. The Adwords system is an automated auction that only charges the advertiser when its link is clicked and your ad's position on the page is related to how much you have bid. Again, this is a complex issue and the Google Adwords site has full details of the options. You can (and are encouraged to) add as many keywords as you like and offer a 'cost per click' via a preset bid. Keep the keywords relevant to the site and the text in the Google ad. The ad text is limited to 95 characters so there is limited scope for explanation or detail.

The best advice is to keep the ads and keywords simple and monitor the responses monthly, once set up. The minimum bids required often increase, and if your bid is lower, the system will automatically stop your ad for that keyword. The Adwords system offers an automated email summary that can help you monitor how the ads are performing.

Geographic keywords can help gain local search results. For example: 'solicitors Norwich' or 'conveyancing Bristol' can help improve the 'click through' rate from your ad and provide local business. However, the Google Adwords system does have some frustrating flaws from the solicitors' website point of view. If the search terms you use are rarely seen by the system, it will not show the ad and often describes it as having a 'low quality score'. It does not matter how relevant, locally targeted and specific you are being, for example, 'head injuries recovery Doncaster', the system seems unable to cope with that level of detail. Be warned that it can become a maddening task to manage and there are suppliers happy to take the frustration away from you for a fee.

A warning is needed at this point. Be very careful to set and monitor the daily budget for the account. This is important because the costs can mount up very quickly if you set an initial high bid and daily limit. Conversely, once the set daily budget is used, the system will stop delivering your ads to the search terms. The effect may be that your ads are served for only a short period during the day and then not available when potential customers get home in the evening. If you increase the daily limit to explore the number of click through you can get, you may find that costs increase sharply, particularly if you are not monitoring the budget daily.

As a management task, monitoring and adjusting the Google Adwords account can be delegated to your support staff. A monthly report is usually enough for partners to manage the strategy, and how it fits in with other promotional spending.

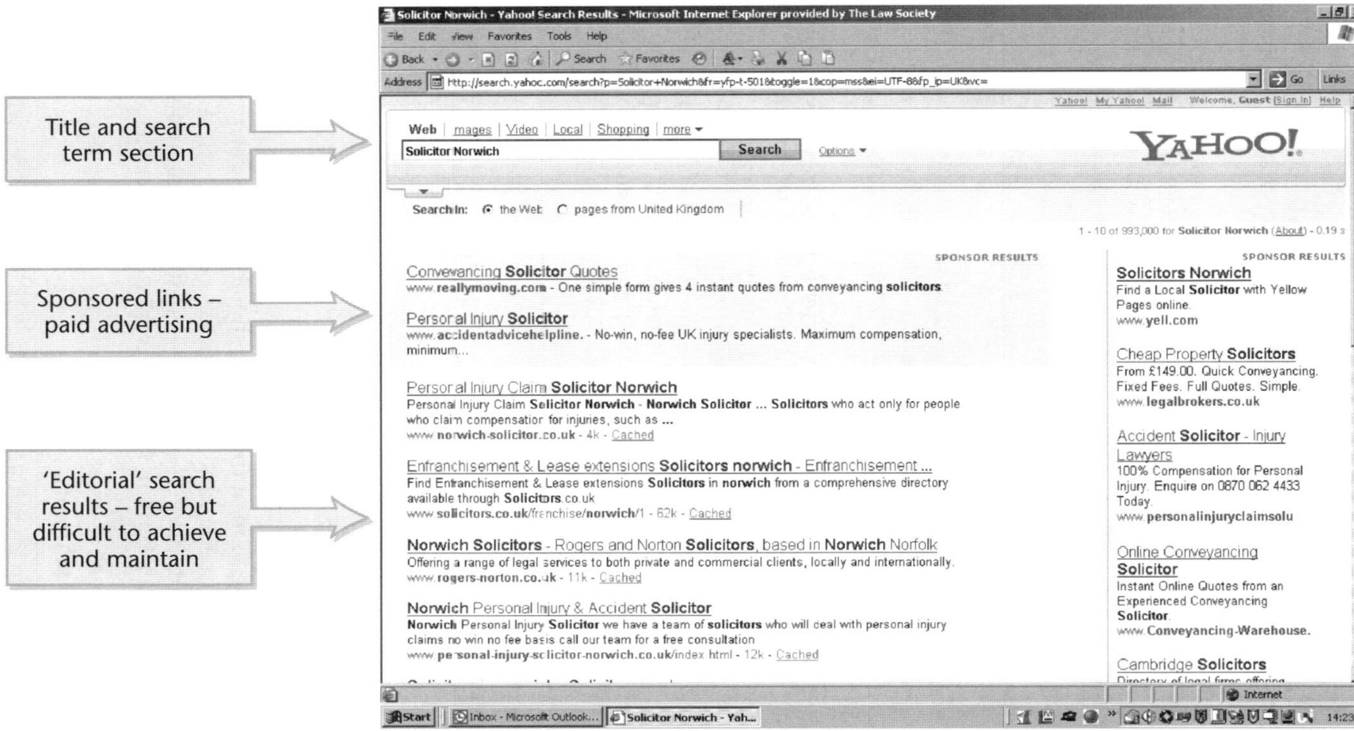

Figure 10.1 Example of the typica layout of a web search results page © Yahoo!

An additional system offered free by Google is a website monitoring and reporting service that can tie in with an Adwords account. You will need to discuss the technical aspects of this system with your website developer as it requires some minimal additional computer code for the website. Once it is set up, the same support staff can easily provide combined reports for a monthly partner review.

This is a very brief introduction to online website monitoring and promotion. It is intended to give you an overview that will help you manage the process and is by no means comprehensive. Your website developer will be able to advise you further on the options that best suit your firm.

Your role in promotion

We would suggest that you take the attitude that to maximise your investment in your website, you cannot leave it floating in cyberspace. You must actively promote it yourself to your clients, prospects and professional contacts.

It is worth considering the subject departmentally, as departmental heads may know more organisations that can provide references or links to your website. Clearly, estate agents would apply to conveyancing, but the PI department may have more luck with the local sports injuries clinic. You should also discuss this with the partners and fee earners of the particular departments in conjunction with the development of their professional contacts register. The more links you have, the more routes of access there are to your website in addition to the search engine ratings.

Promote the benefits to the viewer

- A registered client (see below) may be gaining access to valuable (restricted) information.
- Your past clients will have easy access to your firm's information.
- Prospects will get an impression of your firm's service benefits.
- Professional contacts can access support and information for their clients.

Each departmental section of the website should have its own specific benefits presentation based around each product or service offered. The marketing partner will need to discuss these benefits presentations with each department and develop them from the work done for earlier chapters.

Encourage visits to your site

The onus is on you to encourage visits to your site. Visitors who come by chance are a bonus. The initial promotion should be via word of mouth, and fee earners and staff should be encouraged to promote the website and point out its benefits when they have conversations with clients, prospects, professional contacts or even socially. You need to direct everyone towards your website via your letterhead, business cards and literature.

Your literature kit should have a website dedicated insert, explaining to the recipient why they should use the website. This is one of the few inserts that should go out with every literature kit.

Use your directory advertising, e.g. Yellow Pages, Thomson Local, Butterworth's, etc., to promote the website alongside the telephone number of the firm. All your generic advertising and PR activity should include promotion of the website alongside any social media activity.

And then, there is the 'blackmail budget' (see **Chapter 9**): our rather inelegant title for the type of advertising that is irrelevant, unproductive (though inexpensive) – but refusal of which is likely to cause offence to a client or professional contact. Examples are golfing/theatre programmes, church magazines, rugby club fixture lists and all the other space you feel obliged to purchase. At best, your advertisement will only be glanced at, so there is no point in trying to provide a lot of detail or make a detailed sales presentation. The following is probably the best use of the space, and the most likely to produce results:

> Monk, Moyes and Partners – Solicitors – WEBSITE ADDRESS – telephone number

Make the name of the firm small, the website address enormous and the telephone number legible – and leave it at that.

Listing and price comparison services

As outlined in **Chapter 8**, there are an increasing number of services that provide enquiry services for solicitors in addition to the claims management companies (CMCs) that broker personal injury (PI) matters. While the CMCs use large-scale advertising and web campaigns to attract specific PI work, there is a separate group of general legal services enquiry services filling the gap left unfilled by solicitors. These can be useful as a method of promoting your firm's website, although it can appear to be a complex choice of which is best for your firm. The enquiry services are usually website-based using Internet, web techniques and other advertising methods to gather legal service enquiries on a wide scale and sell them in some way to solicitors' firms. Many such services have been launched and a few have already disappeared. Before investing time, money and effort getting involved with this type of service, it's worth considering how it will help your firm and the service's business approach to the legal services enquiry market. A website offering to connect people and businesses with a suitable solicitor firms can be set up in a few hours, however, how useful this service is to solicitors and their clients is debatable.

Some services simply pass on enquiries in their raw state and leave the firm to sort out the details. Others, like Contact Law, have well-equipped call centres with trained call handlers that qualify each enquiry before sending it on to firms. Quality Solicitors takes the integration further by asking firms to re-brand all, or at least some, of their firm and their website to support a branded approach to gaining clients and matters. While this is moving beyond the subject of promoting your firm's website, it does come down to the same thing. How can your firm attract work through the Internet and other media?

In essence, we are looking at a 'make or buy-in' business management question. Can you manage the process and suppliers to achieve a competitive outcome for your firm at a particular cost or would it be cheaper to use one or a combination of these enquiry services to achieve a similar outcome?

A further option is to try both options for different departments and service groups in your firm. For consumer enquiries, use a combination of enquiry services and your own efforts; for commercial departments, concentrate on doing it yourself.

Enquiry volumes

Quality and quantity of enquiries present an additional aspect to the website promotion. If you launch a website that offers a popular service and you are inundated with enquiries, will you be able to handle them? Promoting your website needs to balance the number of enquiries you need to keep the departments running at their ideal capacity while not generating too many and disappointing potential clients.

In conjunction with other enquiry sources, look at promoting your website through other services and consider these points:

- How many enquiries do you want?
- What quality of enquiries do you expect?
- How many matters do you need to generate for enquiries?
- What flexibility do you need in enquiry numbers?

Other website services – social media

The web continues to develop at a fast pace. In 2011, there was more Internet activity on Facebook social media service than searches through Google. This indicates the change on the web from being a text and information service to a social and personal data system. This presents a complex but enticing opportunity for solicitors' firms to extend the promotion of their services into new realms. However, this complexity presents significant challenges when promoting your firm's services on your website through other web resources.

Social media includes services from:

- Facebook
- Myspace
- LinkedIn
- Viadeo
- Xing
- Twitter
- blogging website (not on your website)
- discussion groups

In **Chapter 12**, we deal with communications plans for identified groups of potential clients and this is worth adding in at this point. Promoting your website that is linked from social media pages is potentially a valuable route to market for specific groups. For example, Myspace is a social media system that is focused on music. If your firm has a set of specialist services in intellectual property or commercial agreements for musicians, then this could be a useful place to promote your services. If you can identify that a target market group of potential clients is using an element of social media, then you will need to plan your approach carefully.

We would caution against using Facebook in most situations as it offer, little immediate return for most firms. It has been used by larger law firms as a social link with younger solicitors or trainees, but that emphasises the point. Facebook is a social medium and any approach needs to encompass that ethos.

There are better business alternatives. LinkedIn, Viadeo and Xing are, respectively, USA, French and German business networking services. LinkedIn is by far the largest and offers both personal and business profiles. Again, using these website services will be dependent on which geographic markets you are active in. For the UK only, you can take your pick; if you have international work in Europe, then Viadeo or Xing may be more appropriate for your market.

LinkedIn has become a general business listing of people active in business and returns a high position in Google rankings when you search for a person's name or business. Often, the name search on Google will show the LinkedIn listing above the details on your own website. This makes it a useful service for promoting both your firm's website and an individual's expertise in specific areas of law.

Blogging, Twitter and discussion groups

Promoting your firm's expertise through other web services that link back to your website does offer useful opportunities, but heeding the warning earlier in the chapter is important. Social media and blogging is very time-consuming and if not managed correctly, can waste many hours and even be counter-productive.

To use these services, you need to be sure that the audience wants to hear what you have to say and will find it in some way useful. General comments in an attempt to raise the profile of your firm will be seen as advertising and may, in fact, damage your reputation by attracting negative comments from other users. These comments have a habit of hanging around on Google and other search services long after the time they were added. Getting adverse comments removed is almost impossible and also very time-consuming. What is worth doing is monitoring relevant blogs, discussion groups and Twitter. This does mean signing up for their services and adding your firm's details to their system. We would suggest listening and watching the discussions and only adding comments when necessary. It can assist you in understanding clients' requirements and needs that can feed back into your own website's content.

Your firm's website and its presence on the Internet is now a vital part of promoting the benefits of your firm's services. While your firm's website remains under your control, you need to be aware of the risks to your firm's reputation in other areas of the Internet where your control is limited or non-existent. The extreme example of this is a website we will refer to only as 'S from H'. More relevant is your firm's Google Local Business listings information mentioned above that appears on Google maps. Anyone can leave a review of your firm on this service and your firm will already be shown on the map. It's important that you take control of this listing to ensure its details are correct and the geographic location is right. As mobile devices and smart phones become ubiquitous, people will rely on information held on map services to guide them to your office and re-assuring themselves that they are making the right choice of firm.

For all areas of social media the main idea to keep in mind is the promotion of the benefits of the services you offer. Keeping a clear policy for all fee earners and staff that outlines the firm's approach to social media is a good starting point. Restricting all access is no longer an option. All fee earners and staff should be proud to work for a successful solicitors' firm and this should be reflected in the business and personal online presences.

The future of the Internet for solicitors

The Internet is dynamic. New and innovative web and mobile services will come along and you need to be able to assess each opportunity on its merits and potential benefits for your firm.

CHAPTER 10 TASKS Developing and improving your website

The completion of the tasks relating to this chapter will have put your firm in a position to create, improve and continuously promote the firm's website, as the first stage of an on-going and systematic programme for communicating with your clients, prospects and professional contacts.

Tasks can be split into three areas of management for a website:

- Development – Using the approach outlined in this chapter provides a framework for assessing and improving your firm's website. Use the outline in this chapter and the forms on the CD-Rom to help you develop your website.
- Management – Appoint a team responsible for delivering your firm's Internet and website services. Appoint a team to deal with each element of the website development and its ongoing management. Each person will need to have that time taken into account alongside his or her other duties.
- Promotion – Assess each available promotional opportunity on a cost versus the tangible commercial benefits for the firm.

Choosing to participate in blogs, discussion groups and the other website promotional opportunities outlined in this chapter may take considerable time to establish and further time to show any return. With the management team appointed to develop the website and other web activities, you will need to plan for 12 to 24 months of development. When considering the costs in time and money for each potential website promotion, compare the alternative such as writing a letter directly to the target market group. List the pros and cons of each approach and use that list to assess their value to the firm.

Ongoing website research and development

List five or more local competitive solicitors' firms for a comparison of their websites:

1.
2.
3.
4.
5.

List five or more regional or national solicitors' firms for a comparison of their websites:

1.
2.

3.
4.
5.

Research alternative legal service providers in addition to the examples listed below:

1. Halifax Legal Solutions – **www.halifaxlegalsolutions.co.uk**
2. NatWest – **www.natwest.com** – business section, employment law services
3.
4.
5.

For each website, note or print the pages that indicate what you like about that website. Note the methods of navigation around the website and how the menus of services and information work. Also, include illustrations of what you do not like or things you do not want on your website. Collate the notes and pages into a rough style guide for your website.

Use the suggested list below to assess the sites. You may want to add categories that are specific to your firm:

- First impressions
- Professional
- Friendly
- Efficient
- Interesting
- Uncluttered
- Easy to navigate
- Benefit-based
- Market specific

Interactivity

Below is a list of common types of interactivity. Consider how these will generate enquiries by easily allowing the viewer to contact your firm.

- Email contact forms
- Helpful downloads
- Telephone call-back services
- Quotations, automated or manual
- Appointment booking
- Text message (SMS)

Comparison with your current site

Using the style guide and the wording and structure from your literature kit, draw together the ideas of what your website would deliver to the person viewing it.

ISSUES TO CONSIDER

- Strategy of vertical and horizontal growth from **Chapter 7** will indicate the types of clients you are attempting to address in the future. What would they like to see, and how can the website help them solve their problem by contacting your firm?
- Database development, client records and your professional contacts register (**Chapter 6**) indicate the primary users of the site. What would they like to see, and how can the website help them solve their problem by contacting your firm?
- The literature kit developed as part of **Chapter 9** can provide the structure and wording. Use that to draft the website pages, remembering that the intention is to have the website viewer contact your firm.
- Interactivity, in the form of news sections, quotations and online information, is useful but should be aimed at generating an enquiry and not too elaborate as your competitors are just a click away and may be easier to use.
- How will your website tie in with other areas of promotional development?

Sitemap example

HOME

Legal advice

CORPORATE

Dispute resolution and litigation

Finance

Human resources

Property and conveyancing

Tax

Technology and commerce

INDUSTRY AND COMMERCIAL EXPERTISE

Employment

Litigation

Contracts and agreements

PRIVATE CLIENT

Wills

Single parent wills

Husband and wife mirror wills

Separated spouses

Cross-life interest wills

Flexible life interest trusts

Wills for cohabitants

ESTATE AND TAX PLANNING

Inheritance tax

Capital gains tax

Tax planning through trusts

ENDURING OR LASTING POWERS OF ATTORNEY

Creation

Registration

Management of affairs

COURT OF PROTECTION

Receivership applications

Accounts

General directions

ADMINISTRATION OF ESTATES

Obtaining grant of representation

Full administration and inheritance tax/income tax

ELDERLY CLIENT

Long-term care funding

Deeds of gift

Trusts

Inheritance tax saving trusts

Protection of asset trusts

ABOUT US

History of the firm

Our partners

Partner profiles

PUBLICATIONS AND EVENTS

Events

USEFUL INFORMATION

Newsletters

Hot topics

Links to other websites

COMMUNITY

Pro bono

Charities

OUR TECHNOLOGY

eBusiness services

eClient services

CAREERS WITH US

Lawyers

Support and secretarial

Graduate

CONTACT US

–

The completion of the tasks relating to this chapter will have put your firm in a position to create, improve and continuously promote the firm's website, as the first stage of an on-going and systematic programme for communicating with your clients, prospects and professional contacts.

11

A client registration scheme and newsletters

This chapter concentrates on the development of a client registration scheme.

It shows how your firm can take an uncleansed mailing list, develop it into a true database and on towards a client relations management system.

It ties together the advice outlined in earlier chapters and illustrates additional ways to use the material proposed in those chapters.

We also introduce the idea of a client newsletter that can be used independently of a client registration scheme, together with some other ideas that can assist you in achieving the aim of being considered as 'my solicitor' by clients.

It is the key to developing client loyalty, which is a major part of overcoming The New Competition.

It demonstrates how target profitability per client can supersede success measured by numbers of clients. It is vastly more expensive to gain a new client than to retain an old one. This chapter demonstrates how.

The way to be a bore is to say everything. – Voltaire

'Saying everything' will also confuse the listener. Providing information that is relevant to the recipient in a regular and steady flow is more likely to ensure the understanding and retention of your proposal. Earlier in the book we talked about psychological needs, and one of these is the desire to 'belong'. It is natural for us to want to belong and feel part of a larger entity that is appropriate to us. Apart from providing security – another psychological need – it also provides us with the satisfaction of knowing that other like-minded individuals have made a similar decision to our own. In essence, a client registration scheme could be considered a club with various membership benefits. Interestingly, people have a habit of being very loyal to their 'clubs'.

In part, the 'club feel' lies in making the past contact or prospect feel special. This is what the huge organisations that are The New Competition can never achieve. Their clients can, by definition, only ever be numbers. Numbers handled by call centres, maybe miles away. Your alternative, what you offer in the face of The New Competition, can be membership: membership to an exclusive, professional, special club – your society of registered clients.

In this chapter we cover how to decide upon the exact format of your firm's personalised scheme, and help the partnership to arrive at decisions, such as the formulation and way of operating your scheme. We will then look at the production of detailed benefit lists, for both the firm and the clients from this scheme. We look at the launch and promotion of such a scheme, guiding you around the potential pitfalls, with examples and anecdotal evidence of both success and wasted opportunities.

Why have a client registration scheme?

Prepared and run properly, your client registration scheme will have a major impact on your business. There are four main reasons for strongly recommending the introduction of a client registration scheme.

1. It replaces the long gone loyalty to the old family solicitor and encourages clients to begin to think of your firm as their solicitor, in the same way as they think of their doctor, their dentist or their bank. If you build a greater knowledge and understanding of each client, it makes serving of that client easier and more pertinent, ensuring you always offer best advice, which in turn leads to increased profits.
2. It enables you to cross-sell your services, despite your likely divisionalisation, whether that be will making to conveyancing, or a private client providing the prospect of commercial work.
3. You can continue your campaign of actively seeking recommendations, with the realisation that a 'card-carrying registered client' is more likely to make a recommendation than one who vaguely remembers using you a few years ago, and who has never heard from you since.
4. A client registration scheme provides the perfect opportunity of turning a mailing list into a true client relations management (CRM) system. This is perhaps the most important objective: the client registration scheme draws together elements discussed in previous chapters on database development, client handling and promotional materials, and enhances both your internal structure of client development and your perceived value to the clients.

Ultimately, your firm will have a significant number of people with whom it communicates regularly, who consider themselves to be registered clients of your firm, and who will feel great security from this new free-of-charge service. The New Competition is using similar techniques. Halifax Legal

Solutions charges a yearly fee for access to its services and others may enter the market with a premium service offer aimed at differentiating their services from high-volume legal work such as the 'conveyancing sheds'.

Your client registration scheme is a pivotal part of bringing together the development of a client database, the growth in vertical and horizontal development, the background promotional activity, the detailed use of the literature kit and website with the development of an ongoing, tailored, targeted and accurate series of promotional campaigns. An initial assessment is required to make sure the promotion of a client registration scheme does not conflict with other offerings, and that your firm has the resources and capacity to provide the services promised as part of the scheme.

In truth, however, the majority of the firms we have dealt with have only a mailing list, and frequently an uncleansed one at that. We know that this scheme does work, with an average of 55 per cent of the people on the mailing list becoming registered clients. This is the start of true database development which, if implemented correctly, will add significant value to your firm.

The future of legal service provision does change the view of the value of a legal service firm. The partners' combined equity is no longer a useful basis for a firm's valuation. As the commercial pressures increase, the value in a solicitor's firm is the contacts database it controls, the amount of data it holds on each potential client and how much future work it can expect from that database. As mergers and consolidation increase in response to the changing market, those firms that can accurately quantify who their clients are will have a far stronger negotiating position. Implementing a client registration scheme will put your firm in that strong position.

What is the scheme?

The scheme involves allocation of a registration card of credit card size, which can either be a privilege card, or most probably a contact card with a slogan similar to 'In the event of accident, please contact my solicitor [name + name of firm] on [number] who holds all my detail's. This encourages registered clients to keep the card in their wallet or purse. It provides a genuine and free-of-charge service, although we must acknowledge that your marketing purpose with the card is to keep your name and contact details always readily at hand when their (derived) need arises.

Registration with the scheme requires completion of a questionnaire by the client. The questionnaire carries all the caveats assuring the client that you do not wish to be impertinent, that the client is in control, they need only fill in the questions which they wish to fill in and at any time they can cancel their registration, should they so wish, and that under no circumstances will information be divulged to any third party.

The questionnaire can be as long or as short as you care to make it, printed and on your website. The example below is only intended to be indicative, and you should consider carefully the information you require for your own firm. The answers provided to you will give an opportunity to be genuinely proactive in the client's interest and to a larger number of clients. You will be able to contact the client with knowledge, and provide relevant information, even if it is simply a letter once a year saying: 'This is the information we are currently keeping about you, is it correct, do you wish to change, add or remove anything?'

The collective details of each registered client, held in a suitable database format, provide a powerful promotional tool. Where previously your firm had a combination of mailing lists and the knowledge of clients from individual fee earners, now you have the ability to aggregate, manage and expand that client knowledge through this system. This helps individual fee earners to provide better service to a larger group of clients through their ability to quickly access full details of the client position and history. It also ties the client to the firm and not only to the fee earner. Since the client information is held by the firm, it is used to introduce other services and presents a 'legal team' approach to the provision of these services. It thereby reduces the ability of fee earners to take clients with them should they leave the firm. Clients are often lost when a contact's fee earner moves on or retires. Again, this approach lessens the likelihood that the client will look for an alternative supplier of legal services.

Clearly, the more we know about the client, the better we can service them and the following indicative questionnaire illustrates that each department will most likely have something to write about to each client during the course of an average year. As you read the questionnaire, we would remind you that the actual form will be 'topped and tailed' with the reassuring messages that clients need only complete the information that they wish. But, remember also that we, the public, are conditioned to answering questions from our lawyers.

Illustrative questionnaire

This is certainly not exhaustive, nor is it suggested that all questions must be included on the questionnaire. This is, of course, a matter for the partners of your firm to decide, and is something that should be discussed fully.

1. Title, first name, last name
2. Date you first became a client of our firm [insert date from firm's records]
3. National Insurance number
4. Surname at birth

5. Address, postcode, home telephone number, home fax number, home email address
6. Employer's name, address, telephone number, position held by client
7. Next of kin's details: name, address, contact details, relationship to client
8. Date of birth, marital status
9. Name and address of bank
10. Name and address of accountant
11. Name and address of doctor
12. Date of will
13. Where is will held? [insert firm's name if you hold that will]
14. Date of last codicil
15. Wealth rating [see list – add list if wanted]
16. Income rating [see list – add list if wanted]
17. Spouse's/partner's name, number of children, name and date of birth of each child
18. Do you have an EPA/LPA or a living will?
    - First attorney's name, address and contact
    - Second attorney's name, address and contact
19. Do you have influence over/need of legal work at your place of business?
20. Would you like to receive details of our commercial services?
21. Which clubs/associations do you belong to?
22. What other hobbies do you have?
23. Where are the title deeds of your property held? [insert firm's name if you hold deeds]
24. With whom do you have your mortgage? Please supply account number
25. Do you own more than one property?
26. Name and address of second property, name and address of third property
27. Do you have any investment property?
28. Do you hold investments in stocks and shares?
29. Have you ever suffered from a serious illness?
30. What is your blood group?
31. Are you taking any long-term prescription drugs?
32. Should we divulge the name of your doctor in the event of an accident?
33. Are you self-employed?
    - Entity of business (sole trader, partnership, limited company, etc.), company name, company's registered office, company's registration number, telephone number, email address, website address, your position in the company
    - Other contacts in the company, year end, areas of activity (e.g. retail, manufacturing, professional, etc.)
    - If part of a group, name of group, group contact, annual turnover
    - VAT number, number of employees, company accountant

This is a general list of questions aimed at private clients. A commercial company list would include more detailed questions on premises and employment issues. There may also be a desire to go on to more specific and specialist questions with, for example, people living in care homes, divorcees, people living abroad, etc.

Again, let us emphasise that it is not intended that you must have all, or indeed any, of these questions. Clearly, the partnership must feel comfortable with the level of questioning. However, it is our experience that the more questions you ask the more response you get and that there is seldom any offence caused provided that it is made abundantly clear on the questionnaire that clients need only answer those questions that they wish to answer. In other words, they answer the questions providing the information that they wish you to hold about them. It almost doesn't matter how little. Each year you have a good reason to write to them again, stating what information you are holding, to ask if it is correct, and whether or not they would like to increase the information that you hold. Clearly, the more we know the better we can target our services, but initially just getting a response, just getting a single answer to a single question, which enables us to send them a welcome pack, a registration card and to write to them personally once a year, is more than most legal practices have achieved since the days of the 'man of affairs'.

Company commercial clients can benefit in the same way, and this is the opportunity to develop and maintain contact with a greater number of small and medium-sized firms. This addresses the 'time poor' element of business managers who have little opportunity for proactive legal issues but need a contact quickly when issues arise. A brief questionnaire followed by a 'business club' welcome pack presents your services in a way that (suitably targeted) is of value to the client.

Although we are focusing on the overt 'club' style approach, this may not suit all types of firms or their commercial clients. The intention is to identify and develop your firm's most valuable clients, look at their needs and communicate to them the benefits of using your services. It may not be necessary to tell the client they are part of that club. Commercial clients may see it as far from beneficial to be part of a collective group if they suspect that many of the advantages will be standard.

Promoting the client registration scheme

We would propose that the client registration scheme is initially promoted via newsletters (see below). It can be hinted at in Issue 1; have the benefits to the client described more fully in Issue 2; and include the actual questionnaire, with encouragement to complete it, in Issue 3.

Our experience is that only 10–20 per cent will respond at this stage. However, sending an additional copy of the questionnaire with a covering letter through the post can at least double this response, and a second mailing of the questionnaire with Issue 4 of the newsletter has frequently brought the total responses up to the 50–60 per cent mark.

This rolling response is no bad thing, as it assists with the work of inputting the information and issuing cards. Once you have completed this process, you should introduce the questionnaire on your website, allowing future clients and prospects to register via email. Clearly, all new clients who come into the firm to see any fee earner should fill in a questionnaire, or at least those parts of it they wish to, if they fit the preferred profile of the registration schemes members. (For example, the partners may prefer not to include clients of the criminal department – unless, of course, the firm is solely a criminal practice.) The registration scheme should also have its own insert in the literature kit.

The client registration scheme and its benefits will probably be unusual in your geographical area and, as such, can attract a lot of PR coverage when the time is right. In developing the scheme, and prior to the production of promotional and other material, the partners need to agree the scheme features and then list the benefits of this 'product' (see **Chapter 5**).

Internal management

The implementation of a client registration scheme needs to be a further development of the ideas already outlined in previous chapters. It relies on:

- fee earners being confident to recommend the services of another department;
- all fee earners and staff having services details to hand;
- having the systems in place to access the client's information quickly when it's needed.

This entails managing the systems for client contact, particularly incoming calls. In the client's mind, you are their solicitor and know all about them. In reality, they are one of several hundreds, if not thousands, of clients who probably deal with one or more of the fee earners. Support staff are crucial to ensuring the smooth flow from the call answering, to the fee earner greeting the client by name and being ready with their client's history.

Clients do not want to hear:

- 'She doesn't work in this branch.'
- 'That's not my department.'
- 'We don't do that type of legal work.'

The client wants to hear:

- 'Hello [firm name], may I take your client registration number?'
- 'I'm not able to deal with that area, I'll find out who is and put you through/have them call you at [time].'
- 'To make sure we can help you with all legal matters, we have arranged for [the legal work you don't do] to be dealt with by our colleague.'

It is worth repeating that clients do not care or understand how you structure your firm, or who does what. They want to talk to a person who can help them solve their problem, knows who they are and what they have done with the firm previously. To achieve this requires a coordinated system of people and IT. It is the essence of client-focused services and is what The New Competition will use. Without it your firm will lose the value of an enquiry.

The value of client enquiries

This is the basic marketing concept of cost per enquiry, and the value that can be attached to the services offered. All enquiries (for services) that your firm receives can have a potential value attached to them and a cost of generating that enquiry. **Chapter 13** deals with specific promotional campaigns and in earlier chapters we have outlined the necessity to set targets for promotions to measure their success.

The basics are that any promotional campaign should deliver an increase in profits, in addition to the profits already achieved by the service being promoted. You are looking for a step-change increase in a service following promotions. In some circumstances, it is not possible to measure returns accurately. Corporate promotions (whole firm, see **Chapter 9**) can have a defined aim with a mixture of profile raising and general services advertising. Your firm would expect an increase in all service enquiries but you may have difficulty showing that the campaign generated clients' interest. When questioned about what prompted a person to contact your firm, often, clients will say where they found your number (e.g. Yellow Pages, website, etc.) and not the real prompt that was a letter or local press promotion.

The cost of generating enquiries can range from pennies for a Google Adwords click via your website, to hundreds, and occasionally thousands of pounds, when dealing with events to attract large commercial clients. The underlying message is that the cost of generating the enquiries should be in proportion to the expected profit from the matters sold.

Once an enquiry is received, the onus is on your firm to retain that client, to become 'their solicitor' by providing access to all the services they may require in the future. Costs can be halved for every additional service bought by the client.

For registered clients this is more important. Your firm should be in a position to profit from the client when they enquire about services you do not offer. Where, for example, your firm does not offer matrimonial services, you should have a reciprocal arrangement with a trusted local firm that can help your client. The basis of these referral agreements can take many forms. However, it is important to retain the client as your client, enabling you to promote services to them in the future. If the arrangement is potentially large in value, or the referral solicitor a direct competitor, then a referral fee may be appropriate. It is important to understand the value in a client's enquiry and to retain that for your firm.

Delivery of benefits to the client

It is not necessary to give away services or provide discounts to registered clients. The idea behind a client registration scheme is to highlight the range of services a client can use. As a firm, you will have established contacts with trusted professional advisers. In addition to the range of legal services (or referrals), the benefits to registered clients can include:

- access to your firm's independent financial advisers;
- business advisers via your local bank;
- accountancy services through recommendations;
- links to a criminal defence firm.

From within your firm you provide:

- newsletters and personalised legal advice;
- access to packaged services;
- named partner as client's legal team leader;
- named individual as primary contact;
- mobile phone and out of hours access to advice;
- evening appointments or late office opening;
- website access to controlled registered client services and information areas;
- freephone number privileged access;
- wills registration.

In essence, anything that costs little more to do, that the client will perceive as better than standard service.

Subscriptions and additional services

Halifax Legal Solutions' services are charged for on a yearly subscription business model. The New Competition will use this option particularly when targeting higher value potential clients. This approach may be worth considering as a development of your client registration scheme. The clients' perception of the services offered is often based on the price charged. A free service, however good, may not be seen as valuable where an alternative paid-for service provides a client with more comfort that they will get what they want, will have the ability to complain and can get their money back.

Commercial clients may offer a more useful route for charging a subscription. Regular reviews of employment contracts and other commercial legal matters can justify a retainer to reassure a small business that its legal matters are covered. A legal health check is a fine promotional vehicle, and this may be the way to make it pay.

More profit from fewer clients and less work

Many of the firms we have assisted consider that they have too much work. The partners dismiss 'marketing' (meaning promotions) since they feel they cannot handle additional matters. Elsewhere in this book, we have dealt with the issues of capacity in a firm and the profitability per matter. A client registration scheme is the overt process by which a firm can start to identify and discard those clients for whom the firm does not want to act in the future. This is a particularly difficult process to achieve without having the background information required to assess each client, each group of clients and where the partnership wants to be in the future. It is also difficult for many partners and fee earners to say 'No' to work when they are unsure of the future supply.

The implementation of a registration scheme provides the internal catalyst for a firm to start that discarding process. Focusing fee earners' attention on excellence of service to a valuable group of clients increases their awareness of client value. The firm needs to have arranged what to do with non-required clients through a referral to other solicitors and services. If it takes two minutes to refer on a 'non-required' client to an alternative, it can release time for the fee earners to concentrate on higher value work; when the referral is done well, it can leave a good impression and potential for recommendations.

Wills registration scheme

As a subsection of your client registration scheme, or even as a stand-alone initiative, consideration should be given to a wills registration scheme. You may decide to use an outside organisation such as 'Certainly' to provide the systems or take on the administration of the scheme in-house. But either way, it should be presented as *your* scheme providing additional benefits to your clients, that *you* have provided or organised for them.

It should be emphasised to your clients that this is entirely different from a wills storage scheme, and unlike many commercial schemes, is totally free of charge to your clients.

In essence, the scheme ensures that everyone concerned is aware that there is a current will, and where that will is. Linked with this vital service is the ability, as with the client registration scheme, to keep details of all other 'life's documentation' so that by the simple enactment of a client registration number, the information is readily available for all those who might be concerned.

A registered will holder is issued with a card which it is hoped will be kept in a purse or wallet permanently with the telephone number of your practice and a slogan similar to 'In the event of an accident or incapacitation, my solicitor's telephone number is . . . and they hold all relevant information about me'. Some clients have even replicated this with an adhesive sticker that can be placed on or near the client's telephone. This is particularly relevant to the elderly client.

Information can be regularly updated via a series of reminders, which not only keeps you in touch with changes to your clients, but also acts as a reminder that you are proactive in their interest. This greatly enhances the relationship with your client and demonstrates your own proactivity. Persuading clients to become registered is not difficult if they are reminded, perhaps through a newsletter on a regular basis, that too often when the time comes to enact a will, there is confusion when family members, friends, executors or others trying to help sort out the matters of the deceased do not know if a will exists or cannot find it or, if found, are not certain that it is a current will and that there have been no updates, renewals or codicils added.

In short, they cannot be certain, at a time of high emotion, that they are actually carrying out the wishes of the will maker. We all assume that a will tucked away with our other papers is going to be found. This can be a misguided assumption. Sometimes a will is not found at all or, perhaps even worse, it is found too late. A wills registration scheme prevents this. It is a promotional activity that provides a very real benefit to your clients.

Newsletters

Many clients use their newsletter as a special benefit for, and communication tool with, their registered clients. It may well be so but, in the early days at least, the newsletter itself can be used to promote the registration scheme and sell the idea of membership to all the past clients on your mailing list.

Even at later stages, the newsletter can have a place in the communications with your professional contacts register and prospects. Perhaps with a covering letter such as: 'The enclosed Newsletter is primarily produced for our clients, but we thought you might be interested in the article on page 2 . . .'.

Why a newsletter?

It is very difficult for us not to be repetitive when something such as The New Competition appears on the horizon. But the message of this book is that things have changed, and a new attitude is needed to compete in this market's changing environment. The key to your firm's future success is to establish a positive brand image, with satisfied clients who will use you again and recommend you, providing you maintain contact with them. So there, we have said it again. But, one of the best ways of maintaining regular contact is via a client newsletter whether traditionally printed or delivered electronically. This is the staple ingredient to the communications plans outlined in **Chapter 6** on databases.

You can prosper in competitive markets by continually presenting the benefits of your firm to your existing client base, prospects and professional contacts. One of the benefits you need to demonstrate is a proactive approach to communications with your clients. A newsletter demonstrates this. As we said, a newsletter provides you with the opportunity to 'tell them what you are going to tell them; then tell them; then tell them what you have told them'. It also provides the opportunity to put a human face on a legal practice that still, even today, is misunderstood in the minds of the public and businesses.

Long before The New Competition, the media were 'knocking' the legal profession on an almost daily basis: arrogant, unapproachable, reactive, hugely expensive, inefficient and antiquated. You have to repudiate this popular press image and a newsletter can do this when carefully targeted and constructed. You do not have to repudiate the media with everyone. Your job is not defending the legal profession, it is promoting the benefits of your individual firm.

A word of warning

Newsletters have, of late, fallen into disrepute. Largely, this is due to the fact that they have become very stereotypical and appear lazy, complacent and dull. This is inevitable if standard material is just bought in, and overprinted with your name. Some firms have recognised this, and simply discontinued the practice of producing a newsletter.

There are many examples of bad newsletters: idly produced, repetitive and offering nothing that the target reader hasn't heard or read before.

Often, the thought of them brings to mind dull, cringingly enthusiastic and irrelevant A4 sheets of nothing. The first one is looked at, the second one is glanced at – all after that are ignored. The most difficult task is making your newsletter interesting. Newsletters need not be in the style of newspaper layout with a little something for everyone. This type is the most often produced and ignored by recipients because it is almost all of no interest to them. A newsletter can take almost any form that is relevant to the client groups it is aimed at. Newspaper style is good for the reception and general promotion. Commercial clients prefer letter style, addressed individually and containing precise details. 'Newsletters' is the best description although letters that contain news is more accurate.

The other reason for disrepute is that people fear being seen to be sending out junk mail. If what you are proposing to send is actually 'junk', don't send it. But it is probably a pretext for inaction – along with the other excuses: Everyone is too busy. Everyone has too many clients. Nobody has enough time. We have got enough work anyway. No one has the skills.

Well, the skills can be acquired or bought in by copywriters or graphic designers. Your own existing printer is sure to be able to point you in the right direction. But as to the rest of the excuses, things are likely to change. The New Competition is coming, and has been estimated by the legal profession itself to have the potential to take 25–50 per cent of the bread-and-butter business out of the high street.

You must not let that happen to your firm!

The many uses of a newsletter

A newsletter can provide detail of the full ranges of services you offer, and the benefits of using them, in a low-key, unobtrusive way. Thus, it can encourage repeat business and recommendations. It can introduce topics such as divorce and will making anecdotally. Other people's stories may make us think.

Further subjects can be introduced, in a similarly conversational low-key way, such as changes in the law and how they affect your clients. The marketing-minded practice will realise that clients do not want a cold description of procedures and changes, they want to know in a simple, jargon free and friendly tone, what it means to them, personally.

The newsletter can be used to publicise the new qualification gained by a member of staff. And even mentioning the birth of a child or a retirement party can be useful ways to present the benefits of the services to a particular group of potential clients. Perhaps you do pro bono work in the community. You could explain it by showing how this adds to the legal experience of fee earners. The newsletter is a perfect vehicle for demonstrating that a welfare legal aid franchise is an accolade that belongs to the whole firm, as it is a quality control reward, and it is impossible to put more than one quality – a high quality – throughout the firm. This might even win over a commercial client who would normally take a negative view of publicly funded work.

If the articles can be written light-heartedly, are suitable and genuinely interesting, this is the place for segments of the history of the firm, its employees or partners, especially if relevant to the geographical area in which the majority of your clients reside.

Commercial and niche market clients are often better served with a 'letter containing news' which can also be delivered via email (an 'Eshot'). For example, in a recent government budget, the chancellor announced unexpected changes to the tax on trusts. This announcement would be a good topic for an article for the next general newsletter. However, your firm will have a number of clients that these proposed changes will affect once finalised. Of far greater value to your firm would be using the client database information on who has (and potentially should have) a trust, combined with a brief letter explaining that your firm was studying the proposal and would inform the client of any changes that would affect their position.

The effect of this letter is to proactively reassure the client that as their solicitor, you are constantly looking out for their best interests and acts as a reminder, or prompt, for them to contact you regarding either that issue or other matters. From the ideas outlined in earlier chapters, the newsletter is the culmination of:

- developing your firm's database to a position where such a targeted letter is simply produced and sent out;
- enabling your department heads and fee earners to have the ability to proactively communicate with clients about their legal affairs;
- providing clear benefits of your firm's services via your website and literature kit;
- establishing processes that capture client enquiries through easy access to fee earners and well-trained support staff.

What to call the newsletter

Many firms struggle for a long time to find a title or name for their general newsletter. Often, this is because of the conflict of having to cover many different areas of a firm's services in a limited amount of space. Here is our recommendation:

> 'THE NEWSLETTER' – written in-house especially for the clients of Monk, Moyes and Partners

For that is what it is, a client newsletter written by you (perhaps with outside help) especially for your clients. It is your demonstration of proactive and additional service to your clients. You have differentiated your 'product'. You have added to your unique selling point. You have demonstrated to clients/prospects/professional contacts and, importantly, your staff, your commitment to the marketing management philosophy.

These methods are already being exploited by The New Competition.

Producing a general newsletter

Consumers of anything need information to make decisions. The customers for legal services – your clients – are no different. Of all the communication tools, your literature kit, your website or other announcement in newspaper, reports, brochures, letterheads, business cards, etc., none is as flexible and useful as the general newsletter.

But, as we said earlier, the reality is that newsletters have been tarnished by badly produced ones. Targeted 'letters that contain news' have not been so tainted so far, but if overused or misdirected, these, again, are no better than junk mail. Your firm should start by implementing a general newsletter and then developing targeted newsletters where you can define a group of clients that would benefit.

A general newsletter should be informative, telling clients about the latest changes in the law and how it affects them, changes in the environment or taxation regimes, etc., but at the same time, it can greatly help in underpinning the existing client base and encouraging those clients to think of your practice as 'their solicitor'. A newsletter can put a personal face to a firm, and demonstrate its ethos or profile via articles about activities within the firm, success of staff, and simply what might be described as 'gossip'.

Also, it can help promote those 'trickier' matter types, as noted above, such as making a will (we are all immortal, aren't we?), trusts (who trusts anybody anyway?), LPAs (something everyone should have?) or matrimonial. A newsletter can tackle these subjects illustratively, drawing attention, without drawing offence. Used properly, a newsletter is a highly effective tool, and one that has consistently reaped benefits for all those who have done it well

But beware: it is essential, before introducing a newsletter, that the partners of the firm commit themselves to a series, probably five or six issues over a two-year period, and undertake to maintain the editorial standard. Once the newsletter is started, your firm must not let it slip in standard, or even worse, peter out. Nor should it be regular, such as monthly or quarterly. Aiming for three a year, unevenly spread, will provide you with more flexibility and a better chance of avoiding rushing out a copy because a pre-declared deadline is approaching.

Layout and style

Layout and style depend on the market to be addressed and the amount of news information you plan to include. Your newsletter should be printed in colour and should include photographs and other graphics. New printing techniques have made this perfectly affordable and economically viable.

Resource, time and costs can be reduced considerably by using a variation of the copy and visuals developed for the literature kit, the website and other printed media within the firm. In addition, articles developed for the newsletter can easily be adapted for distribution to the wider public through press releases.

It is of genuine benefit to use the same or similar illustrations in the newsletter that have been or will be seen later in the literature kit or on the website. Again, this is part of the process of: tell them what you are going to tell them; then tell them; then tell them what you have told them. It should never be forgotten that repetition is a key element in understanding and information retention.

Quality

Quality control and standards usually slip when deadlines approach. Ideally, therefore, the final copy of Issue 2 should be available as Issue 1 is being published. Also, the article list and structure of Issue 3 should be to hand.

By ensuring that you are working one issue ahead, you can greatly improve your chances of maintaining quality standards. Of course, matters of great topicality might arise that require one 'standard' article to be removed to accommodate it, but this article can then be used in Issue 3.

One issue ahead should always be your maxim, and by planning the first three issues and then continuing that process on a rolling basis, you will have a clear view of where the newsletter itself, and the topics within it, are going. However, whoever produces your copy (see below) it is, in our opinion, vital to have the newsletter properly laid out by a graphic designer. Ask your existing printer to recommend someone, although it is probable that you already have a designer on board if you are considering a literature kit and website.

That, however, brings us to the next major problem.

Proofreading

This is a subject dear to the heart of the writer, who was responsible for sending out a piece of print referring to 'enduring powers of atttorney' (i.e. with attorney spelt with three 'ts).

The person who writes the copy, especially if it is an adaptation of material written earlier, cannot proofread it. It is not just word blindness, it is how the brain works. The truth is, when we read normally, not even speed-reading, we do not see all the letters, let alone read them. Anybody who looks at written material regularly, be it hard copy or on a screen, has a brain that has learned to be pre-emptive. We see what we believe to be there, and what is logical.

However you produce your newsletter (or any other written material) you must have someone detached from it who will read the words critically. They need to understand that their role is not to consider content, or even style: just the words, the facts, the layout. And opinion on layout is important. Good graphic design and layout greatly helps understanding and retention. The originator of the copy will not see it at all.

So, at an early stage, decide who your proofreader will be and don't let it be the senior partner's wife.

The recipients

Unless your firm is predominantly commercial, in which case the content of the newsletter will reflect this, it is likely that your newsletter will, at least in the first instance, appeal mostly to private clients. However, you should not forget that commercial clients are also potential private clients in their domestic role. Ideally, the newsletter should be sent to a commercial client by the fee earner most often dealing with him or her, with a covering letter. This covering letter should say something to the effect of:

> I thought you might be interested in the enclosed. It is produced for our private clients, but we hope you will find it of interest, and particularly the article on page 3 relating to our work for the employees of our commercial clients.

Nor should you lose sight of the fact that many private clients, in their business life, may be in a position to influence the placing of commercial work. Every issue of your newsletter should contain some reference to your commercial department (however small or cosmetically created) and the type of work you undertake. The commercial client profile, albeit in a private client newsletter, can help in this respect.

One of the most provocative articles, and the one that produced some of the highest fee earning, was an article in a private client newsletter relating to the potential of criminal prosecution of company directors by (at that time) the Inland Revenue, Customs and Excise, the Health and Safety Inspectorate and private prosecution. Of course, this was in a newsletter from a firm that had a strong criminal department, but you get the idea.

Your newsletter should be welcomed by the recipients and even looked forward to because it is of genuine interest. It is also the perfect medium to build interest and develop a campaign. The development of a client registration scheme (see above) over the course of three issues of your newsletter is an excellent illustration of this.

While your copy style should be light and friendly, it is important, as noted above, that the content is informative and topical. You should never allow the newsletter to become mere advertising 'puff'. This is doubly important when considering the next point.

We have proposed that your 'private clients' newsletter should be sent to commercial clients with a covering letter. This also applies to all members of your professional contacts register. Again, the newsletter should be sent out from the fee earner who is closest to this professional contact, with a covering letter along the lines of:

> This newsletter is primarily written for our private clients, but we thought you might be interested, particularly in the article on page 3 . . .

The principle is to draw the professional contact's eye to relevant articles. These are articles that deal with their area of activity and expertise, for example, an article about conveyancing when the newsletter is sent to estate agents; about inheritance tax planning when sent to accountants, about personal injury compensation when sent to a section of the medical profession.

If a series of newsletters is planned in detail far enough ahead, you can ensure that a relevant article appears in rotation for each departmental section of the professional contacts register. Of course, you do have to be careful. It is perfectly in order to send articles relating to probate to local care home owners, but a little insensitive to send them to the residents.

There is also opportunity for the firm to link, through the newsletter, other promotional activity. If the 'blackmail budget' has been used with the local rugby club, why not include a small article about your support for local sport, perhaps with a replication of the ad from their fixtures list which would, of course, also promote your website within the newsletter.

It is likely that the marketing partner will take responsibility as both production manager and senior editor of your newsletter. However, as with much relating to promotion, it is a departmental matter, and should not be left solely to the marketing partner. The marketing partner should create the overall template for the newsletter, then invite departmental heads and through them, the fee earners, to submit ideas for articles and other material.

The shoebox

Many years ago, when working for a client on their newsletter, the client walked in to the office one Monday, clutching a large box that had contained some shoes he had purchased over the weekend. He gathered his staff together very briefly and said, 'In one month's time, I want this filled with ideas for articles, newspaper cuttings, ideas from magazines and comments relating to our newsletter.' This was exactly what happened (although the large box was only half filled), and for the next five years, we introduced the idea of 'the shoebox' to each of our clients when beginning the process of a series of newsletters.

Now we introduce it to you.

Of course, today, there are email shoeboxes, but newspaper cuttings, magazine articles, together with reports of exam results, births and just simple ideas from throughout the firm, added to the basic material available from the website and the literature kit, will ensure that you are never short of raw material for your next three newsletters.

The copywriter

Copywriting is a skill. It needs to be informative, but not dry; friendly, but not over-familiar; relevant, without being boring; consistent without being repetitive. Lawyers are used to working with words, but not always friendly ones. Perhaps you are aware of somebody within your organisation who has copywriting skills; possibly the skills and interests audit (see **Chapter 2**) may elicit this. If not, do not be afraid of employing the services of an outsourced copywriter. Again, your printer will probably be able to point you in the right direction; an advertising agency certainly will.

If an outside resource is to be used, then the logic is to involve them early in the process and have their input in the overall design and style of your literature kit, website and, ultimately, the newsletter. But, if this has not already been considered, the employment of a copywriter and graphic designer for the newsletter is certainly worth consideration and may in the end save a great deal of time. However, please, please, avoid purchasing a standard, mass-produced newsletter.

A professional copywriter and/or graphic designer will recognise that legal jargon and complicated lawyers' sentences are totally irrelevant to a newsletter. They will inherently understand that the newsletter must explain to the reader the benefits they derive, and if that is not the case, either do not employ this copywriter or brief them strictly. One of the advantages of employing an outside copywriter is that they are not so immersed in legal ethos and jargon that they will consider it the norm. They will be outside your way of thinking, and should produce copy that your clients will understand and approve.

While it is important that your outsourced copywriter or graphic designer understand the ethos of your firm, it is also important to allow them a free rein to use their skills. It is not only a matter of jargon. A good designer will know how to lay out the newsletter in an inviting way; how to use pictures, illustrations and graphics; and the value of 'white space'. Font size and typeface are important, but readability is vital. The designer will choose when to use a summary, bullet points, a shaded highlight box or indentation. As already stated, your newsletter really has to be full colour these days to be taken seriously, but a good designer will know how best to use the shading and subtleties that can be achieved with modern technology.

There is a great value in using what appear to be 'advertisements' in your own newsletter. We, the public, are used to seeing advertisements in newsprint and frequently look at the advertisements first. Therefore, if you don't want to go into great detail, but wish to highlight the activities of the commercial client department, lay out their menu of services as an advertisement and include it on page 2 or 3 of your newsletter. (As a general rule, a newsletter should be gloss paper, colour on A3 folded once to produce a four-sided A4. Therefore, your commercial client advertisement will appear on page 2 or 3.)

In the legal profession you are used to looking at long tracks of print. Most clients are not. The average length of an article should be 150 words. There is place for a longer article, say 300 words, promoting some specific service or dealing with some topical event, but it is unlikely that anything beyond that will fit in a newsletter. A detailed matter requiring more than 400 words is probably better the subject of a separate mailing to a much more targeted audience, and possibly a candidate for a new insert in your literature kit.

Your newsletter on the web

Of course, the majority of your newsletters will be distributed via the post. Some of our clients have overprinted their newsletter envelope to announce, in advance, what is inside. This certainly has a value once the quality and relevance of the material contained in the newsletter has been established. However, it would be sad if an overprinted envelope caused your newsletter to be discarded without even a cursory glance.

Many of our clients have included the local media, local newspapers, radio and in one very successful example, local TV in their newsletter mailings. Again, these should each have a covering letter. After a while a mailing might lead to an invitation to write a regular article or make an occasional comment.

Your website is another way of delivering the newsletter, via PDF. Visitors to your website should be encouraged to download the latest newsletter, and should automatically receive with that details of the content of earlier ones, with an invitation to download those that are relevant to them. As with all downloading, you should ensure that this is monitored, so that it can be followed up. In turn, the newsletter should encourage a viewing of the website, which will reinforce the proposal in the newsletter that the reader should make contact with your firm.

And so we come full circle. Websites have been with us for less than 15 years. Newsletters, at least in the form of pamphlets, have been around for hundreds of years. They both have their place today. They are complementary, they are interlinking and they provide the pincer movement that will be necessary for your firm to overcome The New Competition.

CHAPTER 11 TASKS **Introduce a client registration scheme**

IT and management assessment

Given the details of the questionnaire, you will need to assess what changes are required within your IT system to record and make available the information, when required, by a fee earner. Most legal IT systems will be able to record the information with some changes to the systems interface. Check with your IT systems manager and the systems vendor to assess how much change is required, and how long it will take to implement.

Fee earners and support staff:

- Are fee earners and staff confident to recommend the services of another department?
- Do fee earners and staff have service details to hand?
- Does the IT system provide simple access to the client's information if they call in?

A client registration scheme is about excellence of service to clients, and therefore all partners and staff need to be aware, trained and ready to provide that level of service. Discuss how you will implement this with department heads, the staff and training partner or manager. Assess what training or changes need to occur and how long those will take to implement.

Registered client benefits of membership

Review the list of items and services ('Delivery of benefits', above) to highlight as part of the membership. Your firm may have additional specific services you wish to add.

Literature kit insert

Once you have decided on the initial make-up of the scheme, draft a literature kit insert that explains and introduces the registration scheme under the name you choose. Use the production of that insert as the definition of the service and ensure that all the internal resources are in place to fulfil the clients' expectations.

Name of scheme

Where you choose to have a client registration scheme based on a particular service, you can use that as part of the name. However, don't let that restrict the scheme remit. Avoid a name that indicates discounts on fees. Similarly, avoid anything too grand (privilege, first class, premier, gold) as these may raise the expectations of some clients further than the service will deliver.

Stationery

Several well-known suppliers of paper and office products have 'membership card' stationery available that can be used with A4 office printers to produce registration cards.

Newsletters

Your firm may already be using a newsletter in your firm. Use that as the basis for development and expand the use to other client groups identified as your target markets.

General or specific newsletter ideas for each edition:

- Issue 1
- Issue 2
- Issue 3
- Issue 4
- Issue 5
- Issue 6

General or market-specific newsletters:

- How often should the newsletter be produced?
- Which target clients is it primarily aimed at?
- Who else might be interested in the newsletter?
- Who will produce the articles?
- Which graphic designer and printer should we use?
- What size will the newsletter be?
  - A4
  - A3
  - Folded how?
  - Number of pages?
  - What type of binding?
- What style?
  - Newspaper style
  - Letter style
  - Brochure style

- How will the newsletter be distributed?
  - Post
  - DX
  - Email
  - By hand

With the development and introduction of a client registration scheme along with its attendant promotional activity, the firm will be in a far stronger position to face The New Competition and fulfil its growth aspirations.

While a registration scheme is not the only solution, it is a pivotal part of an attitudinal change which, if maintained, will greatly strengthen your firm's position in the new marketplace by increasing client loyalty, cross-selling and the gaining of recommendations. It will also assist in making you a brand, as clearly understood as The New Competition, in your own, more limited market.

12

Advertising, press relations and other promotion

Early in this book we commented that a large number of solicitors believed that marketing was advertising and promotion. We hope we have established that marketing is far more than this – witness the fact that we have got to Chapter 12 of this book before discussing promotional activity in any detail.

However, in this chapter we begin to do just that. We define the promotional mix and look at promotional budgets. We discuss PR, in terms of both press relations and public promotion, and look at the variety of advertising media available from television to the classified section of your local press. We also discuss sales promotion, mailshots and leaflet drops, but most importantly, outline the process by which you can begin to develop a promotional plan for your practice.

> *The one great principle of the English law is to make business for itself.* – Charles Dickens

Lawyers, it would seem, have been getting bad press since at least Dickensian times. It is unlikely this will change, for the press know that presenting lawyers as greedy, preying on the unfortunate, or bumbling and inefficient strikes a chord (quite unfairly) with the public. It is this outrageous caricature that The New Competition will play on. That, and the perceived expense and inapproachability of the profession.

You cannot expect to change opinion nationally, however ill-founded that opinion is, but you can set out to demonstrate that you are the exception to this rule in your own area, and you must communicate that clearly to your clients.

We have already emphasised the need to define the benefits to the client of instructing your firm, and how to present these benefits through literature kits, your website, your newsletter and in personal meetings. Essentially, we have suggested that you should look first inside your firm, and develop regular communications with your existing client base and professional contacts, using this dialogue, at least in part, to present benefits.

In this chapter, we look at taking this same message further afield by presenting your benefits to a new audience. Of course, it is to be hoped that your client base and, equally important, your professional contacts register, will also see your promotional messages in other media, forming a pincer movement, proving that you, at least, are not tarred with that old Dickensian brush.

Along with 'marketing' itself, the terms associated with promotional activity are often misused, which can cause confusion. From the top down, marketing is a management process by which clients, competition and products are identified and understood by a business (Figure 12.1). From that position, the business can use horizontal and vertical expansion to develop its profitable markets. To communicate the benefits of using a firm's services, there is a need to publicise those benefits. It is at this point that you that start to look at advertising and PR as part of a coordinated promotional campaign that is integrated with the marketing plans. And not before.

The majority of promotional activities are defined below with illustrations of their meaning, use and the hierarchy in the promotional world (Figure 12.2).

'Public promotion', of course, includes advertising, which is usually defined as paid-for space in the media, i.e. newspapers and magazines, including trade or professional press together with directories (Yellow Pages, Thomson Local, The Phone Book, etc.); radio, local and national TV and the Internet (e.g. Google Adwords); plus anywhere else where you

Figure 12.1 The marketing process

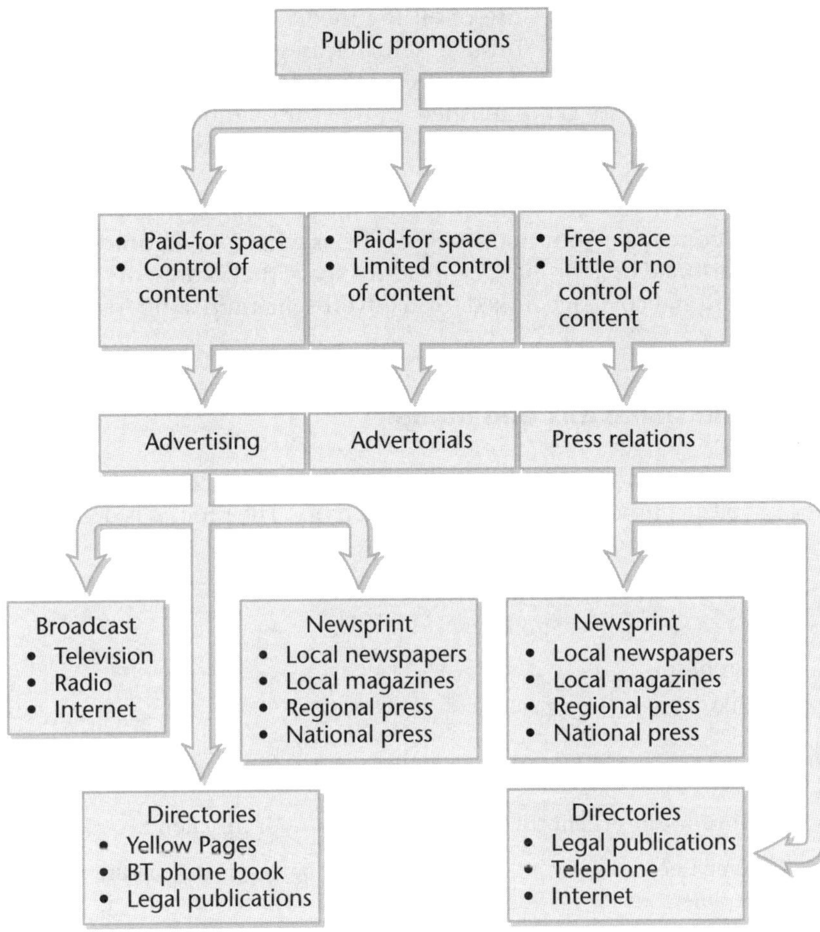

Figure 12.2 Hierarchy of promotional methods

can pay for space and define the content of your message – billboards, buses, blotters, beer mats (and that is just the 'Bs').

In fairness, blotters and beer mats would probably be considered as promotion despite carrying advertising, and rate alongside your literature kit, website and newsletter. Other forms of promotion include seminars, exhibitions, open days and, if not just a junket, client and professional contact entertaining.

But of all public promotion, the most important is personal selling. Indeed, it could be argued that every other form of promotion is geared primarily to getting a face-to-face meeting with a client, prospect or professional contact.

'Press relations' makes use of all the media listed under advertising, but seeks unpaid coverage through news releases. The word 'news release' is worth remembering. They are often referred to as 'press releases', but they are unlikely to get published if they are simply advertisements slightly disguised. They must contain news, and be newsworthy to stand even a chance of publication.

There is one grey area, which applies mostly to local media and trade press, which may be your main target. This is what is sometimes referred to as 'advertorial' or 'aditorial', i.e. paid-for space that is presented as a feature, or editorial coverage linked to an advertisement in a different part of the paper.

The promotional mix and budgets

Steven Silbiger in *The 10-Day MBA* (Piatkus, 2005) links the buying process to the purpose of a promotional activity. The process is defined as:

- Awareness
- Interest
- Trial
- Repurchase
- Loyalty

Already, we can see where many solicitors' firms fall down.

> 'Trial? How can a client try us? They either use us or they don't.'
>
> 'Repurchase? You mean update their will, or buy their next house in seven years' time?'
>
> 'Loyalty? Why that's long gone!'

But if you look at the relationship with the client as being more than a single transaction, if you think in terms of the firm and not just the division or department, if you treat your promotional and selling activity as having the overall objective of developing a long-term relationship with the client, it becomes clearer how this almost alien process applies to your firm.

In addition, when thinking about the five-stage process, it is worth considering the different roles or strengths of promotional tools in the marketing mix. For example, advertising is a powerful tool to create awareness, public relations can foster a better understanding, while sponsorship-based customer events can help create loyalty.

Before embarking on any promotional campaign, it is worth revisiting the theory outlined in **Chapter 5**, and then undertaking a brief review of your current activity and aspirations (see the 'External promotions audit', below, and on the CD-Rom).

Table 12.1 The buying process

BUYING PROCESS	Activity
Awareness	Inform about product, and present a message that prompts a need in the prospect
Interest	Provide a compelling message that provides a solution or resolution to that client need
Trial	Motivate action
Repurchase	Cue to buy – instruct a solicitor – or increased usage of the firm
Loyalty	Reinforce your brand or image, perhaps via special promotions (such as a Client Registration Scheme)

How you plan to retain or underpin your existing client base, target new prospects, cement your relationships with your professional contacts, project your firm and present or promote your various products, and ultimately persuade potential clients to purchase or repurchase from your product range, are the questions that need considering now that we have arrived at the promotional aspect of marketing.

Most of the traditional constraints that were imposed on the profession have been removed, which is a crucial factor when considering The New Competition. The promotional mix of advertising, publicity, sales promotion and personal selling has to be considered on a corporate as well as market level. The overall corporate image exists as a direct consequence of the composition of the corporate promotional mix. The different markets and market segments in which your firm has chosen to compete will require different mixes. What is appropriate for one market segment may not be so for another. The promotional effort required by one product may differ from that required for others during the same time period. All promotional efforts, however different, should be consistent with your firm's chosen desired corporate image and desired competitive edge.

It is a crucial responsibility of the marketing partner to coordinate all the promotional activity to see that it is consistent, and to ensure that the activity of one department does not impinge on or damage the image of another. No doubt you know what promotional activity is going on within your firm, but perhaps a formal audit is worthwhile. In undertaking a promotional audit, you need to consider what activity is being undertaken now, in what form, and who is doing it. Both the audit and indeed, your aspirations need to be looked at from the following points of view:

- the overall firm ('corporate' view);
- the department;
- the individual product and/or its market;
- the individual fee earner.

In the context of departmentalisation, the individual fee earner's activity may seem irrelevant. It is not always so, for several different reasons:

- Some people are good at, and enjoy, promotion and selling – others do not.
- Even today, some solicitors consider that their part of this activity is performed for their clients, and view the firm, in some ways, as a loose collection of sole practitioners. There are cases when solicitors just don't want to share their hard-won client base.
- On a more positive note, there are firms where some practitioners feel that if the firm isn't going to do any promotion itself, then they, the fee earner, jolly well will.
- Add to this the fact that if a promotional opportunity arises, for example, a special feature in a newspaper, it is likely to be passed to, and therefore decided upon and handled by, the department.

As with the majority of lists and questionnaires in this book, there is no intention to suggest that the following is exhaustive. It clearly is not, and is intended only to be indicative. The starting point, therefore, is to review the list, and add to it anything that you feel is relevant to your own individual firm. Many of the questions below will have been addressed in previous chapters, and a review of the work done will provide many of the answers. However, this audit is intended to focus your view on external promotions.

External promotions audit

1. What image does the firm present to its clients?
2. What image would you like it to present?
3. How does the firm currently promote itself and its products?
4. What is the composition of the current promotional mix?
5. What budget has been allocated for the current financial year? (See 'Budgets' below.)
6. How has the firm traditionally promoted its products to existing clients?
7. How has the firm traditionally promoted its products to new clients?
8. For each product that the firm is currently offering or intends to offer in the future, what is the relative importance of each of the elements of the promotion mix (advertising, publicity, sales promotion, personal selling)?
9. Should the firm advertise?
10. If so, what should it advertise?
11. How should it advertise?
12. Which media should it use?

13. Should cooperation be considered with other legal firms for the purposes of advertising?
14. Should cooperation be considered with non-legal firms for the purposes of advertising?
15. How much, if anything, should be spent on paid advertising space?
16. How important is personal selling in the firm's chosen markets/ segments?
17. Who are the people most capable of personal selling?
18. What steps should be taken to support these people and reward them?
19. What steps should be taken to improve the performance of other people?
20. What steps should be taken to improve the overall capability of the firm in the field of personal selling?
21. How important is publicity for the corporate image?
22. How important is publicity to the individual products?
23. What is the real cost of publicity likely to be?
24. What, if any, sales promotional activity should be evaluated/pursued?
25. Which products/markets would benefit from investment in sales or promotional activities?
26. How can the degree of client loyalty be improved?
27. How can you sell more products to existing clients?
28. How can you reach new clients and prospects?
29. How can you best use your professional contacts register?
30. How can you measure the results of time and money invested in promotion?

In a book like this, these questions can only be general. With most of them you can drill down to discover more detail, and undoubtedly there are other questions that relate to your individual firm.

Budgets

One of the main purposes of undertaking an audit is first to ascertain what the firm is currently doing, and second, to decide what it wants to do.

The review of current activity should provide an indication of expenditure currently being deployed. However, we frequently find that a proportion of marketing expenditure is hidden in overall print costs, perhaps linked with stationery, in undefined or unspecified 'client support' or entertaining and various other activities. It is worthwhile pulling together a true picture, and also realising that in the light of The New Competition, this expenditure is almost certainly going to have to increase over the next two to three years.

Recent research on marketing spending by law firms indicated a very low proportion of turnover to marketing spend ratio. While there is no perfect ratio and the ideal ratio will vary from firm to firm, it is worth noting that a recent LawNet survey suggested that 3 per cent of billing would be an appropriate budget. Our experience is that, historically, firms have spent 1 per cent or even less on their promotional activity. In the future, this really is not going to be enough.

Obviously, every activity that you propose will have a cost, and this, by simple addition, can be developed into the first stage of a promotional budget. However, all promotional activity should also have a pre-declared objective, and only by clearly defining this objective and measuring it against the expenditure on that particular activity can you assess whether or not it has been a success.

It is important, however, to remember that most customer/client buying decisions or actions taken are, in fact, the result not of one single promotional activity but of the cumulative effect of a great many. Success comes with a well thought-out, integrated campaign,

Your website may be visited by someone who has heard your name from a previously satisfied client. Having liked what they see, they then enquire for more information and are impressed with your literature kit. They are busy people and nothing happens until they see an article about you in the local paper that stimulates a telephone call. They are impressed by your well-trained and friendly receptionist and the speed at which an appointment can be made. They even like the letterhead and the tone of the letter confirming their appointment. And, regrettably, at any stage, a failure of one of these – or any other – components can make that prospect lose interest.

Lord Leverhulme, the founder of consumer goods giant Unilever, once famously said: 'Half the money I spend on advertising is wasted, and the problem is I do not know which half.' That is a lesson worth remembering when setting budgets.

Public promotion

Advertising

The most obvious form of public promotion is advertising, so let us deal with that first. We hope that, by now, the difference between marketing and promotion is clear.

As you might have gathered from Lord Leverhulme's remark above, publicity, and especially advertising, is very hard to measure in isolation from other promotional activities. In the opinion of the writers, advertising in the general or corporate sense is seldom appropriate for the promotion of a legal practice, although it can be very beneficial when used to promote a specific product to a clearly defined target market, and we give examples below. General advertising, other than in directories, is too scattershot.

People only need solicitors occasionally, and cannot be persuaded by advertising to produce a suddenly derived need. Therefore, your advertising will talk mostly to people who can't use you.

It is only comparatively recently that the legal profession has been allowed to advertise at all, and it is little wonder that it is viewed with some doubt, given some of the examples. These have varied from advertisements that are so bland as to be pointless, to those so aggressive that they are actually offensive. Personal 'knocking copy', as it is known, has no place in the promotion of the legal profession in England and Wales.

Any advertising needs to be, first, legal, decent, honest and truthful, and second, appropriate, recognised as valuable by the target audience and enhancing of the firm's overall image. Ideally, wherever possible, you should have some method of monitoring and measuring the responses, but it must always be recognised that it is only, and can only ever be, a part of the overall promotional mix.

Fairly obviously, good advertisements need to capture the reader's attention from among all the other material in front of them. You will notice that good advertisements are visually exciting because readers will scan pages, particularly in newspapers, to decide what they will read. The attention grabber can be in a graphic, a photograph, a headline or the copy. But there must be an outstanding demand, to be read. Tasteful, dignified advertisements may lack danger, but they are also probably very dull and if so, they are ineffective.

As noted above, the printed media in particular is really only suited to the promotion of products to a specific target market. May we add a gentle reminder that any advertisement, and indeed any promotion, must present and explain benefits and not the procedures or features of your service. Effective advertising will 'speak' to the reader. This can be assisted by the use of 'you/your' frequently.

Why advertise?

Apart from taking many varied forms, advertising is also undertaken for varying reasons. It must seem obvious, but it is important to decide, before you start, exactly why you are advertising, what your objectives are and what your desired results are. The fact that we need to make such an obvious statement should indicate that we have come across many examples where advertising 'seemed like a good idea', was exceptionally well sold by the publication, or was part of an overall package produced by an advertising agency, but was, at best, completely ineffectual. Therefore, to avoid falling into the same trap, decide what you are trying to achieve in advance, and avoid, if at all possible, statements such as 'a bit of flag waving', 'lifting our profile a bit'. One of our clients thought we were being rather rude when suggesting that they should try setting fire to the building to achieve these objectives. After he calmed down a bit, he started quantifying what he was really trying to achieve and, as a result, spent a smaller budget in better targeted media to satisfactory effect – and no risk to life and limb.

Going beyond 'flag waving', advertising can be used to create or perhaps even slightly change the image of your firm. An example would be the advertising of commercial services by a firm that is predominantly a private client operation. Remember that it is very seldom that advertising should stand on its own. It should, almost always, be part of a promotional mix, and part of an overall campaign.

The truth is, however, that you are unlikely to be able to use advertising alone to change your image. It may be a component part in an overall campaign to realign or improve your image, but that is the best that can be expected of general or corporate advertising (as opposed to product advertising). Your firm will already have an ethos, a profile and an image, most probably developed over many decades. A sudden change will be neither accepted nor even understood. More important is to ensure that the 'personality' of your firm matches the 'personality' of your clients, prospects and professional contacts. With thought and the application of the analysis advised in the earlier part of this book, you will know what your firm is, and must ensure that your advertising truthfully reflects that.

Another major reason for advertising is to generate enquiries from a specific group of prospects or clients. You may wish to promote your firm's ability to handle a particularly topical legal issue. A class action for compensation from a particular industry sector would be an example.

In **Chapter 13**, we look at some specific campaigns and consider further your firm's stance. An important part of this 'stance' is the type of person your firm, or more probably a department of it, wants to communicate with. The media, and indeed the whole promotional activity, will be different if you are seeking, for example, privately funded matrimonial work as opposed to publicly funded. If you are seeking to promote immigration services, it may well benefit you to seek out foreign language newspapers, and advertise in those languages. Target the right audience.

You may consider professional assistance in this area and if you have a diverse or niche product offer this could be advisable. As an indication of the array of media available in England and Wales, click on **www.brad.co.uk** – the website of publishing specialist BRAD Insight. It contains details of the 13,500 publications you can buy advertising space in, and this alone illustrates how easy it is to make an expensive mistake.

Looking at rate cards can be quite daunting at first. Make sure with printed media that you understand the difference between circulation and readership. For example, some magazines are read by just one person, others by an entire family or office. It is possible to compare different media by looking at the 'cost per thousand' – the cost of reaching 1,000 people. The lower the cost, the more efficient the paper or magazine is at reaching your audience.

Advertising can assist in maintaining brand loyalty. In *Creating Value* (2001) S. S. Mathur and A. Kenyon use Harley Davidson as an example. In the 1970s, Harley Davidson and BSA Motorcycles managed to retain their social status long after they had been technologically overtaken by Japanese rivals. One explanation for such a lasting competitive advantage was that early customers formed a commitment to the brand and were encouraged, at least in part by promotional activity, to stick with it.

This may be more relevant to your firm than is immediately obvious. We are not suggesting that The New Competition will be more professionally able than the legal profession – far from it. Quite the reverse in fact. But The New Competition will use a lot of innovative means to persuade the uncommitted away from traditional providers of legal services.

However, with a little effort, your firm could produce an argument as mighty as any Harley Davidson for people to stay with the provider they and, indeed, their families before them, have known and trusted. There are some people you certainly will lose to The New Competition; conversely there are others who would never consider going anywhere other than to a solicitors' practice when the need for their services arises. But the battle will be fought in the middle ground, where your clients need reminding that they are better off with an established, reliable supplier rather than the new branded service providers, for all their high revs and flashing lights. Or, in this case, continuously promoted, price point services, presented as good value, easy to access and to use, help yourself websites and call centres available 12–18 hours per day.

It is important, therefore, to remember that promotion does not only draw attention to the existence of your firm and what it is offering; it should also seek to influence the way your firm is perceived by clients, prospects and professional contacts with regard to its image and its positioning.

Therefore, all promotion, including advertising, has two distinct strategic purposes. First, to draw attention to a new offering. Second, to direct the shaping of clients' perception and preferences.

And don't forget that one of the most successful motorcycle advertisements in history was right in the middle of California, which one would have suspected was 'owned' by Harley Davidson. It simply said:

> You meet the nicest people on a Honda.

Brands and branding

Many marketing manuals will talk about using advertising to enhance 'branding'. It is worth reiterating that whereas these manuals are, of course, talking about national advertising and 'big brands', your own objective is likely to be the establishment of your firm's name as a 'brand' within your own immediate geographical area. Within that constraint, all the efforts in establishing what the brand means, the brand values, the image and accessibility are precisely the same. Only the cost is different because where bought media is used, it will, except on very rare occasions, be local media.

Part of what we are trying to achieve with your 'brand' is the reassurance for your clients that they have made the correct purchasing decision, the advertising of 'added values' to prospects, and the desire to be associated with your firm by your professional contacts.

The New Competition will be made up of a number of businesses that already have a substantial brand image. Effectively, what they will be doing is little different from the reaction of retailers to manufacturers when retail price maintenance was abolished in the UK. First, they are likely to stimulate demand by cutting the price of their services at the expense of margin, but in the knowledge that they can sustain a low profit scenario far easier than the traditional supplier of legal services. But they may not have to for long. For they are also concentrating demand by creating larger and larger units of production that should give them economies of scale. Finally, just like the supermarkets all those years ago, they are differentiating demand by creating Tesco Legal, Halifax Legal Solutions, etc. By doing that, they are effectively producing another subset of their own brand that will enable them to compete with traditional suppliers on more than just price alone.

Buy one get one free?

Although it is unlikely that The New Competition will employ the 'BOGOF' approach to sales promotion (buy one get one free), there is every likelihood and some evidence already that they will use various forms of sales promotion. The limited time discount offer is not unusual, even within the legal profession where autumn will writing initiatives have effectively promoted wills and probate for many years. However, they are likely to be used with much more power and, frankly, forethought, than before. While not strictly BOGOF, we are likely to see the advent of 'buy one product and get a discount on another'. This already exists in some areas – the obvious one being legal expenses insurance tagged on to car insurance. Conveyancing with will writing seems likely and LPAs with wills another possibility. There is then the option of a base price plus optional extras: a basic (and highly advertised) low price for conveyancing with add-on charges for other needs, e.g. a mortgage, the redemption of an old mortgage, a leasehold agreement, a flying freehold agreement.

Strangely, this approach is more logical than it seems. An example from our own experience is a firm on the south coast where many of the large regency buildings had been turned into small flats. The result was that the actual purchase price of the flat was very low, but the annual maintenance charges very high, and the title deeds extraordinarily complicated involving, as they did frequently, covenants, unusual obligations, liaison with management companies and numerous penalty clauses for failing to comply. As a result, an enormous amount of work was done, for very little reward, because 'the type of people who buy this property can't afford to pay big fees'. The question really should have been: can the firm afford this type of work? You may be certain that without an 'optional extras list' this type of work is very unlikely to attract The New Competition.

But there seems to be little difference between the normal offer of 'free fitting' when you purchase a carpet in this month's sale, and a free conveyance if you purchase your mortgage through The New Competition. The New Competition already has dedicated teams thinking up promotions, advertising and special offers. They are well practised at tactical deployment of promotion as the need arises, are extremely well funded and, most importantly, have massive databases through which they will have access to at least part of your client base.

So let us now look at how advertising can help us overcome The New Competition. As with so much else, the key to using public promotion successfully is targeting. Although we start with the use of newspaper advertising, we would reiterate that this is extremely unlikely to have value in establishing an image or developing your corporate promotion. We are therefore looking purely at product promotion through advertising.

Newspapers

National

Very few solicitors have used national newspaper advertising. A few firms tried it some years ago with highly discounted 'bucket shop' conveyancing and, more recently, for PI compensation. On the whole, such campaigns have not been a resounding success because the available advertising spend was too small to create the impact that was necessary to sustain it, and the back-up service. The exception has been class actions (asbestosis, etc.) and highly targeted legal services through the business sections of the broadsheet newspapers.

Generally speaking, national newspapers are far too expensive for the average legal practice to consider.

Regional

Many national newspapers produce regional editions, which can provide an apparent national presence at a lower cost than a true national advertisement. However, even this would be very expensive and, like the national editions, the regional offspring are very short lived – daily in most cases, weekly in a few – and have a very widespread readership, even when that readership has been demographically segmented and defined.

It is important to remember that the instructing of a solicitor is a derived need. People do not want to buy solicitors' time, they want to move house, make a will, get divorced, etc. Therefore, their desire to purchase from you is subservient to some other action and is, at best, infrequent.

So, as they are expensive, too scattershot, in terms of both readership and the frequency of likely interest, it is probably best to avoid even the regional editions of national newspapers.

Local

Now this is a different matter. There are many reasons to cultivate the local press, and the purchasing of advertising space can obviously assist in that. Ideally, as noted above, all newspaper and magazine advertising should be for the product not the firm. But if there is an image enhancement role, it can be best executed by local press. First, it is likely to be produced weekly. Second, you are likely to be able to buy a specific space within the paper on a regular basis, through which readers will know where to find your details when the need for a solicitor arises. Local advertising can be used in addition to product promotion, to draw attention to events, seminars and other promotional activities. It can also be linked with editorial and 'advertorial' and may well have a part to play in your promotional mix. One of the problems with local papers is their distribution area. Depending upon your own location, you may find the need for a presence in more than one publication, as it is unlikely that one publication will cover your declared geographical area. The various options available to you are easy to investigate and, indeed, to review over a period of time. The media you select must obviously enhance the profile of your firm and you need to be sure that the readership is predominantly the type of people you are seeking to attract to the practice.

Free press

A number of local papers will be hand-delivered 'freebies'. Historically, these have had a very downmarket image, and the general impression within the legal profession was that unless you were promoting publicly funded work, they were best avoided. This now seems a somewhat harsh criticism. Of course, it does depend on the style of the publication and its circulation area, but, if it is local to you, it is likely to be read by people who are also local to you including, potentially, your clients, prospects and professional contacts.

Local press tends to be very full and perhaps somewhat 'cluttered'. Remember the two key pieces of advice are:

1. Make your advertisement visually attractive with the prime objective being to persuade the glancer to read it.
2. Buy a consistent spot in the newspaper, rather than what is called 'run of paper' (ROP), where your ad may appear anywhere in the publication.

In this way, local and free press can become, in effect, another directory, where prospects look up your details, when they have decided to use you.

Magazines

National

Any visit to the local library or newsagent will illustrate the astounding number of magazines available, on practically any subject or interest.

In many ways, this can make magazine advertising more attractive than newspaper advertising to the legal profession. Generally speaking, magazines have a much longer life than either daily or weekly newspapers. As a result, they are seen by far more people than buy them, and frequently lead to discussion between the purchaser and other people. Second, they are, by definition, specific interest publications, which mean if you are setting out to advertise a particular service to a specific segment of the population that can be defined by an interest, there is almost certainly a magazine to cover it.

In **Chapter 2** – the skills and interest audit – we mentioned the discovery in an audit of a solicitor with nationally recognised sporting achievements, and the success this conveyancing solicitor had by targeting people with a similar interest to his own. This campaign combined direct mail to clubs and other sporting venues, with advertising in the low-circulation, high readership, monthly magazine devoted to that sport.

The problem is, of course, that such magazines are, almost without exception, national, and decisions have to be made (before placing advertisements) about how you would service enquiries on a national basis.

Regional

Regional magazines usually cover a geographical territory that extends beyond a town, city or county. They are usually stand-alone publications, and are not, like newspapers, regional editions.

Local

As with local newspapers, local magazines can offer a well-targeted audience. Of these, the 'county' colour magazine has proved particularly successful for products such as 'upmarket' conveyancing, last-time conveyancing, inheritance tax planning and divorce.

Trade and special interest

'Trade' publications are directed (usually nationally) at specific interest groups either involved in a trade, or for people interested in that subject. There are your own profession's publications, such as the Law Society's *Gazette* and *The Lawyer*, and other professional and business titles like the *Estates Gazette* and *The Lancet*. In addition (see BRAD) many hundreds of magazines cover all aspects of business and trade and, in most cases, there will be two or three to choose from in each market. It seems unlikely that you would wish to advertise your services in the professional press; however, these magazines do have a part to play in press relations (see below).

However, the trade publications of your commercial clients are a different matter. It is almost certain that your clients and other members of that industry will at least skim-read these publications on a regular basis. The best examples of these types of publications are actually considered vital to the industry in maintaining contact with developments and news within it. They can be of particular importance and relevance to commercial practices wishing to develop a niche market centred upon clients in an industry that they are already serving. Obviously, one must avoid a conflict of interest or confidentiality, but the national coverage of these magazines makes that more manageable.

A good example, and one to emulate, is Marketlaw's own advertising. We provide consultancy services nationally, but only to the legal profession. Our main promotion is direct mail and seminars, backed up by advertising in the *Gazette* and other professional press.

Types of advertisement

The type of advertisement accepted will, of course, depend upon the make-up and printing process of the chosen publication, and publications use a variety of labels for the paid-for space. Generally, they can be divided as follows:

1. Display advertisements
2. Lineage and classified

Within those types you will also need to consider:

- Colour
- Dedicated sections
- Directories

Display advertisements

These are full-page or part-page advertisements that are part of the main body of the publication alongside the editorial section. As we said earlier, if you buy a consistent spot, rather than ROP, you can define the position on the page (and in most cases even the page) where your advertisement will appear. It is usually worth paying the extra. The advertisement should include colour, as a black and white advertisement often looks out of place.

Lineage and classified

Lineage and classified ads are by far the cheapest form of viable advertising in either newspapers or magazines. It is not usual for a solicitors' practice to do this sort of advertising, although it would be fair to say we have seen some success with lineage ads, for example, among property advertising, obviously promoting conveyancing services. Similarly, a lineage advertisement appearing regularly over a period of time headlined with 'Why pay the Chancellor of the Exchequer £100,000 more than you need to?' produced considerable success for one inheritance tax planning department.

Classified advertisements are most often associated with selling motor cars. However, one firm with a specialist in driving licence totting-up offences developed a very inexpensive and successful campaign by appearing every Saturday morning in the local paper's Cars for Sale classified advertisement section. Classified advertising is effectively linage style, with the ability to put in 'display' or 'semi-display' ad that include pictures, bold type or outline boxes in an attempt to make them stand out from the others. This should not be confused with display ad in the editorial section as defined above. The position of the ad within the classified section usually depends on the first line wording.

Colour

The numerous changes in printing techniques in recent years have made the use of colour, in the appropriate publication, very much easier and less expensive. The use of colour will obviously highlight any advertisement, assuming that it is not a full-page colour ad and even the use of spot colour – a single colour on a small part of the advertisement-can help highlight it.

Dedicated sections

Newspapers and magazine supplements dedicated to a particular subject have both a positive and a negative facet. They are, obviously, aimed specifically at a type of person within the publication's readership, and therefore you can be sure that you are targeting the right people for a specific product. However, a feature of this type will also attract your competition, both traditional and, potentially, The New Competition, which means that without care, your advertisement can appear of the 'me too' category. Space in these features is frequently offered at the last moment. Beware. You will not have time to produce a specific advertisement, and even if you are offered a discount, why should you want to fill a space that the salesman has failed to sell to one of your competitors?

This type of feature is planned long in advance. If you have been made an offer of space a few days before publication, you can be certain that the publication's prime targets have successively turned them down.

Directories

This is the one form of advertising that we believe is still essential to all legal practices despite the staggering growth of search engine use on the Internet. By directories, we mean Yellow Pages, Thomson Local, The Phone Book and, in some cases, even those laminated cardboard directories that are often given away with local papers, promoting local services. (If you do use the latter, try to ensure that you are the only local solicitors' practice on it.)

Of course, these directories have become increasingly irritating. But they can only get away with this because they are so successful and valuable. Yes, they do continually reduce the geographical coverage, forcing you into more than one directory, to cover your obvious geographical area. Yes, you find there are ever-increasing numbers of business categories so that, in addition to 'Solicitors', there are 10–15 other categories in which you could advertise your services. But the directories are where people go to get your contact details when they have decided to use you, or at the very least, to use a solicitor.

Many firms find, when they do an introduction analysis, that a disproportionate number of people come to them as a result of Yellow Pages. This is misleading. When they were asked 'Where did you hear of us?' they say 'Yellow Pages' because that is where they looked up your telephone number. In fact, as with so much promotion, it is usually a 'pincer movement'. A past satisfied client or a professional contact may have recommended you, which resulted in the search in Yellow Pages. They may work for one of your commercial clients with the same result. Or they may simply have walked past the beautiful new signage of your premises.

Certainly, some people, though a lesser number than generally suspected, will have thumbed through the directories and chosen you from the vast array available, but whatever the reason, you need your presence there, because that is where your prospective client is looking for you.

Your firm's website is an important element for directory listing. All the major directories have website search facilities and often include your firm in these for a small additional cost. People using them to look up a local solicitor's telephone contact details will often use the website links included in the listing. For the foreseeable future, notwithstanding the inroads of the Internet, directory advertising must have the first bite of your advertising (not to be confused with promotional) budget.

Professional directories may also have a place in your advertising budget where you have a specific specialisation worth national or international promotion. Legal 500 and similar legal listings can be useful for developing professional contacts or attracting new employees, but you should be aware that this type of publication is used by your competitors. A large and detailed listing may flatter your firm, but the costs of such are more useful when spent on attracting clients.

The 'blackmail budget'

This is also related to the purchase of space, usually in printed media.

You may remember the term 'blackmail budget' from **Chapter 9**. We use the rather unflattering term 'blackmail' because it is media that is usually bought at the behest of a friend, a client or a professional contact. The space is purchased, not because there is any real or measurable chance of gaining meaningful additional business, but because to say 'no' would cause embarrassment or potentially damage the relationship with an important client or contact.

As we advised, the most sensible use of this space is to encourage people to your website, by simply including in the advertisement your name, the fact that you are a solicitor, your website address as large as possible and your telephone number smaller. The same principle could apply if you were persuaded to take a pitch-side advertisement at a football club, or put up a banner at the village fête.

To be more positive for a moment, the use of the blackmail budget will almost certainly be in your core geographical area. Therefore, within that area, the exposure of your brand is no bad thing. It will, at least, demonstrate that you are active in, and care about, the community and this impression can be enhanced by reference to the sponsorship or support of local activities in local newspaper press releases, and importantly, in your own newsletter (see **Chapter 13** for the example of sponsorship of the local under-10 football club).

Remember what Lord Leverhulme said, 'Half of my advertising . . .' etc. And the trick is to get as much as possible out of all your efforts, even the blackmail budget.

'Advertorials'/'Aditorials'

As mentioned above, advertorials are either advertisements in paid-for space that are set out to look like articles, or articles written about the firm or the subjects it is advertising linked to an advertisement, but in a different part of the paper.

This practice is covered by specific legislation, rules and codes of practice. For example, an advertisement set out to look like an article must have the word 'advertisement' at the top or the bottom of it. In some ways, this rather defeats the object. Better, by far, is to have a genuinely interesting article written by either your firm or the newspaper itself. The key to this is to ensure that the material is newsworthy per se and of interest to the publication's readers, and not just advertising 'puff'.

Another area worthy of consideration, simply because it is really used by the professions, is the type of column that could be entitled 'Wendy recommends you use . . .' or 'We survey the local providers of goods and services and recommend the following . . .'. If your 'brand' has sufficient impact in your geographical area, this type of unusual promotion, providing that it is product-led, can be surprisingly effective.

Billboards and posters

Again, if your brand image is strong enough within your own geographical area, these unusual forms of advertising, providing they are product-based, can be effective. They are likely to be part of a campaign that is being featured in other media at the same time, and must be clearly understood with a specific, easy 'call to action'.

Above all else, they must have a clear and unambiguous proposition such as 'Fixed price conveyancing', 'Ring us for a free half-hour interview', 'Need advice on divorce? Ring 01243 790632 FREE advice' and, of course, 'No win – no fee'.

Poster advertising can have considerable effect when displayed on the premises of a professional contact, especially if it ultimately leads to a conversation in which a recommendation to visit you can be made. The most obvious example of this is PI promotions in accident and emergency hospital waiting rooms, but poster advertising can also lead to matrimonial work if placed in Citizens Advice Bureaux or women's refuges, etc. As with many facets of advertising and promotion, it is probably best considered departmentally.

It is of paramount importance, however, to ensure that this type of advertising does not damage the image of other departments of the firm. The promotion of 'welfare services' rarely sits comfortably with a serious commercial firm.

On the buses

Transport advertising is really only another place to display billboards and posters. It does have the advantage of maintaining the reader's attention as they are stuck in a traffic jam behind a bus or sitting in a commuter train carriage. However, if this form of promotion is to be considered, all the advice relating to billboards and posters applies, with the additional consideration required about routes. There is little point in advertising on a train or bus if it is going to spend 90 per cent of its time outside your logical geographical catchment area.

Radio

Local radio can be difficult because the profile of the audience changes almost by the hour. The stations are also often unrelentingly cheerful and childish. But they do maintain an extraordinary degree of listener loyalty with items such as phone-ins concerning local or national issues creating a great deal of interest.

It is unlikely that commercial work will be attracted by local radio, but we have seen success with matrimonial, PI and some litigious matters. As with billboards, the advertisement needs specific offers and a clear call to action such as 'telephone us now'.

A client of ours in the Midlands ran a very successful campaign for their full range of legal services in Urdu, on the local Asian radio network. The key to their success was in defining and then supplying what their clients wanted, in this case, a professional who would listen to them in their own language. It is precisely the same principle as that applied in printed media by the firm employing the conveyancer who was a national sport champion. It is all a form of market segmentation and targeting that segment with a specific and appropriate message.

It is why the skills and interests audit (see **Chapter 2**) is important. It is why it is genuinely worthwhile looking at your client from the point of view of market segments and niches. It is why brainstorming all the benefits applicable to your firm is so worthwhile, and it is why marketing will be so important to you in the light of The New Competition.

Public relations

Public relations (PR) covers a wide-ranging number of specialist disciplines including media relations, customer communications, investor relations, government lobbying, staff communications and even the unnervingly titled 'Crisis PR'. Probably the most relevant aspect of PR for the high street practice is media or press relations.

Unlike advertising, this is the attempt to get unpaid editorial coverage in the local media. Properly done, it is a potentially valuable tool in the marketing mix but the ground rules of dealing with journalists need to be understood. Moreover, unlike advertising or 'advertorials' where the message is fully controlled by the advertiser, there is no certainty that either your press release will be used at all or, that if it is used, that the final story comes out the way you had hoped it would.

To avoid the pitfalls and disappointments you need to have some insight into how an editor or journalist works. First, you must appreciate that the typical local papers and magazines are deluged with press releases – hundreds a week. The main problem for the journalists is filtering through the junk, spam and general corporate 'puffs' to get to something worth reading.

That said, if you get media relations right, it could provide you with fantastic 'free' coverage that boosts your firm's profile, helps existing and potential clients understand what you do and gives staff a boost. Remember, people mostly buy newspapers and magazines to read the news, not look at the advertisements, so a story about your practice is more likely to be noticed than an expensive ad! It is also more likely to be believed as more credibility is given to impartial editorial.

Not only do relevant press releases create positive awareness, but they also stimulate invitations to provide information for other articles. By building confidence with the individual editors and journalists you will also be asked to comment on other stories that don't start from you. Your senior partner and head of department can become reliable 'pundits' on topical affairs once credibility has been established.

So it is well worth learning a few basics about writing a successful press release.

Some press release tips

Journalism is more an art than a science and you may well wish to employ a specialist (see **Chapter 13**). However, while there are some naturally more gifted writers than others, an effective press release can be written by most intelligent laymen with a little thought and practice. So whether you are writing the release or approving one someone else has written, put yourself in the busy editor's seat wading through the pile of releases he receives every day. There are key criteria he is looking for: relevance, timeliness, readability and presentation. Relevance to the publication and topicality is essential. The editor is thinking 'Are my readers interested in this?'

To do this you must learn to grab the attention of the editor or journalist (and ultimately that of the reader) quickly. Well-written news stories and press releases start by providing the essence of the story in a nutshell. The enduring press release mantra runs: Who? What? When? How? Where? Why? The headline and first paragraph should answer all of those questions. After this immediate summary of the story use the next three or four paragraphs to expand upon events and use one of those to include a quote from the relevant partner or spokesperson. This is an opportunity to convey the firm's wider vision and ambition.

Within four or five paragraphs you should be able to tell a full story. Keep the tone neutral and do not resort to corporate 'sales babble' – a press release is not an advertisement. End the piece clearly by saying where and from whom the journalist can get further information. Always date your release.

Traditionally, releases are typed with 1.5 or double spacing allowing the journalist to insert, edit and modify, although this is becoming less common with the use of email.

If you use email, which is very acceptable, do not use complex formatting. Clarity is king and the journalist wants the ability to cut and paste easily. There is no need to send an email with a separate word attachment though an attached jpeg is acceptable.

Finally, of course, make sure you send it to the right person (worth checking beforehand) and don't be afraid of following up with a courtesy call. Despite their reputation, most journalists (particularly local ones) do not eat solicitors for breakfast!

Sales promotions

Sales promotions are designed to complement and reinforce other promotional efforts, especially advertising. In the world of trade and commerce there are two types of promotion: those directed towards the consumer and those directed towards distribution channels. They are most often seen in the manufacturing of goods that are sold by retail outlets. The obvious examples are coupons, refunds, samples, premiums, or trade-directed sales promotions such as displays at point of purchase and dealer or employee incentives. In the professions these are unlikely to have much relevance, but closely linked to them are business gifts, and perhaps these are relevant.

As with retailing, there are two potential targets for this type of sales promotion – the client and the professional recommender. Business gifts are a multibillion pound industry and the variety of items that can be used in this way is almost limitless. However, generally, the profession will stay with the traditional gifts, namely calendars, diaries, pens, notepads and, surprisingly, T-shirts.

Let us start with those T-shirts.

It seems an extremely unlikely gift for a solicitor to consider. Our experience, however, is completely the opposite. Several client firms have taken part in such events as charity runs, charity bicycle rides and even the climbing of notable mountains. One of our clients trekked across a desert and another took part in a round-the-world yacht race.

Every one of these clients used the event to gain publicity through press releases, their own newsletter, their website, and as all of these are enhanced by photographs, produced special promotional T-shirts. The twist (one well worth considering) is that they also produced replica shirts that they gave away to clients or professional contacts. For example, the partner who sailed the world was a conveyancer. More than 100 estate agents received T-shirts with the firm's logo and that of the round-the-world race on them. They were accompanied by an invitation to view progress on a dedicated section of the firm's website. A breast cancer charity was supported by the matrimonial department of a client firm, and every member of the Citizens Advice Bureaux and other organisations received replicas of their T-shirt. The same applies for most of the other events noted above.

The aim must always be to try and gain that little advantage from what you are doing – that little bit extra attention. For example, why not an 18-month calendar and send them out in June? (How many calendars do you throw away in November and December?) Or produce your own calendar.

A client of ours sponsored a local children's hospice by running a competition in the local press inviting children to draw a 'Christmas scene'. There were three prize winners and nine runners up. Each received a prize, and a written judgement from a celebrity artist. The overall winner was used as the firm's Christmas card and all 12 chosen pictures were used for the firm's calendar. The publicity that was received was priceless and the value of the exercise to the hospice enormous. From a marketing perspective, this was a perfect example of an integrated campaign.

Mailshots and leaflet drops

In keeping with the principles of using different methods of promotion collectively and 'telling them what you are going to tell them; telling them; and telling them what you have told them', it is worth considering other uses for the material you have created during the production of your literature kit. We have already seen how copy, graphics and photographs from the literature kit can be used on your website and in your newsletter. As an aside, the material can also be used with minor alteration in press releases, advertising and other public promotions. But here we are concerned with mailshots and leaflet drops. What is the difference?

- A mailshot, or direct mail, is when the postal service is used to distribute promotional material about a specific product or offer to clients, prospects and professional contacts.
- A leaflet drop is when a piece of print is incorporated into a local newspaper and distributed with it, or is hand-delivered individually via other means.

A hand-delivered leaflet drop is most appropriate if you wish to promote your services to e.g. a specific housing (or possibly, industrial) estate, or all estate agents in your geographical location. Clearly, you are able to target very specifically. And delivery by hand allows for personal contact and a limited form of dialogue. It also avoids the need for producing a specific mailing list and labels, etc.

By contrast, a mass leaflet drop via newspaper or other hand-delivered means will cover a far greater area at a much reduced cost per 1,000 than any other method. But, it will be very general or non-specific in its coverage.

Whether it is a mailshot or a leaflet drop, the content will almost inevitably have to be based upon 'product promotion', and will, most probably, be part of an overall campaign. Clearly, the firm is likely to be talking to non-clients and should therefore encourage as quick a contact as possible – for more information, tickets to a seminar, to make an appointment for a free half-hour interview, or whatever. It will also reinforce your other promotional activity and provide that old 'pincer movement' to existing clients, who with any luck will be pleased to see that 'their solicitor' is being proactive.

The most refined form of mailshot will use the postal service, be personally addressed and probably take the form of a covering letter with some pre-produced printed leaflet. This, too, should contain a 'call to action' that specifically tries to elicit a response, possibly through some form of incentive.

If your mailshot or leaflet drop is a stand-alone promotion, or possibly a test promotion, it does need care. Particular attention to the image being projected is essential, as is planning. The exact offer needs to be understood, the recipient identified, and thought given to both why that recipient has been chosen and what level of response is to be expected.

It is, of course, possible to buy lists, but it is essential to ensure that the information contained in them is current. Your own database will provide you with information regarding your current client list; it should also (see **Chapter 6**) have details of your prospects and professional contacts.

Some manuals recommend the use of an incentive, via free gift, competition or discount, etc. While this is normal practice elsewhere and may well be a tool used by The New Competition, we are a little uneasy when this type of promotion is related to the legal profession. Far better, in our opinion, is the offer of free service or initial interview. The exception to this rule may well be parts of your professional contacts register. For example, with estate agents, incentives simply to read a mailshot have proved extremely worthwhile.

And now, two very important points that most people seem to forget at planning stage.

1. Be absolutely clear what your internal action will be when you receive a response to your mailshot. Frankly, this also applies to every other promotional activity, but especially when you are specifically asking your client or prospect to do something. You must be clear who is going to do what in your response to their response.
2. Make sure that all your staff know about this mailshot (and again, all other forms of promotion) in advance of them taking place. It is most demoralising for a receptionist to hear first from a client about a special offer, event or mailing. All your staff, not just those who have obvious client contact, should be made aware, be given a sample of the mailing, and should be told in detail what it is for and when it is going out. Perhaps it would even be worthwhile to give them a few copies of the mailing (in case any of their friends would be interested).

CHAPTER 12 TASK **Plan your marketing**

Using the contents of this chapter the partner responsible for marketing should coordinate promotional planning with department heads. The CD-Rom contains a copy of the audit.

The most important action following the reading of this chapter is to draw up, department by department, a promotional plan for your firm. This chapter is intended to assist you in producing this, coordinated throughout the firm, together with the necessary budgets, action plan and monitoring system.

13

Tying up the loose ends and specific campaigns

Having discussed in Chapter 12 in general terms about promotional activity, we now look at some specifics that could be considered by your firm.

We look at sponsorship and charities, consider seminars, exhibitions and local shows, and reinforce again that personal selling is of prime importance, and is in no small way the objective of all promotional activity.

We consider the problems surrounding the appointment of a PR or advertising agency and how to get the best results out of a consultant.

Finally, we discuss some specific campaigns that have been undertaken by Marketlaw clients that will, we hope, act as a spur for you in developing your own individual campaigns.

Explain. Clarify. Simplify. – Lord Northcliffe

Alfred Harmsworth (Lord Northcliffe) used this exhortation in developing his newspaper empire.

In many ways, this maxim applies to everything we have suggested in this book. In face of The New Competition, solicitors need to explain, clarify and simplify their proposition to their clients, partners and employees, and to their professional contacts. The maxim could also be applied to the firm's product range and, specifically, to all promotional activity where the message must explain the benefits to the prospect (and even an existing client is a prospect for a new service). Clarify the proposition by clearly explaining to the prospect why they should follow your recommended course of action, and simplify the message you are putting across. Of course, in the case of promotion, one also needs a 'call to action' and a pre-prepared follow-up.

Lord Northcliffe's words also apply to your product range and will assist you to get the best out of your staff. Define and understand the difference between the first-time buyer and the last-time buyer, and provide each with an appropriate service, not just conveyancing. Explain to staff their position in the overall scheme of things. Clarify their job description and way of working. Simplify the lines of communication by removing 'them and us' barriers and reducing red tape.

In fact, there are few areas in the running of a legal practice and the facing up to The New Competition that could not have the Harmsworth maxim applied to them.

We will now look at some specific promotional ideas, activities and campaigns. We hope these will provide food for thought and background information to assist you in developing your own promotional activity and campaigns. That said, unless you know that a campaign using the following has already been run in your area, there is no reason why they could not be lifted and used by your firm, as they will be unique, at least to your own area, and your own client base. However, adaptation and innovation are probably best.

Sponsorship and charities

It is not intended to appear, or to be, cynical when we link charities, charitable donation and sponsorship to promotional activity. It is also more than the 'blackmail budget' referred to in **Chapter 9** and elsewhere. Supporting a local event for a school, hospital, hospice or other charity is clearly worthy and worthwhile, especially when the activity is an actual event rather than a publication (such as the programme for that event) because activities such as the local church/school fête do provide an opportunity to talk, face-to-face, with clients, prospects and professional contacts. You might also gain press coverage that should, of course, be covered in turn in your own newsletter.

If it is considered worthwhile giving up one's time to attend such events, it is doubly important to ensure that the objective is clearly understood and that an aide-mémoire in the form of leaflets, literature, newsletters, etc. is available to be handed out at the event. Too often people consider the presentation of their business card sufficient. It is not.

Sponsorship

Of course, sponsorship and events can be a form of public promotion, especially if they are linked to such things as advertising, PR and newsletter articles. They can be very valuable as they are directed at a chosen section of the public, be that geographical, demographic or by interest, and as this is predetermined, you can ensure that the literature you provide (from your literature kit, of course) is appropriate. Sponsorship and events are therefore worthy of serious consideration, because they can be used to promote your 'brand' in your area, establishing you as a local and caring organisation in the face of the national, faceless New Competition.

EXAMPLE **Team players**

A very inexpensive but highly successful form of sponsorship worked because the whole campaign had been thought through, rather than being dealt with irritably just to get it off the desk. A client of ours sponsored a local under-10 football club. This sponsorship was no more than providing a new set of kit for the team and the occasional tea. The team's kit was, of course, emblazoned with the firm's name. Photographs of the team were taken at the beginning of the season, and press releases were sent out. It was a genuinely newsworthy and interesting story that was published under the by-line 'Local solicitor sponsors under-10s'. That solicitor, anonymous in the copy, was clearly identified by the logo emblazoned upon the kit.

The same photograph, albeit with much more upbeat copy, was reproduced in the firm's newsletter, and the team's results were printed in subsequent editions. The family division used the photograph under the slogan 'Childcare matters to us' and even the commercial department adopted it when emphasising teamwork and the valuable part the department had to play with their commercial clients.

The team members were invited to a garden party that the firm had organised and played a 10-minute demonstration five-a-side game for which they were rewarded by a trip to a local theme park. It was no accident that the trip itself gained coverage in the local press. It is sad to report that the team came almost bottom of its league – but no matter, it had been great fun, and at the end of it all, the whole team was entertained to an end-of-season barbeque that, once again (unsurprisingly), gained local coverage.

Your authors suggested a slogan 'We'll support you when you're down', but this was rejected by the client. Pity!

We have seen many forms of sponsorship from rally cars and racehorses, through hot air balloons, to a specific animal at Marwell Zoo and a tree at Sheffield's botanical gardens. The successful ones have a local connotation and a link (which must be demonstrated if not obvious) to the firm, or the firm's department. Sponsoring the senior partner's racing Aston Martin or his wife's equestrian efforts, while understandable, should not really be part of the promotional expenditure.

Charities

Support and donations to charities are worthy, worthwhile, have potential promotional value, demonstrate a caring face in the community, debunk the 'fat cat' image and do good. Today, more and more charitable activities involve active participation – fun runs, moon walks, etc. – that can be used positively from team building to being a promotional vehicle. Again, this activity goes further than the 'blackmail budget', in that it reflects well on the firm and may even lead to additional business.

But charities can also be clients – very valuable clients. There is a strong case for doing charity legal work at a discount, in return for permission to use the story. Perhaps it seems cynical. How can we use a charity like this? How can we make a profit or take a promotional advantage of a charity? The answer is really straightforward. Without doubt, the best deals are those that benefit each party. In this particular case, the charities will benefit from receiving expert legal advice less expensively. The target of the charity's operation will therefore receive the benefit of additional funds being available to serve their needs. Your firm receives the promotional benefit, and it must ensure that it does. This is a genuine win-win situation and you should not be dissuaded by the cynics.

In addition, despite a 'discount', charity work need not be unprofitable. It is complex, and is known by the charities themselves to be so. Therefore, those who can demonstrate an experience in this area are likely to be able to expand upon this particular niche market.

Seminars

In *Marketing Your Law Firm* (2002), Lucy Adam details very fully what seminars are, how to organise them, how to stage them, monitor them and manage the responses. In fact, she takes the same detailed approach to sponsorship and charities (see above).

However, for the purposes of this book, we are assuming that you know how to organise a seminar, have identified the people within your firm that can present one, and have decided, as part of your marketing programme, which areas of activity you want to highlight through seminars. What we want to deal with in detail is the two areas where, in our experience, the legal profession falls down in its organisation of seminars that frequently (yes, frequently) fall into disrepute and are never done again.

These areas are:

1. Getting people to turn up.
2. Following up those who do (and don't).

Let us assume that you have a brilliant seminar organised and a superb range of speakers. This is something that has been developed at not inconsiderable cost. You are ready to present it. How do you get people to attend?

First, remember the old promotional maxim we talked of earlier: 'Tell them what you are going to tell them; then tell them; then tell them what you have told them.' This is the basis of a campaign. This is why professional marketers plan campaigns rather than one single hit.

Tell people that you will be holding a seminar and why they should attend (i.e. benefit presentation) well in advance, via articles in your newsletter, direct mail and the enlisting of the appropriate part of your professional contacts register. Then tell them again. If you are embarrassed about simply saying the same thing twice – and there is no need to be – find a different form of words to impart the same information. Now find the best person in your organisation on the telephone, and give them a short-term extra 'marketing' job to do. Don't forget to explain the importance of your activity to them, and the appreciation of the partnership for taking it on.

Now resolve to present the same seminar twice on the same day. Send out formal printed invitation cards, along with an explanatory leaflet if necessary, to your invitation list. But on the invitation card itself, as well as the times of the two presentations, include the following slogan (or similar):

> To establish numbers for catering purposes, we will telephone you during the week prior to the seminar to establish which session you would like to come to, and to confirm the numbers of people you will be bringing.

Your telephone follow-up person will usually get through that guardian of all portals, the receptionist, and be put through to the invitee, or at least their secretary. We would propose that the seminars are held at, or around, 12.30–2.00 pm with a light buffet lunch included and 6.00–7.30 pm along with aperitifs, which will result in one of three responses:

1. Lunchtime session.
2. Evening session.
3. Can't make it.

The 'Can't make its' can be followed up with a letter and either an invitation to a later seminar, or the handout from the existing one. This will also apply to those who said they were coming, but did not. As a result of this activity, a list of names and numbers expected for each session will be available prior to the presentation of the seminar, and can be checked off against it. Our experience is that this, or a similar approach, will ensure that your seminar is attended by an increased number of people with a much more targeted quality response.

Occasionally, your telephone person may come up against the 'I'm not interested' response. If your staff member is confident enough, it is extremely useful to find out why they are not interested. But, sometimes it is worth accepting that you cannot win them all, and move on.

Alone or joint venture?

There has to be the assumption that somewhere within your firm there are people who are capable and willing of making public presentations at a seminar. It is practical, and we have undertaken this for clients, to have the seminar presented by someone from outside the firm, as long as a sufficient number of firm members are available to talk to attendees. However, it must be remembered that one of the prime objectives of any seminar is to provide proof to the attendees that your firm contains a particular expertise; this can only be watered down if you do not present the seminar itself.

However, technology, with specific reference to PowerPoint, can help greatly. Well-produced visual aids not only stimulate the audience, but also greatly assist the nervous presenter in their task.

Another route is, of course, a joint venture, where a skilled presenter from an associated field can lead the seminar with your less able or shyer legal colleagues providing back-up support. An example of this would be a financial adviser (usually good on their feet) presenting investment advice, or perhaps an accountant-led business seminar on, for example, improving profit, led by the accountant, with the solicitor providing the legal back-up. There are, of course, many other examples from each legal discipline.

In the case of a joint venture, the selection of a seminar coordinator or leader is of particular importance. Strangely, this can be a more comfortable role for the less-experienced speaker who can remain centre-stage while simply introducing topics and fielding questions. But, as a general rule, the more you can do in-house with your own people, the better. The more you can lead the seminar, the higher your firm's profile. The more you instigate the seminar, the more it will be 'yours'. As with much else in marketing, the starting point of seminar organisation is to define not only the subject, but specifically the objective, which should be quantified if possible.

A seminar should also be part of a campaign using other promotional vehicles, to ensure the success of the common goal. An important area related to this is press and PR, coverage in the newsletter and even mailshots relating to the content and success of the seminar. A seminar should not be an entity solely in its own right. It should be a focus for a whole range of other promotional activity.

Follow-up

We have discussed above how to follow up and keep in contact with those who are unable to attend your seminar despite your tailored invitation. If there are sufficient people who would have attended if they could, but were genuinely unable, you should run the seminar again.

Indeed, most really successful seminars are repeated. They can be reported in the newsletter and elsewhere so people feel that they have missed out. The announcement of an additional date 'due to public demand' can reap considerable attendant benefits, not least of which is that the firm is seen to be putting itself out for its clients and prospects. This does, of course, presume that the seminar was worthwhile in itself. But if it is not, quite frankly, you should be reconsidering presenting it in the first place.

Now let us look at how to follow up those who did attend.

Every delegate should leave with an aide-mémoire. Your firm's folder with the appropriate inserts from the literature kit, maybe with a covering letter, is the ideal and inexpensive way of producing this. It might be appropriate to include a questionnaire, along with a call to action, depending on the subject being covered at the seminar. To achieve a response from those who have attended is the prime objective, almost irrespective of what that response is. Therefore, a questionnaire to be returned is a good start.

If this is inappropriate for your seminar, you will have to be proactive. If the seminar was attended by a large number of people, a standard follow-up letter may have to suffice. If, on the other hand, the delegates were a small number of highly targeted individuals, then a telephone follow-up either from a fee earner, or perhaps your original telephone person, would be more appropriate. Once again, define the call to action. What are you expecting from the person you communicate with? Define the objective and quantify it, and then measure the success of the seminar and its follow-up by these standards.

Other presentations

Aside from formal seminars, there are numerous opportunities to give talks, presentations or speeches. Whatever the size of audience, from a handful of people through to hundreds, there are two basic rules. First, the speaker needs a thorough grasp of their subject, especially if there is to be a question and answer session afterwards; second, the topics must be of genuine interest to the audience. There will be plenty of groups within your area for whom the chairman is actively seeking qualified speakers. Some of the solicitors for whom we have worked have developed a range of speeches or presentations on varying themes. Local organisations know that they can call on these people for an interesting and informative session. It takes considerable time to develop a good presentation and therefore it is sensible to seek more than one outlet for it.

Once again, this is a departmental matter. The private client department may well develop a presentation of caring for the elderly, while the commercial division should be looking for subjects that will appeal to local trade associations, chambers of commerce or even less formal groups such as sports clubs or associations if the audience is appropriate.

It is worth noting at this point that, with little extra work, a speech can be converted into a press release, which can be of interest to the local paper; an article for your own newsletter, which should, in any case, cover the event and indicate to the readership the willingness of the firm to make these presentations; and even perhaps an insert for your literature kit.

Exhibitions and local shows

If there is a trade exhibition, an agricultural show, a local consumer exhibition (of the Ideal Home type) or any similar function in your geographical area, attendance by your firm is well worth considering.

Exhibitions and local shows are the perfect opportunity to present the human face of your firm. Attendance is not arduous, it need not be expensive, and you might even enjoy it. You will be demonstrating your interest in the local community, and providing an opportunity to introduce yourself to prospects and professional contacts, while reminding your past satisfied clients of your existence. You will also be demonstrating your firm's interest in the local community and will be in a position to answer questions without placing clients or prospects under any obligation. This is not a question of giving free legal advice. It is presenting, to interested parties, what your firm does, and how it can be of assistance. If there is a genuine matter to be discussed, of course, an exhibition stand is not the place and an appointment should be made at the office.

Many people, even today, still hold solicitors in awe, are diffident about entering the firm's offices, and concerned about cost. For them, going to see 'that nice lady at the exhibition' or 'that helpful commercial solicitor from the trade show' alleviates these fears, even the unfounded ones. In many ways, it is similar to holding an open day at your office, in that people will not feel under pressure, and are more likely, therefore, to ask questions and demonstrate their actual needs.

Personal selling

Although this activity has been mentioned elsewhere in this book, it is worth revisiting at our conclusion. Not everyone is able or willing to promote the firm in personal interviews. It was not intended that solicitors should be salesmen. But fee earners will, in the course of their work, have face-to-face meetings with clients, and must adopt the promotional stance when seeking opportunities for cross-selling the firm's various services.

The introduction of the concept of personal selling is not a revolution. In most practices of our experience, it boils down to persuading people to do what they are already doing, but more professionally, more often, and in a more formal way while giving recognition to the importance of the sales task. Selling, however you wish to describe it, is very important to your firm. Consideration should be given to incentives, referral fees and other rewards. It is also not unreasonable for the marketing partner to set sales activity targets that should then be monitored.

It is, however, worthwhile defining the 'finders, minders and grinders'. Those capable of finding new work and clients for the firm should be supported, perhaps rewarded, and certainly allowed time to do so. There can be few fee earners who are not minders. It is part of the job to take care of the client. But, where you do have a grinder, someone excellent at a particular area of work, but perhaps best described as a 'backroom boy', they should not be forced into a position where they are expected to undertake work that they cannot perform. As with so many other areas, it is better to support strength, rather than bolster weaknesses.

It is often said in industry that the best salesmen act as their own sales managers and constantly review their own efforts. This self-development often brings success, and it is obviously true that success leads to success as confidence builds. Selling is a lonely and exposed activity. Perhaps here more than anywhere else, a 'thank you' and the publishing of success (telling the staff about a new client, for example) is of major importance.

Appointing a PR or advertising agency

An advertising agency or PR company is often seen as a portal giving access to graphic design, copywriting, media and print purchasing plus commercial and marketing advice. Some years ago, with the advent of deregulation, advertising agencies saw the legal profession as a potentially lucrative new market. Of course, one must not generalise too much, but overall, the results were not a great success. A lot of money was spent on inappropriate advertisements, bulky brochures and a whole swathe of swanky new corporate images. Why was this?

It was partly to do with the advertising industry's lack of understanding of the legal profession's uniqueness, and partly the inability of many partnerships to brief an agency properly. Perhaps a third reason is that the majority of partnerships confused marketing with promotion – a misunderstanding that we hope this book will clear up.

The legal profession is hard to understand for those outside it. If you are to brief an outside agency, it is imperative that you provide sufficient detail of the profession's characteristics to ensure that those bidding for your account can demonstrate an understanding of it. One of the biggest problems facing any legal firm, and their advisers, is the variety of people (clients and prospects) they have to serve and communicate with. As a minimum, there are commercial and private clients, plus all the subdivisions based upon departmentalisation. Additionally, there is a range of services within each department all with varying client benefits, most of which are a 'distress purchase' or at the very least, a derived need.

Then, the firm's promotion needs to match the firm's aspirations that need to be clearly understood, not only within the firm, but by the agency being briefed. It is essential that anything that is proposed does not damage the existing recognition or the client loyalty that you are trying to build. To defend the agencies for a moment, they are dealing, perhaps for the first time, with possibly the worst structure available for making emotive decisions and subjective choices – an equity partnership.

So the odds are that an agency, more used to an industrial structure, will not get everything right. At the same time, currently, the profession is about to go through an enormous upheaval with the Legal Services Act 2007, the Carter report and various other changes, all of which will assist or precipitate The New Competition.

All in all, it will take an excellent brief that, ideally, should be presented to an agency that already has an intimate knowledge of the legal profession and the challenges facing it. In our experience, it is often most effective and always less expensive for the marketing partner to deal directly with a skilled graphic designer. However, even graphic designers need briefing. First, they need to understand the three tiers of promotion.

Corporate

Corporate promotion is used to raise the profile of the firm and demonstrate who you are, what you do and how to make contact.

A designer also needs to understand exactly what type of firm you are. Are you a one matter-type practice, such as a criminal practice? A private client, non-contentious firm? A full service (including litigation) private firm? Are you a private client firm that also works for 'owner driver' businessmen? Are you a full service firm providing a wide product range for both the private and commercial client? Or is your firm purely a commercial or corporate practice?

Once this is understood, the firm's geographical market needs to be included within the brief, along with the firm's ethos or profile, and its current standing in the marketplace (a market leader, or a market follower?). In addition, it is essential to be clear about the stance the firm will take. Where on the scale of work and charges does the firm stand? Is it a high quality, high fee practice or high volume, low fee practice? These extremes are fairly straightforward. The difficulty with the majority of practices is that they are somewhere between the two and the subtlety of defining exactly where is extremely important.

Perhaps the hardest of all to brief an outsider on is the 'personality' of the firm. Every firm, indeed every commercial entity, has a personality. In every field, there are those who demonstrate a young, 'trendy' and even flash personality. Then there is the traditional, dignified and even dour other extreme. Like attracts like, and the personality of the firm will be reflected in the clients who have associated themselves with that firm. But it works the other way around too, and clearly in these extreme examples, each personality would be alienated by the other. A brief that does not establish this may well assist the alienation, or more likely, fall between the two extremes – becoming safe, boring and ineffectual.

Market specific/product specific

A design brief should also take into account the other tiers of promotion: market and product specific, even if there is no intention of taking either approach at this time. An understanding of niche markets and the full product range is essential from the beginning.

Making a choice is difficult. It is essential to view earlier work by your designer or agency and to compare their 'pitch' with others. It is important to listen properly when they are making a presentation to ensure that they have fully understood the brief. Once you have appointed your outsourced assistance, you will find, as has long been established, that you will get the best results from them if you trust their judgement. And don't water down their ideas. It is important to keep the agency and, importantly their staff, enthusiastic about you. You know for yourself which clients you prefer dealing with. And in truth, do they not get priority? It is the same with agencies. Aim to be their favourite client, and you will be the one they work the hardest for.

Campaigns

As we are 'tying up loose ends' a word about campaigns may be helpful.

Several years ago, a client said to us in response to what we thought was a pretty good idea, 'We've tried that. It didn't work.' The subject under discussion was a legal advice helpline for selected commercial clients. 'It didn't work', as it turned out, referred to a single mailshot, which had elicited a poor response.

Nevertheless, the idea was liked by the commercial department and eventually we were given permission to proceed, which we did by organising a campaign. The first thing a campaign must acknowledge is that people have to have a recognition factor before they respond. Because of this, anything done as a one-off seldom works in the promotional field. As we have said before in the book, people need to be told what we are going to tell them; be told; and then be told what we have told them. This applies almost universally, because people are so busy and have such crowded lives. People need to be reminded, even about things they thought were a good idea in the first place. I saw it – I liked what I saw. I saw it again – and decided I must do something about it. I saw it for a third time and was reminded to take action.

Our advice line campaign took the following route. We wrote to the target audience to announce that we were starting a paid-for advice line. We announced it again in the firm's newsletter, which was, of course, automatically received by the target audience. We wrote a personalised letter again, outlining the details of the advice line, and placed a small but prominent advertisement in the industry's trade press. We then wrote again to those members of the target audience who had not responded, outlining how successful the advice line was, and recommending that they registered to join it. We gained editorial in the trade press, and wrote a second time in our own newsletter. Finally, we wrote once more to non-respondents announcing that there were a limited number of vacancies left to register for this helpline and enclosing a prepaid envelope for the return of the registration form.

It can be seen that a campaign of this sort is relatively inexpensive and far more likely to succeed that any one-off promotional action.

The principle outlined above can be applied to any promotional advertising activity and is highly recommended. The most successful marketing companies know that a campaign can succeed where one-offs seldom do, and that a successful campaign should bring in many promotional elements (including, as did the above example, a limited telephone follow-up) and should not simply be a continued repeat of an advertisement.

Specific campaigns

This part of the chapter outlines actual promotional campaigns that we have been involved with over the past few years. Perhaps they are not campaigns that are appropriate to your firm, but they are reproduced here primarily to illustrate the thinking that needs to go behind the promotion of legal services and the inclusion of different elements within each campaign.

'Planning ahead'

Our client started their campaign by publishing a well-presented booklet entitled 'Planning ahead – for a comfortable later life'.

As you might imagine from the title, the subject matter was retirement and beyond and covered such things as wills, probate, inheritance tax planning, powers of attorney, advanced directives, care home provision, along with advice on such matters as equity release schemes and funeral bonds. The booklet included a freepost tear-off coupon, which elicited a surprising number of replies. The firm concerned had, of course, remembered to put in place a swift and careful response system, which was also used for monitoring the success of the campaign. Initially, the firm's very good client database was searched for appropriate clients, who received a free copy of the booklet with a covering letter signed by the fee earner most recently in contact with that client.

The booklet was then featured quite heavily in the next edition of the firm's newsletter, which resulted in additional requests for a copy from other members of the current database. The newsletter was also sent to the appropriate section of the firm's professional contacts register, again, with a covering letter, but this time with an offer of the provision of a quantity of booklets for distribution around the contact's own client/customer base. The booklet was well thought out, well presented and of genuine value to the reader and the take-up from the PCR was considerable.

An editorial about the booklet was obtained in the local weekly newspaper and because of the response to that, a series of advertisements was placed. While the advertising was relatively cheap and probably worth doing, it is important to note that in terms of cost per enquiry, this route was by far the most expensive.

The firm then ran a series of seminars based upon, and distributing, 'Planning ahead'. The first in the series of these seminars was held for the firm's clients and prospects but the same material was also used in a series of joint seminars with a financial adviser that took 'Planning ahead' to a far wider audience. These seminars were reported both in the local press and in a subsequent edition of the firm's own newsletter, enabling the firm to keep alive the message about 'Planning ahead'.

Armed with the interest and success that the booklet had achieved, the firm then approached the local radio station and, following a meeting with its commissioning editor, gained a weekly slot in the station's afternoon show providing answers to listeners' questions, initially based upon 'Planning ahead', but subsequently moving into many other areas of law.

We have used this example of a true campaign at many seminars. Most people who have attended have grasped the concept and admitted that their own firm would most probably have printed a leaflet, done one mailing with it, and then left it in reception.

Eventually, 'Planning ahead – for a comfortable later life' became so well known that the commercial partner felt able to discuss it with some of his commercial clients. At the time of writing, two industrial concerns and one large call centre have had special editions printed incorporating their company's logo alongside the firm's name and address. The management of these concerns like the kudos of having done something extra and provided information proactively to their staff, and the practice concerned has spread its name effectively along with a recommendation to hundreds of additional prospects. To date, many thousands of copies of 'Planning ahead' have been distributed and this campaign shows no sign of abating.

There was one more vital component to this campaign. The senior partner was so proud of the booklet that, prior to its launch, he closed the office for a lunchtime, invited the entire staff to a light buffet and presented the booklet and the campaign to everyone. In fact, he sold the campaign to the staff, who all went away with their own copy of 'Planning ahead', enthusiastic about it and their firm's proactive stance and were then kept involved by being informed via email of the outcome, numerically, of each component of the campaign.

A divorce helpline

Following the Carter report, a client firm of ours resolved to give up legally aided family work and concentrate upon privately funded work. It narrowed the target market further, to 'reasonably wealthy people'.

The campaign centred upon establishing a divorce helpline. It should be noted that it was a helpline, not an advice line. As soon as it became evident that legal advice was needed, it was obvious that an appointment should be made, and easy to encourage the client to come into the office. The helpline had its own dedicated telephone line with a separate and memorable telephone number. This line was only answered by one of the three members of the family department who had been trained for this campaign.

The principle behind the helpline was that anyone could use it to discuss matters with a trained professional without the obligation of giving their name or contact details. The line was truly confidential and free of charge.

Bearing in mind the target market, a series of large format advertisements was placed in the upmarket county colour magazine. This type of publication is produced to 'coffee table' book quality and, as such, has a very long life indeed. The advertisement was placed in the same position on the same page in each edition. As a result, it became almost like an ad in a directory. It is also worth noting that the response for the first three issues was very low, but has been increasing steadily ever since. The reason for this is simple. People need to see something and think about it before taking action. Particularly with divorce, there is a concern that visiting a solicitor will start the ball rolling irrevocably towards a marital breakdown. This was not the case with the helpline. Of course, many enquiries did turn into matrimonial work, some of it very valuable. There were other callers who did not proceed, at least with their divorce. But we do know of other callers who use the firm for different work because of the way they were handled by the divorce helpline.

In addition to the placement in the colour magazine, the divorce helpline was advertised in other local publications (with a markedly lower level of success) and was promoted via the appropriate section of the firm's professional contacts register. The divorce helpline had its own section in Yellow Pages and other directories, its own insert in the firm's literature kit, a page to itself on the firm's website and was, of course, featured in its newsletter.

While the firm has avoided the mistake of trying to promote the firm in its entirety and its various services through a single advertisement, there is no doubt that the advertisement for the product that is the 'divorce helpline' has lifted the profile of the firm as a whole, and has demonstrated a considerate and caring approach which is very much the ethos of the whole firm.

Subcontracting litigation

This campaign came about because of the recognition of two separate sets of needs. On the one hand, there was the continued pressure on sole practitioners and smaller firms, constraining them from offering the full range of services that a certain section of their potential client base demanded, resulting in the potential and actual loss of clients to other (usually bigger) firms.

At the same time, our client's practice found that it had perhaps expanded its litigation department too quickly, and as a result had excess capacity. There was a real reluctance to downsize the department again, and an even bigger resistance to being seen to do so. The resultant campaign had three prime component parts – direct mail, personal selling and the production of third party promotional material.

The direct mail was confined to the large northern city in which our client's firm practised. It took the form of a personally addressed letter from the partner in charge of the litigation department, who was a high-profile character, well known within and beyond the profession. The letter proposed a joint venture that could expand the range offered by one party while maximising the production resource of the other.

Importantly, the mailshot was followed up by a personal telephone call, which resulted in a face-to-face meeting in four out of five cases. However, this meeting was not allowed to be simply a chat between professionals. It was a planned, rehearsed and well-equipped sales presentation.

It was recognised from the beginning that the commitments of the partner in charge of litigation would preclude her from making all the presentations personally. Therefore, her assistant was trained thoroughly and undertook 50 per cent of the work. Interestingly, the assistant's success rate was only marginally less than her boss's, which may well have been due to the division of the prospect list.

The presentation included visual aids; a graphic illustration of the way of working; a draft contract guaranteeing that the referring firm would maintain and own the client for both this transaction and all future legal work; an illustration of the referral fee structure; and visuals and dummies of the promotional campaign that the litigation firm would produce for the referring company. In other words, the idea was presented as a rounded, well-thought out and comprehensive business system.

The promotional material to be used by the referring firm included a series of three announcement letters to the existing clients, posters, leaflets plus a leaflet dispenser for the referring firm's reception and a series of letters similar to the client letters announcing the availability of litigation services through the referring firm to be sent to their own professional contacts.

At the launch for each referring firm, all members of that firm were introduced to the campaign and the campaign material by the litigation practice and met with and discussed the way of working with departmental members of the litigation firm.

The Negotiator's Friend

Whether or not an estate agent recommends your firm, there is no doubt that they can put people off from using you. Research has shown that most agents will try to direct a client to a solicitor they favour. Perhaps this is for some form of reward, but as often as not, it is simply the solicitor with whom they find it easiest to deal.

Recognising this, and the fact that nobody gets paid until everything is completed, we came up with the slogan 'Helping the transaction rather than hindering it', for a client firm in the Midlands. The problem now was how to demonstrate that claim and get the message across. We hit upon a weekly 'transaction report'. When we first instigated this campaign, we used the fax machine to provide the information, although these days, of course, it is more often email. The transaction report simply listed the matters we had on with that particular estate agency and the current state of play at the end of each week or, more usually, the beginning – Fridays being what they are for completions.

As an aside, part of our campaign was to fax or email a blank transaction report to those firms with which we had no current work, illustrating how proactive we were in providing information, how we understood the estate agent's problems and how we 'helped rather than hindered the transaction'.

We then hit upon a gaudy newssheet not dissimilar in size and colour to the *Racing Post*. In this piece of print, we introduced the transaction report, although we did also follow it up with a more formal and dignified letter. The newssheet was supposed to be a light piece of fun and, as such, we called it 'The Negotiator's Friend'. It contained competitions, anagrams, crosswords and a draw for six bottles of champagne. The introduction was quite open.

'We know you are busy, we know you probably won't read this unless you are given a good reason. But if you do read it through and answer the three simple questions on the returnable form, you could win a bottle of champagne.'

The response was really quite remarkable.

Other coupons asked for the names and addresses of colleagues that had not received 'The Negotiator's Friend', and a third one invited them to join our 'users circle'. This was a discussion group over a light lunch that at least got a few agents into our office, and put a face to the voice on the telephone.

On average, we would publish three issues of 'The Negotiator's Friend' a year, and we would always hand deliver them. There were two reasons for this. First, solicitors just don't go out to estate agents – but we did. Second, we wanted each negotiator to receive a copy, not just the manager or, as so often with mailing lists, the address. Hand delivery gave us an opportunity to ensure we knew the name of every negotiator in every office.

The sceptics would claim it was pointless knowing names, as negotiators moved around so much. This logic has always escaped us: unless they go out of estate agency completely, they will take their knowledge of your good service to their next job.

As already noted, this was a fun piece of print, and is not suited to all practices. We have already acknowledged the danger inherent in the promotional material of one department damaging the image of another. However, in general terms, this light-hearted approach does work, and is in keeping with the ethos and feel of most estate agencies.

Local PI promotion

This is the name we gave to a campaign we devised for the PI department of a client some years ago. It refers to the number of surgeries we were able, at the end of the campaign, to consider referrers of work.

This campaign came about because we had experienced little success with NHS doctors' surgeries; they genuinely are too busy and the receptionist is there to protect her doctors, not promote solicitors. By contrast, we had considerable success with private clinics, sports injuries clinics and secondary medicine such as chiropractors, osteopaths and, on one memorable occasion, acupuncturists.

Again, the firm produced a booklet and provided posters, leaflets and a leaflet dispenser for the surgeries. Surgeries were persuaded via direct mail, personal selling and recommendation. In fact, recommendation was of considerable importance and was one of the reasons that it was necessary to keep the campaign running consistently for a period of time, despite its apparent lack of success in the early days.

Direct mail led to a telephone follow-up and, wherever possible, a face-to-face meeting. Who actually undertakes this campaign will depend entirely upon who you have available within your own firm, but on one occasion, we were able to run the entire campaign without taking up any fee earner time. This firm had a receptionist who was very happy to take on the running of the campaign and well able to undertake the selling side of it. In this case, it was she who made all the presentations. The pitch to the surgery owner centred upon the experience of the firm and its caring, capable ethos. We developed a whole range of ways to demonstrate that these solicitors were not just 'ambulance chasers' and that having someone on your side, seeking financial compensation, could genuinely assist the healing process. Our receptionist sales lady maintained contact with each of the surgeries, not, of course, dealing with the legal matters, but merely managing the promotional side and the way of working. On her own initiative, she built up a collection of thank you notes, complimentary remarks and even letters, and persuaded several people to talk to other surgeries about the success they had enjoyed in the association with the PI department. She took great pains not to overuse referrers, ensuring they were never asked to act in that capacity more than twice.

The message, again, was that a campaign is not a one-off shot, but a series of activities that are maintained at a constant level over a sometimes lengthy period.

The university card

One of our clients acted as the solicitors to their local university. The senior partner persuaded the academics that his firm could offer an improved, enhanced and cheaper legal service to all employees of the university. Once it had been acknowledged that it was only employees, and not students, and the conflict of interest surrounding employment law was resolved, the campaign went ahead based upon a registration card.

In many ways, this was the forerunner of the client registration scheme referred to in **Chapter 11**. The card was numbered and came on a bearer with an outline of the services available and the privileges offered to the university employees. There was a private, dedicated telephone line. A newsletter was introduced specifically for the university staff, although, of course, the material was not dissimilar to that used in the firm's general newsletter.

The result was an increase by 4,000 to the firm's prospect list. And, as it was a true campaign, it was not left simply at cards, telephone numbers and newsletters. The firm held a weekly evening clinic on the university campus, which was so successful it developed into one day and one evening a week. Then, to keep the profile high and cement relationships further, the solicitors sponsored the annual graduate show and funded a travel bursary.

This scheme has been adapted for several other clients. We know of no other university target, but several of our client firms have taken this approach with the staff of their large commercial clients.

The licensed trade

One of our clients in the south west had a highly experienced and respected licensing department. Coincidentally, the firm was also the solicitor to a firm of accountants who had on its client list the local Licensed Victuallers Association, several public houses, a nightclub or two and a small chain of hotels.

At our instigation, the two formed an association to offer a full range of legal and financial services to the entire licensed trade in their area. The campaign comprised mailshots, a newsletter, a helpline (which, in this case, was, in fact, run by the accountancy firm), seminars, pre-emptive advice and a financial/legal health check.

Finally, on this subject of campaigns, we would suggest that the marketing partner looks at the firm's current promotional activity and selects those that have really been a one-off that could be developed into a true campaign. Perhaps you should look back also at some of those ideas where it has been said, 'We've tried that and it didn't work'.

Getting the best out of consultants

An increasing number of firms are using outside marketing assistance. This outsourcing is not unusual, even in the legal profession. Solicitors employ neither accountants nor auditors, and it is almost certain the IT support is outsourced. With the production of work and accounts now taken care of, it is essential in the face of The New Competition to look at marketing and decide how best to provide that resource.

It should be partner driven, hence our advice to appoint a marketing partner. The consultancy you invite for consideration must have an intimate knowledge of the legal profession, and ideally of The New Competition. You will need advice, but you also need access to action. Your consultancy firm should be a resource doing things for you as well as a consultancy telling you how to do them. This is particularly important in the matter of graphics, print and media buying. A good marketing consultant can act in exactly the same way as an advertising agency and should have access to graphic design. Used properly, the result will be far less expensive than the alternatives.

However, you do need to brief your consultant fully on your own requirements and ensure that these are understood and acted upon. A proposal that does not recognise your firm's uniqueness, despite its similarities to other legal practices, should be rejected. Part of the proposal should include a dated work/action plan and accurate costings though, in addition, it will need to be flexible and the consultancy able to react swiftly to opportunities.

Once your consultancy is appointed, you need to be both supportive and realistic. One of the problems facing consultants serving the legal profession is the need to be able to demonstrate they are doing something for each of the partners and all of the departments. In fact, this may not be the best answer for either party. Prioritisation is vital.

Your firm should appoint one person, presumably the marketing partner, as the interface, who will relay the consultancy ideas and actions to the partnership and the partners' requirements to the consultancy. However, approximately quarterly, but certainly twice a year, the consultancy should attend a full partnership meeting where marketing matters can be discussed openly with everyone. Incidentally, marketing should always be on the standing agenda of partners' meetings.

You need to monitor the consultancy against the agreed work plan; like any other supplier, consultants will sometimes need to be kept up to scratch. That said, the relationship must be one of mutual trust and respect and, ideally, a feeling of success shared.

Finally, you must give your chosen consultant time. Marketing is not a quick fix. It is a permanent series of management tasks.

One last loose end

We hope that you have accepted the idea in the introduction to this book to read it through, and then return to the beginning to begin implementing the tasks given, and adapting them specifically to your firm. If you think we can help, our contact details are given in the Preface.

EXAMPLE **And finally, another true story from David Monk**

In this last section of the first edition of our book, I wrote of a young lawyer who was unable to defend herself against a fee level-based attack on her profession. Essentially, she talked only about the length of training, the difficulty associated with providing the procedures, and the cost of running a town centre practice. Never did she list the benefits provided by her profession nor her practice. I don't know if she ever read this book, but if she still fails to overcome common objections like the price-based one, it will be she, and those like her, who drive clients towards what we then called The New Competition, but which we should now simply and more properly term, The Competition. This last 'loose end' comes from a much older solicitor who I know read the book in its first draft stage, and who I have known personally throughout our somewhat lengthy careers. This is what he had to say to me the morning after his retirement party.

> 'You know David, they [the clients] will never appreciate what we do for them, because they don't understand it. It is all very well for you to say 'explain the benefits to them' but they don't listen. Who was it who said the English know the price of everything but the value of nothing? (Oscar Wilde) Well, that is your average client. When I started, my profession was

just like that of a doctor – no one asked us how we wrought our miracles, they just thanked us for doing so. Oh, how things have changed.'

He went on to say that he still felt his profession had an important job to do – important to 'ordinary' people, not just the good and the great, not just those who need defending or seek justice. The ordinary people, who need help in the simple matters and advice on the increasingly complex day-to-day tasks of living.

'. . . those who really, although they would never admit it, need a friend – a friend in difficult times. No computer will ever give them that.'

We were then joined by his son, himself a successful city commercial lawyer.

'But will they pay for it?'

'They pay you well enough for what you have described as 10 per cent law and 90 per cent common sense. It's the same throughout. 10 per cent law and 90 per cent common sense. And friendship.'

'Yes, it's support I guess' said the son, 'No computer can give them that' these two wise lawyers laughed together.

And they are right. No big shed operation of The Competition can ever replace that accessible, personal touch of the traditional solicitor. It is what people want, what they need. All you have to do is tell them . . . that you can provide it.

I hope that it will help you too. We really do need an independent legal profession, free from government, big business and the multinationals.

Bibliography

Adam, L. (2002) *Marketing Your Law Firm: A Solicitor's Manual*, Law Society.

Bartram, P. (2006) *How to Write the Perfect Press Release*, New Venture Publishing.

Bresler, F. (2000) *Law without a Lawyer*, revised edn, Century.

Denney, R. W. (1984) *How to Market Legal Services*, Van Nostrand Reinhold.

Drucker, P. (1994) *Managing for Results*, Butterworths-Heinemann.

—— (1999) *Management: Tasks, Responsibilities and Practices*, Butterworth-Heinemann.

Humphrey, G. and Hart, N. (eds), (1990) *The Professional Adviser's Guide to Marketing*, Mercury Business Books.

Kotler, P. (1999) *Marketing Management: Analysis, Planning and Control*, 10th edn, Prentice Hall.

McGregor, D. (1960) *The Human Side of Enterprise*, McGraw-Hill.

Mathur, S. S. and Kenyon, A. (2001) *Creating Value*, 2nd edn, Butterworth-Heinemann.

Moore, M. (1997) *Marketing for Lawyers*, 2nd edn, Law Society.

Silbiger, S. (2005) *The 10-Day MBA*, 3rd revised edn, Piatkus.

Townsend, R. (1977) *Up the Organisation*, Coronet Books.

Additional resources

GfK NOP Social Research for the Solicitors Regulation Authority (2010) *Consumers' Attitudes towards the Purchase of Legal Services*.

YouGov (2010) Legal Services Reports Legal Services Consumer Panel, Legal Services Board (June 2011) *Tracker Survey 2011*.

Fieldstone Associates (2006) Research on ABS investor expectations.

Index